GREAT SOUTH CAROLINIANS

The voting ticket used when James L. Petigru ran for the State Senate. It is decorated with the English rose, the Scotch thistle, and the Irish shamrock.

Great
South Carolinians

From Colonial Days to the Confederate War

By Helen Kohn Hennig

Essay Index Reprint Series

Originally Published by
THE UNIVERSITY OF NORTH CAROLINA PRESS

BOOKS FOR LIBRARIES PRESS
FREEPORT, NEW YORK

First Published 1940
Reprinted 1970

STANDARD BOOK NUMBER:
8369-1658-1

LIBRARY OF CONGRESS CATALOG CARD NUMBER:
79-117806

12-11-74

PRINTED IN THE UNITED STATES OF AMERICA

To

LENA WITCOVER HENNIG

Foreword

By Professor D. D. Wallace

MRS. HENNIG has given us, in this series of biographies, history in one of its most attractive forms. She has taken advantage of the fact that biography is history teaching by example, in selecting a group of the best examples of character and service among great South Carolinians. While this is not the whole of history, it is a part that has a strong appeal to young readers.

Mrs. Hennig has assembled her material with enormous research and careful judgment. She is constantly under the necessity of restraining the very abundance of her material. The various aspects of history and character have received attention. We have here the lives of educators, scientists, engineers, artists, agricultural pioneers, and leaders in industry as well as politicians and soldiers. By the industry and care by which she has made conveniently available such a useful body of material on how our great men and women lived and worked in helping to make the state, Mrs. Hennig has done a lasting service to the teachers and school children of South Carolina and to the wider circle of readers who, it is to be hoped, will avail themselves of such an agreeable means of learning something of our past.

Wofford College

Preface

"History is but the record of the men who made it."

THE STORIES of the men and women who have builded a state or nation comprise in their essence the whole of history. These biographies of South Carolina's unforgettable sons are presented by the author in the hope that they will make the history of the Palmetto State become vibrant and alive. Through the lives of these men the story of the State is told, for through them history was made. How they lived, what they did, and the crises they met have become the framework on which the history of our nation is woven. In this first volume is presented the period from colonial days to the eve of the Confederate War. The second volume will give the biographies of the men from the beginning of the war until the present.

The men whose lives are depicted are the heroes of the birth of a state and a nation. It was necessary to leave out many, but they are not forgotten. Those who were included were selected by teachers who have expressed the need for such a book of biographies. To them a list of names was sent, and the forty-five which will be presented in the two volumes were the ones for whom the greatest number of votes was recorded. The other men to whom South Carolina owes a great debt of gratitude have either been adequately treated in other easily accessible works or, the limits of space being as they are, are left for some day in the future, when they too will be presented to the young people of South Carolina.

With deep gratitude I express my thanks to those who have helped in the preparation of this book. Many have offered the use of their rare family treasures and to them, too numerous to mention, goes my deepest appreciation. I greatly appreciate the assistance of the teachers who commented in detail on the sketches submitted to them. They tried them in the classroom and their findings proved of great value. My thanks are extended also to the teachers who allowed me to sit as an observer in their classrooms.

It is difficult out of so many who helped to mention the names of some and not of others, but I must express my especial gratitude to Miss Alice Blanton Carter, of the English faculty of the Columbia High School, for reading and correcting every manuscript; to Mrs. Martin Young, of the Richland County Library, for reading the material with the eye of the children's librarian; to Miss Wilma Lois Price, of the faculty of the Chester Schools, and to Miss Helen Drum, of the faculty of the Darlington Schools, who have edited each sketch from the point of view of the class-room teacher. Mrs. Jules W. Lindau 3rd has been far more than a stenographic assistant. All of them have undertaken tedious tasks and have done them with great care.

The great historical and educational knowledge of Dr. D. D. Wallace, of Wofford College, has been at my disposal. He has read the manuscript and has checked on the historical facts. Words cannot express my thanks to him.

I am also deeply appreciative of the valuable advice and constant encouragement given me by Mr. J. H. Hope, Superintendent of Education of South Carolina.

Miss Mattie Thomas, Director of the Division of Elementary Education of South Carolina, has given me the benefit of her interest and technical knowledge. From the first suggestion that this book be written until now she has advised and counseled me, and I am truly grateful. Mrs. Arney Childs, Dean of Women and member of the history faculty of the University of South Carolina, gave me valuable aid.

The amount of assistance I have received from libraries and museums cannot be calculated. Certainly this work could never have been completed had it not been for the service rendered me by the staffs of the many libraries whose manuscripts and books have been constantly consulted. I express my especial appreciation of the service, "beyond the line of duty," of the workers in the Richland County Library and the University of South Carolina Library, particularly in the South Carolina Room. I have also received valuable aid from the Charleston Library, the Gibbes Art Gallery, the South Carolina Historical Society, and the Charleston Museum, as well as from the New York Public Library, the Library of Congress, the Metropolitan and the Boston Museums, and the Frick Art Reference Library.

It is earnestly to be hoped that this volume will be the means of introducing South Carolinians to their heroes, men who have builded, both in war and in peace, the great State in which we live. Not all the heroes of the world fought in battle; many of them were painters and artists, industrialists and statesmen. All kinds are needed to make a State. Here are included some of each—the heroes of war and the heroes of peace.

HELEN KOHN HENNIG

COLUMBIA, SOUTH CAROLINA
June, 1940

Contents

GREAT SOUTH CAROLINIANS

A late sixteenth-century ship of the kind in which Joseph West may have come to Carolina.

From a drawing by GORDON GRANT, *in Grant and Culver's* The Book of Old Ships.

LET US imagine ourselves in London, over two hundred and fifty years ago, at a council meeting of the Lords Proprietors. We are sitting around the table on one of London's famous foggy days, unseen by the eight men to whom King Charles II had given the land of Carolina. This royal gift extended from the Atlantic to the Pacific, and from Virginia to Florida, and the eight Lords Proprietors expected to make a very good business of it. After all, they had heard glowing tales of this land of wealth. It is true that in 1665 they had sent an unsuccessful expedition to settle this vast territory. Sir John Yeamans, of Barbados, had led a group of people to Cape Fear, North Carolina, but they had stayed only a short time. Was it because the colony had not been carefully planned? Or was it because the colonists did not have the right man to lead them?

As we imagine ourselves sitting around that table in London, we can almost hear the brilliant Lord Anthony Ashley Cooper, Earl of Shaftesbury, explaining to his partners that just because they had failed once they had no reason not to try again. Perhaps he even named the man who could lead them to success. Perhaps he said, "It's true that we must have just the right person to make the colony succeed. I've been looking for that person, and I am certain that I've found him. He's a young man with an excellent personality. He's very ambitious and anxious to make a name for himself. I've sounded him out and I think he will go. Gentlemen, I suggest that we send the second expedition to Carolina under the leadership of Joseph West."

It took a lot of money—in fact, about two hundred and forty thousand dollars, as we count money today, to buy equipment and boats. Two long years went into seeing that every little detail was complete. Joseph West, the leader of the colonists, knew very well that he was on trial, and that if he failed in this big undertaking he might never have such a chance again. But he had no intention of failing. He was a hard-working man, and it did not frighten him when he thought of all the hours, months, and even years which must be spent in gathering provisions of every sort for the colonists who would cross the Atlantic Ocean with him and for whose safety, happiness, and success he felt himself responsible.

At last the great day came. On August 17, 1669, three little boats, the frigates *Carolina* and *Port Royal* and the sloop *Albemarle*, lay at anchor in the Downs on the east coast of Kent, England. Complete reports sent by Joseph West to Lord Ashley have been saved, and it is from these that we today can find out about the first successful settling of Carolina and the beginnings of Charles Town.

The Lords Proprietors could not decide whom they wanted to be the governor of their new colony. They finally agreed to let Joseph West go directly to Barbados to pick up additional settlers. He carried with him an appointment for a governor of Carolina, the name to be in-

A smaller ship of a kind which may have brought colonists to the New World.

From a drawing by GORDON GRANT, *in Grant and Culver's* The Book of Old Ships.

Port Royal.

From an engraving by DE BRY.

serted later by Sir John Yeamans, who had had great
experience in this sort of thing. Sir John named William
Sayle as governor.

It was no easy journey that this band of about one hundred and fifty pioneers made across the Atlantic. Wind,
storm, and high waves did their worst, and it seemed at
times that none of them would live to claim their land and
begin life in the New World.

The Proprietors told West that when he stopped at
Barbados he should supply the colonists with certain roots
and seeds, which they would plant in their new home and
which would bring wealth to them and to the Proprietors.
Their instructions were that the colonists should be fur-
nished with cotton seed, indigo seed, and ginger roots.
They even provided that the ginger roots were to be

planted in a tub of earth so that they would not die before arrival in Port Royal. They suggested to West that he also take shoots of sugar cane, some vines for the growing of grapes, and some olive plants. The Proprietors were taking no chances on having their agricultural program fail; so they wrote out detailed instructions about how many times a day these plants should be watered and exactly how, when, and where they should be transplanted to the soil of Carolina.

Perhaps it might be fun to invent a game of history called, "What would have happened if—." In South Carolina one of the first questions might be, "What would have happened if, when the party landed at Port Royal, they had not met the clever Indian cassique of Kiawah?" This Indian brave came to the settlers with a hair-raising story that the Westo Indians near Port Royal were cannibals and that if

Exploring a river in the New World.

From an engraving by DE BRY.

the white men remained in that part of Carolina they might some day find themselves in the cook-pot. But if they settled near his home, which was by the two great rivers which we now call the Ashley and the Cooper, they would be entirely safe, and he could promise that the beautiful country of the Kiawahs would welcome them.

True or not, his story made a deep impression on the minds of these people, who were not any too certain of their safety in this strange, vast, wooded land, inhabited only by red men. They sailed to the western bank of the Kiawah or Ashley River and there in 1670 established the first English settlement in South Carolina. This settlement was called Charles Town in honor of King Charles II.

It was a hard task to settle the new country. Governor Sayle was an old man, and although he did the very best he could, most of the work was done under the leadership of the strong, healthy young Joseph West. The settlers had to build homes, plant crops, and clear the land. They cut the trees so that they could have enough space for farming and also so that they might use the logs to build houses. They had to take care of all the things they had brought from England, and one of the first tasks which Joseph West set them was building storehouses, one for arms and the other for food, which they called victuals.

Everyone had to work hard, but none of them worked harder than did Joseph West. Governor Sayle was an excellent man for his job. He and the Council held court, encouraged the workers, and punished where it was necessary. With the assistance of Joseph West, he taught the people how to make homes in the New World. He saw that every man did his fair share and received his part of the food, which, unfortunately, at times was very, very short.

Indians attacking a fort at night with flaming arrows.
From an engraving by DE BRY.

He took care of the interests of the Proprietors and wrote to them about every small, unimportant or important detail of the founding and building of Charles Town.

Governor Sayle was about eighty. He had worked hard, and age and his labors finally wore him out. In order to protect the colonists and to have a governor on hand if anything happened to the one they had appointed, the Lords Proprietors had given to Governor Sayle the right to appoint a governor in his place, if for any reason he felt that he could not carry on, or if he felt he was about to die. Just before his death, Governor Sayle appointed Joseph West. West was to serve as governor until word could be received from the Proprietors about what they wanted done.

Not only did the colonists have trouble in finding enough to eat; not only did they have to learn by bitter experience how to tend their crops so that they could grow enough of the right kind of food; not only did they have to work long and hard building their homes, their storehouses, forts, and roads; but they had also to fight the Kussoe Indians.

Perhaps the Indians would not have given trouble if the Spaniards had not stirred them up. Spain claimed all of Carolina as part of Florida. The Spaniards saw that if they could make the Indians give enough trouble to the English colony, they might get rid of these unwelcome neighbors. Things became so bad that Joseph West decided he would have to go to war and teach the Indians a lesson. This he did quickly and with as little loss of life as was possible. The Lords Proprietors were of course interested in trading with the Indians, for in this way they could make a great deal of money. As soon as West had defeated the Kussoe Indians, he again began plans for the trade of the English with their Indian neighbors.

We must remember that the Proprietors were more interested in the business success of this Carolina province than in anything else. They tried to understand what was going on. They really wanted to do what was best for the settlers, but that was naturally hard for them. These great gentlemen lived in fine houses, and their coaches were drawn by decorated horses. It was a matter of great importance to them that their brocaded breeches fit exactly right and that their lace knee-cuffs be of just the correct length, and that the drooping feathers on their hats be at exactly the right angle. Of course it was difficult for such men to understand all of the troubles which came to the English settlers in Carolina. Joseph West explained over and

Anthony Ashley Cooper, Earl of Shaftsbury, one of the Lords Proprietors and the friend and patron of Joseph West.

From an engraving in Courtenay's Genesis of South Carolina.

over to the Proprietors the difficulties of life in Charles Town. He tried to do what was best for the settlers and what was best for the Proprietors.

We have one interesting example which shows that the Proprietors could not imagine what was going on over here. At the very time the Indians and Spaniards were giving West the greatest trouble, Thomas Colleton complained to his brother, who was one of the Lords Proprietors, that the interests of these eight gentlemen were being neglected while "the timid colonists are concerned about two or three Spaniards and a few Indians." How differently he might have felt if he had been one of the settlers, living in constant fear and ever ready to protect himself, his wife, his children, and his fellow settlers from the savage Indians who were being pushed on by the jealous Spaniards!

Although Sayle had appointed West governor, the Lords Proprietors made Sir John Yeamans governor on April 17, 1672. Yeamans was a landgrave (which was the title given to the nobility of Carolina), and West was not. Yeamans did not succeed particularly well in his governorship, and even before his death in August, 1674, the Proprietors had decided to make West governor again. West was made a landgrave one day before he was named as governor.

In the meanwhile things were happening in Charles Town. It was decided that the first site chosen for Charles Town was not the best that could have been found. Some time before, Sir John Yeamans had written to the Proprietors advising that they should have the settlers move to a safer and more convenient place which Governor Sayle had selected. In 1679 Lord Ashley finally wrote to Governor West that it was the wish of the Proprietors that the town be moved to Oyster Point and that the name of

Document showing a grant of land to Joseph West in 1680. It is written on parchment, hand-colored and elaborately decorated with the English rose, the Scotch thistle, and the Irish shamrock. West's coat-of-arms is in the upper left-hand corner.

Charles Town be kept. This, of course, is the present site of Charleston, South Carolina.

For eight years Joseph West served as governor of Carolina. It was during these eight years that the greatest strides were made in building up the province. Although he often had to be stern with the people, they were grateful for his work and saw that what he did was for the good of all the settlers. Sometimes he had difficulty in making the Proprietors see that what he was doing was for the best, but they appreciated his work and trusted him with the handling of about fifteen thousand dollars a year and the management of all their lands. This business venture was costing the Lords Proprietors a lot more than they had planned! Perhaps the Proprietors had a right to complain when they had spent $90,000 and had got nothing in return.

West did not know it at the time, but all the hard work he put into the building up of the Proprietors' plantation finally came back to him. For a long time the Proprietors had not settled their money accounts with West. So later they gave him this plantation and certain other lands and raised his salary from £60 a year to £100 a year.

Certainly the Proprietors were pleased with West. Perhaps, then, it will seem surprising that on May 18, 1682, Joseph Morton was appointed governor. The Proprietors were anxious, of course, to bring as many settlers into this country as possible. Joseph Morton had a great deal of influence among certain Scotch and Irish people. It was thought that, if he were made governor of Carolina, these people would come to the province. Governor Morton's term of office lasted only two years. Then, for the third time, West was given this high office, but he was not anxious to be governor of Carolina again, and in about ten months he gladly withdrew in favor of Robert Quarry.

At last Joseph West left Carolina, and we know that he spent some years in Massachusetts and New York, because Judge Samuel Sewall, of Boston, mentions in his *Diary* at least five times that he had met Governor West of Carolina. Joseph West died in New York, and his will is dated there, May 6, 1691.

Little is known of Joseph West's family. For a long time it was thought that he came of rather ordinary people, but the original grant by which he acquired some of his land in South Carolina was recently discovered, and in one corner can be seen his coat-of-arms. This shows that he came from the branch of the West family in Sussex County, England, and that his family had some distinction.

We do not know who his parents were. In fact, all that we do know about his family is that he had a wife, for in his letters to the Proprietors he asked that his pay be given to her. A Mrs. Joanna West came to Charles Town in August, 1671. Was she the wife of Governor West?

It is a pretty good guess that Joseph West had no children, for he willed his entire property to two cousins.

It seems sad that this great man, whom many think to have been the most valuable in the early history of South Carolina, and who three times served as governor, should have died in another colony.

Both the Proprietors and the people trusted, admired, and honored Joseph West. Through his attention to duty and his stern but fatherly care of the new, struggling province, he laid the foundation for a thriving colony which was to become a famous American state. He was a wise, just, God-fearing man, who well deserved the name conferred upon him—"The Father of South Carolina."

Robert Johnson
1676 (or 1677)–1735

YOU HAVE to be some-
thing more than merely
good to earn such a title as "the
Good Governor Johnson." This is especially true when
your father, Sir Nathaniel Johnson, has also been governor
of South Carolina and an excellent governor at that. But
Robert Johnson did earn that title, and he has gone down
in the history of South Carolina as "the Good Governor
Johnson."

Thrills and excitement seem to have followed Robert
Johnson wherever he went. He was always landing in some
dramatic situation. This son of Sir Nathaniel Johnson was
born in England in 1676 or 1677. As a little boy, Robert
went with his parents to the Leeward Islands, where Sir
Nathaniel was governor. After his resignation as governor,
Sir Nathaniel sent his wife and children home to England,
while he came to Carolina to establish himself on his lands.

Portrait of Governor Johnson. This portrait is believed
to be authentic and is attributed to Henrietta Johnston.

He expected to send for his family in a very few months.

On the way to England, the Johnsons had a dreadful adventure. They were captured by the French, who were then enemies of England, and were held prisoners for about a year. During this time Robert's mother died. She was a very beautiful woman, as is shown in a portrait of her, painted by an unknown artist, now in the possession of the South Carolina Historical Society. The Gibbes Art Gallery has a portrait of Robert's father, Sir Nathaniel Johnson, which shows him as a man of strong character.

When Sir Nathaniel Johnson came to Carolina, he expected to spend the rest of his life planting on his very large land holdings here. He did not plan to take any part in public life. But the Lords Proprietors realized that he was far too good a man to retire, and they appointed him governor, the highest office in the province. He served as governor until 1708. Affairs in Carolina did not look any too bright to the Proprietors, and they needed a man who would be a strong governor and who would succeed in making the province a paying proposition for them. Sir Nathaniel did his best for the province and for the Proprietors.

When Nathaniel Johnson's son, Robert, finally became governor of South Carolina in 1717, he found himself in the very middle of trouble. Even then, the discontent between the colonists and the Proprietors was rising to a climax, and two years later, in 1719, the Proprietors were to lose Carolina entirely. It was certainly not a happy time for Robert Johnson to arrive as a proprietary governor of South Carolina.

There were many causes of discontent in the province at this time. The most serious of these was that blood-

Blackbeard as he appeared on the Carolina coast.

From an old engraving

thirsty pirates were preying upon the shipping. They stole the cargoes, sank the boats, and murdered the people. The colonists had asked the authorities in England, again and again, to aid them in this serious problem, but the authorities, as usual, turned a deaf ear. Then the colony undertook, on its own account, to rid the sea of pirates, and it wrote into the history of America one of the most thrilling chapters in all of its wonderful story. You have read of the adventure of Rhett's expedition against the pirate, Stede Bonnet. Perhaps you don't know, however, that Governor Johnson felt that Rhett had been too soft in offering easy terms to Bonnet and that the Governor himself led the second expedition, which cleaned up the nest of pirates off the coast of Carolina.

Imagine yourself having to decide this: What would you do if the villainous "Blackbeard" Teach (or Thatch) had captured Mr. Samuel Wragge and his son and had sent to you (the Governor of South Carolina) the following message: "We have captured the eminent Mr. Samuel Wragge and his son. My men are sick and need drugs. If you send me the drugs, I'll not kill the Wragges, but if you don't send me the drugs no one will ever see Mr. Wragge or his son again?"

Would you allow a fine citizen of Charles Town to be sacrificed while you tried to capture the pirates who had been weakened by illness? Or would you send the drugs which would make the pirates well and at the same time save the lives of your friends?

Perhaps you would have done just as Governor Johnson did—send the drugs and then go after the pirates. Johnson had decided to put an end to piracy and to make shipping safe for Carolina. No amount of begging, no "deals" could turn him from his plan; Stede Bonnet and twenty of his men were publicly hanged in Charles Town. Thus Robert Johnson did more than plan to rid the Atlantic of pirates; to him goes the glory of actually leading the expedition which captured these terrible robbers and put an end to their attacks on Carolina shipping.

The misunderstanding between the people of Carolina and the Proprietors had been growing for a long time. Perhaps each nursed a grudge against the other. The Governor tried to make the Proprietors understand all the hard conditions in the New World and at the same time to make the colonists see the troubles of the Proprietors. No one man could make peace between these two groups, and in 1719 their grievances worked up to such a climax that the people of South Carolina [1] declared themselves to be under the protection of the King of England and not under the Lords Proprietors. The Proprietors did not agree to this arrangement, at least not until they had been paid for their province. The business details took a long time, and meanwhile the government of Carolina was in confusion. The people would not pay any attention to Governor Johnson's efforts to help the Proprietors, but they let him know definitely that they had no personal quarrel with him. In fact, they regarded him with deep affection and respect. When he read to them a statement regarding the rights of the Proprietors, they answered, "The paper you read and delivered to us we take no notice of, nor shall we give any further answer to it but in Great Britain." They softened this, however, by adding, "It is the greatest satisfaction imaginable for us to find throughout the whole country what universal affection, deference,

[1] The name South Carolina was used as early as 1685, and "had doubtless become common long before it was legally adopted."—D. D. Wallace, *The History of South Carolina*, I, 124.

and respect the inhabitants bear to Your Honor's person, and with what passionate desire they wish for a continuance of your gentle and good administration."

The people meant what they said. They honestly wanted Robert Johnson to continue as their governor; but he felt that he must be loyal to the Proprietors who had appointed him. Feeling this way, Johnson returned to England, but before he left Carolina, he was involved in several thrilling adventures.

The Spaniards realized that this would be an excellent chance for them to take a slice of Carolina. Therefore, the province was seriously in danger of an invasion from the south, and prompt measures were taken by Governor Johnson and the other men responsible for the public safety.

During this time, the people really did not know who was governor, and this had its amusing side. People wishing to marry had to have a license signed by the governor, and the clergymen refused to marry a couple who did not have a license from Governor Johnson. Some people, however, refused to admit that Johnson had a right to sign marriage licenses. The young people who wished to marry were greatly bothered by this. They thought that it was all very well to have a political turnover, but they did not see why a stumbling block should be put in the way of their romance.

The act of the Carolinians in refusing to have anything more to do with the proprietary government is known as the rebellion of 1719. Even after this rebellion was successful, and James Moore had taken over the control of the government, Robert Johnson stayed on. In fact, he lingered in Charles Town until he was convinced that Francis Nicholson had received a legal appointment from the King and was to become governor of South Carolina.

But Robert Johnson was again to be governor of South
Carolina. In 1729 the rights of the Proprietors were purchased by the King and South Carolina actually became a
royal province, as the people, ten years earlier, had wanted.
For three years before 1729 Robert Johnson had been ask-

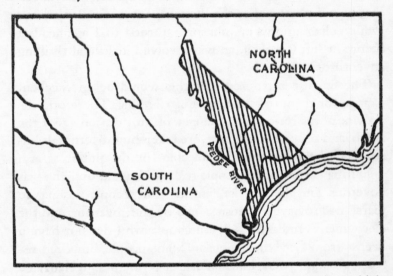

The shaded portion of this map shows the region which
Governor Johnson saved for South Carolina.

Based upon a map in Paullin's Atlas of the Historical
Geography of the United States.

ing that he be appointed as royal governor. Supporting his
claim, he had presented to the King a most interesting paper.
In this he had shown that the rebellion of 1719 had been
due to the acts of the Proprietors, against his advice. He had
realized and warned them that what they were doing was
not wise. He made the interesting point that as a large land-
owner in Carolina he was naturally deeply concerned in the

welfare of that province, for its success or failure would affect him personally. Perhaps he felt that his best argument was the fact that when he left Carolina, after having been governor and "admiral" of the fleet which rid it of pirates, he was exactly £1,000, or $5,000, poorer than if he had never gone to Charles Town. Of course we don't know which of his arguments was most effective; but on November 22, 1729, Robert Johnson was appointed royal governor of South Carolina. He was thus the last of the proprietary governors and the first governor after the King's purchase of Carolina.

One of the most important tasks set for the new governor was the placing of a line between North and South Carolina. In this he was not entirely successful, although he did manage to save for South Carolina a very important part of the seacoast. The governor of North Carolina wanted the Waccamaw River to be the line, but Johnson insisted that it be the Cape Fear River. Governor Johnson gained for South Carolina part of what he claimed, about eighty miles of seacoast. If you will look on your map you will see that the land between the mouth of the Waccamaw River at Georgetown and the mouth of the Cape Fear River at Southport, North Carolina, forms a crescent, dotted with wonderful fishing and bathing beaches. It was this section which Governor Johnson saved for South Carolina. The actual and final settling of all South Carolina boundaries did not take place for almost another hundred years.

Now that South Carolina was a royal province, Governor Johnson, in his first speech before the Assembly, urged the members to forget their former quarrels and to put aside any petty misunderstandings. He pointed out to them that the only way they could hope to build a successful royal province was by working together. The members of the Assembly had one very unpleasant task before them. They had to pay the public debts, which had fallen four years behind. It is bad enough to have to meet the debts of a government year by year, but it is terrible to have to pick up the debts of four years and pay them, as well as those of a current year.

Governor Johnson understood the needs of his people, and he did not hesitate to tell the authorities in England what should be done and how to do it. If the people of Carolina had thought in the past that they were forgotten and neglected, they had no cause for complaint now. The royal government was as eager to assist Carolina now as it had seemed to want to forget her in the past.

It is true that Governor Johnson had not been born in Carolina, but in every other way he was like a native of the province. He was a son of a former governor and he owned about 19,000 acres of Carolina land. He had served the province in the troublous days at the end of the proprietary rule. He knew its problems; and his advice on such difficult subjects as paper money, rents, immigration, and land grants, counted for a great deal in the royal councils. On March 7, 1730, Governor Johnson presented to the government a carefully-worked-out plan for the establishment of ten or eleven townships along the frontiers of the province. In this way he hoped to ring Carolina around with a protective circle of settlers.

Governor Johnson was not the man to neglect Indian relations, for he fully understood how necessary it was to have the red men as friends of the English. He showed honor to their chiefs and head men, hoping in this way to keep them away from the French and the Spanish. On June 18, 1718, while he was still serving as a proprietary governor,

The Cherokee chiefs when they visited London in 1730 with Sir Alexander Cuming. Johnson is credited with having suggested this method of advertising Carolina.

he had written that he had concluded a peace with the great nation of the Creeks, although he was not at all certain that it would last. He felt this doubt because he knew that the French and the Spanish were giving the Indians as many gifts as he could give, and it was almost a case of which nation could pay the biggest price.

When Sir Alexander Cuming took the seven Cherokees to London, they stirred up an interest in Carolina which was very helpful. People to whom Carolina was only a name, saw these Indian braves in their paint and feathers, or read about them and their strange doings, and became interested in the far-away province where they lived. Governor Johnson is credited by some with having originated the whole idea as an excellent peace move toward the Indians and a better advertisement for Carolina. A treaty was made with these Indians, the like of which had not been known in England in many a day. It was something like a good Wild West show, with the finest, most colorful pomp and ceremony of England. It pleased the Indians, entertained the English, and made Carolina the most talked-of province in America.

Governor Johnson wrote to England that "nothing is needed in Carolina so much as white inhabitants," but, not content with writing, he decided to do something to bring in settlers. First, he arranged to have independent military companies stationed at the frontiers so that the people living in the outlying districts could feel free to continue their work. It is never a pleasant sensation to be afraid that if you leave your house you might find your wife and children dead or kidnaped when you return. Governor Johnson had had some experience of this himself, when his mother and her children had been seized by the French, and he planned to protect his people from the fear of invasion of the French, Spanish, or Indians.

In order to populate the country, he invited into Carolina a group of Swiss immigrants under the leadership of Pierre Purry. Under his encouragement these Swiss people established Purrysburg, on the lower part of the Savannah River. This little town enjoyed some prosperity for a while, but it was finally abandoned. Johnson did not give up the idea of getting groups of foreigners to settle Carolina; throughout his term of office he helped to bring thrifty, intelligent, hardworking foreigners into the province.

Governor Johnson could hardly have picked more difficult times in which to earn his title of "the Good Governor Johnson." He was so popular, under both the proprietary and the royal rule, that even those who did not agree with him politically spoke of him with affection; and he almost did what had never been done before—he almost succeeded in getting the salary of the Governor fixed by law, as the King wished. The nearest that the Assembly ever came to doing this was in 1731. Then the Commons failed by only one vote of settling the Governor's salary, as the popular Robert Johnson had asked them to do. It was for him that the Commons wanted to settle this question. They were very much pleased with him and gave him annually £3,500, currency, which was £500 more than they had given Governor Nicholson.

Coat-of-arms of the Johnson family, showing pistol, which is rare on coats-of-arms of this period.

Governor Johnson's father, Sir Nathaniel Johnson, had successfully experimented with the growing of silk on his plantation, "Silk Hope." Sir Nathaniel had planted many mulberry trees. His son's home plantation, "New Keblesworth," was next to the plantation of "Silk Hope," and the two plantations made a large tract of land owned by the Johnsons. The Governor's will shows that he was a man of great wealth. His wife, Margaret (probably Bonner) had died of fever in Charles Town. His estate was left to the three sons and two daughters who survived him. His eldest son, Robert, received the larger part of the property. The other two boys, Nathaniel and Thomas, shared most of the rest of the estate. The daughters had to be satisfied with an annual income, a few personal slaves, and a sum of money which should be paid to them when they became twenty-one or upon the day of their marriage, whichever should happen first.

Do you know what a mourning ring is? Have you ever seen one? Probably not, unless your great-great-grandmother pulled it out of her treasures in the old jewel box. The mourning ring was very popular during the seventeenth and eighteenth centuries. A beloved friend or relative wore such a ring, in which were engraved the initials of the dead person. The ring was usually of some black material. It might range from a very simple black stone to a very expensive black pearl and was a sign to the world at large that the wearer was grieving for the dead person whose initials were engraved inside. Rich people often left items in their wills providing for the purchase of these mourning rings. Governor Johnson's will provided that one pound of British money should go to each of his British trustees, or men who managed his affairs, and ten pounds of provincial money to each of his American trustees, so that they could buy mourning rings to wear in his memory.

Governor Johnson's daughter, Margaret, married Henry Izard, "Eldest son and heir apparent of Ralph Izard." To them was born a son, Ralph Izard, later to become famous as an American leader of the Revolutionary War.

If he had been asked, it is probable that Governor Johnson would have wished to die just when and as he did, for his death took place in his beloved Charles Town while he was still serving as governor of the province of South Carolina.

A page from the *Gentleman's Magazine* for June, 1753, showing St. Philip's Church, Charleston, grouped on same page with a poem by Dr. Watts, a rare beetle, and a lady with a fashionable headdress. This page is typical of the custom of using unrelated pictures in one engraving.

The South-Carolina Gazette [1] of May 3–10, 1735, gives an account of his passing. "Between 12 and 1 o'clock, May 3, died after a long and lingering illness, his Excellency Governor Robert Johnson . . . in the fifty-ninth year of his age and the fifth of his governorship." The whole community grieved at his passing and his funeral reflected not only the honor due to a governor but the love of a people, "who looked upon him as their common father." His coffin was carried to a vault near the altar in St. Philip's church, Charles Town, by the gentlemen of the Council.

Johnson had asked to be buried in St. Philip's church "as near my beloved wife, as possible." Here the Assembly erected a monument in his memory, a cold stone which tried to tell something of the gratitude of the people of Carolina for the far-sighted vision, the unselfish devotion, and the devoted service of their "Good Governor"—Robert Johnson.

[1] *The South-Carolina Gazette* is the important newspaper which first appeared in Charles Town in 1732 and continued to appear until 1800.

Mourning rings typical of the period of Governor Johnson. The first is an elaborate ring by which George Washington was honored. The second is a smaller type generally worn by women.

James Glen
1701–1777

"MARY, MARY, where are you? I've something to tell you!" James Glen called out as he rushed into his home in Linlithgow, Scotland.

"Why, Jamie, what on earth is the matter with you? I don't think I've ever seen you quite so excited."

"Madam, I would have you know that you are gazing upon the newly appointed Governor of South Carolina. Madam Governor, I greet you in the name of the royal province in which you shall soon be the first lady!"

"Oh, Jamie, I'm so glad, but I knew you'd do it. How did it happen? Was it because Duncan Forbes, the Lord Advocate, spoke in your behalf?"

"Perhaps it was, but I'm just too good a man for them to overlook! After all, the government is interested in any man who can collect taxes from those fighting liquor-dealers. I took an awful chance when I was sheriff and called out the

---

Governor James Glen.

From a miniature by an unknown artist.

militia against them. Do you know, Mary, I think that's the thing that made the impression."

"It'll be a great help to you, won't it, being a lawyer? And I understand that quite a few of those provincials have been to Leyden University, where you were graduated. That'll be a bond in common."

This conversation might have taken place between James Glen and his wife in the year 1738, for it was then that he received his appointment as the thirtieth governor of South Carolina.

Five long years passed before Glen was to take up his duties as governor of South Carolina. They were crammed full of study, plans, and constant visits to the colonial offices. He, James Glen, the Scotch governor of South Carolina, was going to make a model province of this land across the sea. Though he'd never seen it, it was already close to his heart. With all his planning and studying, the time went slowly, for Glen was an impatient man and he was eager to assume the dignity of his new office.

At last the great day arrived. The warship *Tartar* was put at his disposal by the government. On December 19, 1743, *The South-Carolina Gazette* gave the entire center of the front page to the announcement of the arrival of Governor Glen. The new governor liked pomp and ceremony, and the province was certainly going to see that he got it. Cannon boomed, and two lines of soldiers, dressed in their finest uniforms, made a brilliant aisle for His Excellency. Every man was at salute as the new official walked between them to "Mr. Shepheard's tavern," where his commission was read amidst shouts of joy. Everyone enjoyed a holiday and an entertainment fit for the occasion. Glen thoroughly appreciated all the excitement, for he knew that after the terrible fire which had swept through Charles Town not long before, it took a lot of enthusiasm and courage for the people to receive him with such delight. They needed all the business success which he could bring to them.

The people, too, were expecting great things from their new governor. If he had any ideas on making friends of the Indians and on enlarging Indian trade, they were only too eager to hear all about them. And hadn't someone said that the Governor was planning to invite Protestants from Europe to settle in South Carolina? He had the right idea—to offer them freedom to worship as they pleased, and a chance to make a good living. South Carolina would be the gainer. Of course it was silly to suppose that the speech he had made would ever come true. Why, he had actually said that in a few years there would be many thousand white people in the province! Frankly, that was too many people for Charles Town to take care of! But you couldn't stop Governor Glen. No, sir! He announced that he was going to make the back-country (or up-country, as it is sometimes called) safe for white people. Men in Charles Town had actually heard him say that he was going to arrange matters so that the back-country would not be attacked by Indians, even if he personally had to carry gifts and make friends with every Indian chief and warrior in the province.

Just as soon as the excitement of his arrival had worn off, Governor Glen studied the affairs of the province and saw how it was being run. He did not think that the governors who had held office just before him had been strict enough in carrying out the King's wishes. In fact, he wrote to the British Ministry that the actions of these gentlemen had been so lax that they had "unhinged the whole structure of government."

It wasn't long before Governor Glen found himself in the very middle of a quarrel between the two important groups of the Assembly, the Commons House and His Majesty's Council. Both groups wanted to make sure that no

Fire insurance plate attached to the outside of insured houses in Charleston. Fire-fighting companies, which were partly maintained by insurance companies, had orders to save first those houses which had such plates attached. These plates were in use in the time of Governor Glen, who was particularly interested in fire prevention.

power should be taken away from them, and each group urged the governor to settle their dispute. Thus the poor man found himself in the very unpleasant position of the innocent bystander who never meant to get mixed up in a family squabble.

One of the first things that Governor Glen did was to try

to stop the terrible fires that frequently broke out in Charles Town. To do this, he went to the fires himself, and one time, when the fire company was not doing as well as he thought it should, he joined the "bucket brigade" himself and helped to pass buckets of water to keep the flames from spreading.

Maybe the leaders of Charles Town didn't always agree with him, but they realized that this rather stubborn Scotsman, who was their governor, didn't just sit and wait for things to happen. He went out and made them happen. For years there had been a movement for better fortifications at Charles Town; but fires, hurricanes, and the constant threat of the French, who had a greedy eye on Carolina, made it hard for the English to take the time to do anything about it. When Glen arrived, he decided that something should be done right away to improve the fortifications. He was so determined about this that twice he paid from his own purse to bring John William Gerard de Brahm to Charles Town. De Brahm was an excellent engineer who had worked out complete plans for the proper protection of Charles Town. These plans he presented to the Assembly, who would have none of them. For, said they, "It'll cost a lot of money to do the things Mr. de Brahm suggests, and where is the money to come from? Besides, we don't need all these fortifications. There's no man-made fort in the world that could possibly be as good a protection as the Charles Town bar, which was put there by nature."

But they decided that even nature needed a little help when, in 1755, it seemed that the French were going to attack Charles Town. De Brahm was recalled, his plans were accepted, and Governor Glen had his way. Charles Town was properly fortified.

We mustn't forget that all this time a three-cornered

game was being played. The French, the English, and the Spanish were bidding against one another for the friendship of the Indians. Sometimes if one white nation couldn't win the friendly coöperation of the Indians, it stirred them up against the other white nations. Each governor had to be cleverer than his neighbors in holding the friendship of the red men. Frequently that was the final test of the success or failure of a provincial governor.

In this respect Governor Glen was clever indeed. He went direct to the Indian chiefs. After all, what better way could be used to impress the red men with the power, the wealth, and the friendliness of the great English King than to have his own representative, the governor of Carolina, come in person to visit the camp of the red men?

Governor Glen realized that no mere traders' journeys would make the right impression on the Indians. So in 1746 he set out, accompanied by "four companies in the public pay and about two hundred gentlemen of their own charge, with their servants." It cost a lot of money—impressing your neighbors usually does! But Governor Glen did not begrudge the £200 (about $1,000) that he himself spent to arrange the meeting with a hundred Catawba Indians at the Congarees. The Indian emperor and his sixty head men were properly impressed by all this show, and they were greatly pleased that such a body of white men should come so far to seek their friendship.

Governor Glen liked to have his office given the dignity which that high position called for. In fact, sometimes he was inclined to be a bit too pompous. But he could be very human, too, when it paid; and in his dealings with the Indians he cleverly combined the dignity of the governor of the royal province of South Carolina, personal representative of

the King of England, with the friendship and human qualities of James Glen, the friend of the Indians.

We who live in Edgefield, Abbeville, Laurens, Newberry,
Union, Spartanburg, York, Chester, Fairfield, and Richland counties owe a particular debt of gratitude to Governor Glen. He purchased from the Cherokee Indians thousands of acres of their lands "south and east of Long Canes
creek." The Indians were not used to having their land paid
for. Usually it was taken by force. Therefore they appreciated greatly the attitude of Governor Glen. In fact, as
early as 1745 Glen had been going deeper and deeper into
the back-country, extending friendship to the Indians and
making it easier for the white and the red men to live together in peace. The Indians needed forts to protect them
from unfriendly whites as well as from enemy tribes. Glen
promised that he would have the colonial government provide these forts, and though he was not able to fulfill all of
his promises, it was not because he did not try.

In 1753 it was a great joy to Glen to start out from
Charles Town to keep a promise to the Indians. When he
arrived in the mountains he explained to the Indians that he
would have to await an order from the King to build the
fort they wanted beyond the first mountain ranges, among
the "Overhills," but he could buy land for a fort "among
the lower towns" immediately.

Glen relates, "As I refused to accept the land as a gift,
they crossed the river to Keowee for a great consultation,
and then came back, sold me the land, and went around it
with me. I paid them in goods of a cost in Charles Town of
near £100 sterling. The tract contains many thousand acres
of rich soil. I told the head man who rode round it with me
that we had a custom of giving a handful of earth on selling

land. He dismounted, gave me the earth, and being on the bank of the river, he gave me some water in his hat, adding that I was now master of better water there than in Charles Town. He told me that the trees and everything else were mine, but that he must recommend me to care for the graves of some of their head men who were buried on the top of the hills, and carrying me up to them, he showed me several great heaps of stones under which he said they lay. I accordingly promised that they should never be violated and gave orders that they should be railed in."

In the same year Fort Prince George was built on the land Glen had purchased. Later Fort Loudoun was built, carrying out Glen's promise of a fort over the mountains in the "Overhills." It was located on the Little Tennessee River in what is now the state of Tennessee. Both these forts were built at the request of the Cherokee Indians to protect them from the Choctaws, who were friends of the French, and from the French traders to the south of them who wanted to break up the Cherokee trade with the settlers in South Carolina.

It is small wonder that Glen wrote with pride that the Indians called him "Father instead of Brother." When a hundred Creek Indians were in London to be received by the King, they were further honored by having Governor Glen make a speech to Malachi, the Indian King.

Perhaps it sounds as if everything went as Governor Glen wished. Unfortunately for him, this was not true. He was too fond of show and a bit too proud of his position as governor of the rich province of South Carolina.

Perhaps the members of the Council might say, with truth, that Governor Glen couldn't or wouldn't take a hint. One time, feeling that the governor's presence interfered with their rights to make the laws, the Council went into the attic to get rid of His Excellency, while they were engaged in law-making. Glen felt that he had a right to attend the sessions of the Council at all times, and so he sat and sat, but the Council did not come back until it had finished its business of law-making.

If the Assembly and Council thought they could disturb Governor Glen's good nature or make him fly into a temper, they were greatly disappointed. Throughout all the squabbles he stayed good-humored, and the government of the province really improved because of the differences of opinion between the governor and the Assembly and Council. Things which had been taken more or less for granted were definitely settled, until each branch of the government knew exactly what it was expected to do.

Some people might say that Governor Glen was the kind of man who catches a minnow and calls it a whale. He did like to boast about what he had done and how clever he had been in helping the province out of its troubles. In this, he was almost like a child. But that can easily be overlooked when we think of his excellent record during his governorship, which lasted about thirteen years.

That the Commons appreciated Governor Glen's service and didn't mind his boasting is shown by their action when the news arrived in 1754 that a new governor was to be appointed. They went on record as appreciating his mild manner of governing the province and his friendly spirit toward all people. They were particularly grateful for his service in the matter of the Indians and for his long, hard work in building up the back-country. He had shown that he understood and was sympathetic towards the difficulties which the pioneers faced. He had planned and worked that their

Bishop Roberts' plan of Charles Town in

lives should be easier and their homes protected, and their rights guarded in every way. Feeling that any man who lived in South Carolina needed his care and protection, he frequently traveled around the province. These trips took him further into the back-country than any colonial governor had gone before.

Glen realized that the people needed forts; but he knew that they also needed court-houses, so that justice could be done. He himself chose the sites for these important buildings, though many of them were not built until after his day.

Governor Glen discovered that it cost a lot of money to uphold the dignity and the honor of such an office as that which he enjoyed. He wrote to the Lords of Trade that his fees had never exceeded £300 a year, although before he

1739, dedicated to Governor Glen

left England he had expected to get at least £1,000. Perhaps some of the men who had dreams of making great fortunes by the dishonest selling of arms to the province knew of his financial difficulty and hoped that, if they offered him money, he would shut his eyes to what was going on. In fact, he might even work with them and issue paper money, which would be dishonest but extremely profitable to him. If they had any such thoughts, they must have been unpleasantly shocked when he refused with scorn to have anything to do with such men. Instead, when he left the province he was a comparatively poor man.

We know that the Glens lived in at least two homes in Carolina. While Charles Pinckney's family were living in England, they leased their beautiful home in Charles Town

Eighteenth-century Chippendale chair, quasi-throne of the colonial governors of South Carolina. The left arm has been restored. Originally the chair had a canopy, with almost certainly the royal arms of Great Britain on it.

to Governor and Mrs. Glen, who occupied it for some years. This is why we call it "the Governor's Mansion." Governor Glen's plantation, "Belvedere," had a history which it would be hard to match throughout the state. It was the home of three of Carolina's colonial governors, Craven, Johnson, and Glen. Governor and Mrs. Glen entertained very largely and very beautifully. Their parties were described in the diaries of the ladies and gentlemen of that day.

Mrs. Ann Manigault was one of those ladies who kept a diary and in it she put many things that happened in her life. This is very fortunate for us, because by reading her diary we can learn much of the social life of South Carolina in the early days. On April 28, 1761, Mrs. Manigault wrote, "Mr. & Mrs. Glen to take leave. I dined with them at Gordon's." Perhaps the Glens had to do as much official entertaining as they did unofficial. At any rate, *The South-Carolina Gazette* of Thursday, November 13, 1755, gave a glowing account of the supper and ball which the Glens gave at "Mr. Poinsett's," to celebrate George II's seventy-third birthday, which was "observed with the usual demonstrations of joy."

Although Governor Glen was a leader in society, he probably felt that the living conditions in Charles Town were a bit too fine for that day. He wrote that the quantity of luxuries and fine things was too great and the quality far too fine for any infant colony. He must have realized the interest of the Carolinians in art, literature, architecture, and beautiful things in general. His own secretary was a Scotch artist named Alexander Gordon. Some day perhaps you will recognize in "Sandy Gordon" of Scott's *Antiquary* the man who so easily fitted into Charles Town society as

Alexander Gordon, secretary to His Excellency, Governor James Glen.

Even if Glen had not been such an interesting and excellent governor of South Carolina, we would still be interested in him as the author of an excellent book, *A Description of South Carolina, Containing Many Curious and Interesting Particulars Relating to the Civil, Natural, and Commercial History of that Colony*. Glen felt that the people of Great Britain did not know enough about this colony of theirs, and in his book he tried to give them a fair and just picture of the province, which he considered the most promising in all America. It is a curious little book, for the governor spared no details. He told his fellow countrymen all about the settlers, the boundaries, the soil, and the crops and how they grew. The climate came in for a very large share of his attention, and he recorded readings of wind, temperature, and tides for the years 1737 to 1740. He put in some interesting tables which had been prepared by a man whom the governor called "a very curious gentleman," Dr. Lining.

Did you know that oranges had ever been an important export of South Carolina? Governor Glen says they were. With indigo, corn, barley, and rice, they balanced the imports from Great Britain; but unfortunately "the principal purpose of fine peaches was to feed the hogs." He thought that in a few years there would be at least thirty thousand white people in the province. He believed this because there was so much uninhabited territory, a great many wide and glorious rivers, a fertile soil, healthful climate, liberty of conscience, equal laws, easy taxes, and (here he couldn't resist paying himself a compliment) a mild administration of the government. The governor was very anxious to have his dream for South Carolina come true, and so he made a particular point of having the book distributed among the Protestants of Germany, who were badly in need of a new homeland.

Governor Glen did not feel that his job was completed when he turned over his office to Governor Lyttelton, who arrived on June 1, 1756, but he had reason to be pleased with what he had accomplished, for his term of office was, on the whole, successful. He had done much toward settling the Indian problem and had opened up the back-country for white settlers. Perhaps his greatest value lay in his ability to make the officials in England see with the eye of America. He presented to them a fine picture of the life of Carolina and made them appreciate what a glorious future it could have if they handled affairs properly.

Governor and Mrs. Glen had had a happy life in their official service to South Carolina. Probably they were eager to remain here, for they did not leave the province until June 21, 1761, which was actually five years after Governor Lyttelton had taken over Glen's office. Perhaps Glen did a little trading among the Indians during those five years, for sometimes he is mentioned as having been an Indian trader. He could not have gained this reputation earlier for he did no trading during his term as governor. He felt, and surely it must have been true, that being governor of the province of South Carolina was a full-time job and demanded all the energies a man had.

When he left Carolina, Governor Glen returned to Scotland, where he made his home until his death on July 18, 1777.

Inside the State House in Columbia there is a most unusual monument, which well expresses the affection of the people of Carolina for their Scots governor. It is Governor Glen's coffin plate attached to a tablet on the wall—a sign that his prayer, which he wrote in 1748 to the Duke of Bedford, came true: "For I shall reckon it my greatest happiness to be able to say with truth of Charles Town and this province, that I found them in Ashes, Defenseless, Declining. I leave them Fair, Fortified, and Flourishing." Governor and Mrs. Glen were not fortunate enough to leave children, but their kinsmen throughout South Carolina have done their share toward keeping this state "Fair, Fortified, and Flourishing."

William Bull, II
1710–1791

"IT'S A shame, that's what it is. Five times they've let
William Bull serve as governor of the province, and yet
they've never given him the official title but call him 'lieutenant-governor.' "

"Yes, just because he's an American by birth, I suppose
they think he doesn't deserve the full honor of being governor of South Carolina. I don't see why we stand it."

"Well, it's true that Lord William Campbell, our new
governor, is handsome and gallant, but I see no reason why
we had to have an Englishman sent here again. Oh, after all,
he did marry Sarah Izard of South Carolina, and that makes
him a little closer to us."

The usual excitement at the time of the arrival of a new
governor was strangely lacking as the people of Charles
Town expressed their annoyance that their beloved William Bull was again being replaced by an Englishman as
governor. When Lord William Campbell arrived in Charles
Town, June 18, 1775, it was not exactly a joyous occasion
for anyone, except, perhaps, Sir William.

Since 1760 the royal government had been making William Bull lieutenant-governor and acting governor of South

Sketch by Charles Fraser showing Ashley Hall, the country home of William Bull. The house was destroyed by fire a few years after this sketch was made.

Carolina. Five times he had served and each time with such patience, understanding, and ability that everyone thought he would be rewarded by being made governor in his own right.

William Bull was truly a son of Carolina. He had been born on his father's plantation, Ashley Hall, near Charles Town, September 24, 1710, the second of the five children of William and Mary Quintyne Bull. He had a splendid family history to live up to. His grandfather, Stephen Bull, had come to Carolina in 1670 from Warwickshire, England, and had been of such service in the first years of provincial life that he was ranked as one of the three most important men in Carolina. William Bull's father had twice served as lieutenant-governor of the province and had been highly successful in that office.

We do not know a great deal about the early education of the young William Bull; but it has been recorded that he was good in his studies, which were conducted at home. Those early studies must have been very thorough, for on April 13, 1734, he entered Leyden University Medical School in Holland, and just four months later, on August 18 of the same year, he received his degree as a doctor of medicine. Even for a very bright South Carolinian that was something to be proud of. His graduation essay was on "lead colic," which he thought was to be found very generally in his own home province, probably because of the lead bottles in which the liquor drunk by the gentlemen of Carolina was stored.

William Bull, by his graduation from Leyden in 1734, became the first native-born American to receive a medical degree. Other Americans had been graduated in medicine, but they had not been born in this country.

Perhaps William Bull used his medical knowledge only among his friends and among those who lived on his plantations, for there is little record of his having had a general practice. He was, however, referred to as Dr. Bull, until the more imposing title of "Honorable" was given him when he became lieutenant-governor. He never was called "Your Excellency," however, because he never became a full-fledged governor.

Instead of practicing medicine, William Bull became a very busy planter and an even busier politician. These two occupations were natural to young Bull, for all his life he had been surrounded by people interested in agriculture, science, and politics. In fact, his father's house had been open to every well-known scientist who visited America. Here the great English naturalist, Mark Catesby, was en-

House in Charleston, in which William Bull lived. Piazzas at the left were added at a much later date.

tertained. All the important men in South Carolina gathered at the Bull home, and, as a boy, young William must have heard many discussions of politics.

After his return to South Carolina, William Bull did not have to wait long for his opportunity to take a part in public life. He was elected justice of the peace.

In 1736 he was sent to the Commons House of Assembly, which corresponded to our present House of Representatives. Here he served until 1749. In 1740 he was made speaker of the House, and in 1749 he was appointed to His Majesty's Council.

If you are curious enough to look up the laws of South Carolina for the period of 1740 to 1749, you will find the signatures of two William Bulls, father and son. Both had to sign an act to make it become the law in South Carolina. The elder William Bull was lieutenant-governor, and the younger was speaker of the Commons House.

Of course all young men of that day had an opportunity in military service. William Bull was not a fighter by profession, and he was always far more eager to make peace than to win wars, but he served as captain, colonel, and brigadier general in the colonial troops.

In his dealings with the Indians, Bull was highly successful. In 1752 he was asked to serve on an Indian commission which met at Albany, New York, to settle peace terms between the Catawbas of South Carolina and the Iroquois of New York. In this service he showed himself to be a level-headed friend of the Indians, and they appreciated his interest in them. This feeling toward the Indians was responsible for the advice which he gave to Governor Lyttelton as to the best way to handle the Cherokee Indians in South Carolina. If his advice had been followed, the South

Carolina-Cherokee war might never have happened. But Governor Lyttelton did not take Bull's advice; and, strangely enough, Bull himself finally had to carry the war through to an end. This he did with system and strength, not forgetting to be merciful in the white man's victory.

A governor had to report every move he made to the Lords of Trade in London. In his letters to these gentlemen, Bull wrote that he hoped the Cherokees would be punished for the wrongs they had done, so that they would understand that they could not commit crimes without punishment. On the other hand, he thought that it would be very unwise as well as cruel to kill them out, and he thought it would be almost as great a mistake to push them into the arms of the French, who were only too eager to use them as allies against the British.

The Lords of Trade might have found it a bit hard to understand some of Bull's military plans. On one occasion he wrote that he was going to win the war with bits of ribbon and pots of paint. He realized that the Indian women, like all other women the world over, liked to dress up, and that they were particularly fond of ribbons and paint. So he engaged two men to carry each a package of ribbons and paint, which they would exchange for corn, hogs, and fowl. The Indian women would use the bright-colored ribbons, and the food would save from starvation the troops quartered at Fort Loudoun. The Governor figured that a man might live for a month on the food that could be bought from a squaw for a yard of ribbon. On June 17, 1760, he reported that Captain Demeré in Fort Loudoun had already bought fourteen days' provisions for his men in exchange for the ribbons.

With the help of the colonial and British troops, peace

was finally made between the English and the Cherokees. The head of the Cherokee nation, Attakullakulla, came to Ashley Hall, Bull's plantation, to sign the peace which was to make the Cherokees and the English of South Carolina friends. While there, the Indian chief learned some ideas of fine table manners. Later, when he was entertaining white travelers, he served every piece of food on a separate clean piece of bark, which was then thrown away. His guests

Small frame building at Ashley Hall in which the treaty with Attakullakulla was signed by Governor Bull. This little building is still standing.

From Walker's Romance of Lower South Carolina

were so interested in this way of serving that they finally asked why he did it, and he told them that he was following the pattern set by his great friend, Governor Bull. He had noticed at Ashley Hall that each item of the menu had been passed on a separate clean platter. Knowing that Governor Bull would do only the things which were highly proper and admirable, he, Attakullakulla, had decreed that all of his company dinners should be served on platters of bark.

William Bull was a strong believer in education. He realized that if South Carolina was to be successful, it must work out some plans for the education of its people. He personally gave to the College of Philadelphia, which has since become the University of Pennsylvania, a gift of about $500. This was done in the hope that a good college could be developed in America so that young men students of this country need not go abroad for their education. On January 30, 1770, Governor Bull presented to the Assembly a remarkably fine plan for free schools and a college supported by South Carolina. His ideas of education, expressed nearly two hundred years ago, still hold true. He said: "I must further observe that grammar schools alone are not sufficient as they lay only the Foundation of the education of those who are to be employed in the learned professions. . . . It must be acknowledged to be a work of time and expense to build, endow such a seminary [college], but the benefits which the province will thereby receive will overbalance all considerations of that nature." The Assembly voted in favor of Bull's plan, but so many exciting things were happening in the province that nothing was done with it for a long time.

Governor Bull was concerned not only with education, but also with the welfare of the settlers in the back-country. He pushed plans to give them forts, jails, and court-houses, and begged that good lawyers be sent from England to act as judges, so that the rights of the people might be taken care of and every man, whether he lived in or out of Charles Town, should receive equal justice.

Bull was interested in so many things and did so much for the province that we cannot tell it all here. He had the very modern idea that libraries play an important part in education, and for many years he was president of the Charles Town Library Society.

His interest in science led him to help in starting the present Charleston Museum, which is the oldest in America. At a meeting of the Library Society, he moved that a com-

A certificate of membership in the Charles Town Library Society, signed by William Bull as president. It is issued to Charles Cotesworth Pinckney and is dated October 4, 1796.

mittee be appointed "for collecting materials for promoting the natural history of the province." This collection later became the basis of the Charleston Museum.

On March 1, 1765, Bull reported that he had recommended to the General Assembly a continuance "of the post [mail] through this province—as at all rivers in this province where roads pass there are bridges or ferries where houses are already."

It may surprise us that South Carolina had a mail service at such an early date, but, even earlier than this, on February 17, 1692, permission had been granted to one Thomas Neale to establish post office deliveries in North America. Bull approved of the outlined plan of His Majesty's deputy postmaster general (who in 1765 was Benjamin Franklin), and, in order to help in the matter, he enclosed a map of the roads in South Carolina. He saw all sides of the question, as is indicated when he asked: "What about ship posts . . . at Charles Town—within the last twelve months have arrived 360 sail from different countries. At Beaufort, 40, Georgetown, 21." Even today the carrying of mail by ship is a very important part of our postal service.

In the period when Bull served five times as governor of South Carolina, about sixteen years passed. Eight of these years he spent in first-hand running of the affairs of the province. The last four of his term of office came during the very trying period between 1764 and 1775, the years leading up to the American Revolution and the break with England.

Any governor would have found the successful administration of his office then almost impossible. Certainly it tried William Bull to the limit. He had been born and reared in America, and he was a loyal American. On the other hand, he was a British subject and had sworn to support the King who had appointed him to office. His nephews and his brothers-in-law were among the hottest of the American rebels, and a very strong tie of family affection bound him to these relatives. Many arguments were given to show him that his selfish interests might be better served if he would throw in his lot with the patriots who were bringing on the American Revolution. But there was a loyalty even higher

According to an old print, this is what brought on the Revolutionary War.

in the heart of William Bull. The King had appointed him, and he had sworn to remain true to the King.

Once his dearly beloved nephew, William Henry Drayton, had, in his enthusiasm as a rebel, made speeches which could not be overlooked by the King's government. It became William Bull's very unpleasant duty to suspend his nephew from the King's Council. The governor himself had no sons, and this young nephew was as dear to him as his own child; but duty came first, and William Henry Drayton was suspended by the acting governor, William Bull.

Bull tried in every way possible to stop the rising anger against England, but this could not be done when England insisted on taxing the American colonies against their will. There was great commotion in Charles Town when the news arrived that the hated tax stamps were coming from England. Bull did not want any clash, and so he quietly stored the stamps in Fort Johnson. That he did not succeed in keeping the people calm, we shall read in the lives of Henry Laurens and William Henry Drayton, but he certainly tried to avoid trouble.[1]

[1] See note on the Stamp Act, p. 72.

Types of Stamp Act stamps which Governor Bull stored in Fort Johnson. The shilling stamps were for general use. The penny stamps were for pamphlets and newspapers. The small stamp showing the crown was pasted on the back of the paper on which the two shilling six pence stamp was stuck.

He had better success in the matter of the tea. *The South-Carolina Gazette* of May 30, 1771, reported that the inhabitants of Carolina, assembled under the Liberty Tree on Thursday, December 13, had agreed that "tea was not to be imported into this province as long as the duty [tax] on it continued." Governor Bull tried to avoid trouble by having the tea seized and stored. However, there was really nothing he could do to stop the people. They had seen a vision of liberty. The word "independence" rang in their ears. The summer of 1774 saw South Carolina hurrying toward her part in the Revolutionary War.

This matter of being an acting governor, torn between love for your native country and loyalty for your King, was no easy matter for William Bull. The King was not too pleased with the way things were going in South Carolina and vigorously expressed his anger that the Commons House of Assembly had given money "for the hated Society for the Support of the Bill of Rights," which, as everyone knew, was trying to take his power away. Every day found a new trouble for the beloved William Bull to handle. He really was greatly beloved, and perhaps if he had been governor of South Carolina, instead of acting governor, the people might have remained loyal to the King, instead of being among the first to press for freedom and independence from Great Britain.

The Bull family was a distinguished one, and we find it throughout the history of South Carolina. Perhaps you don't always associate the name of Bull with that of the beautiful old Sheldon Church, but here a great many of the Bull family worshiped and are buried. Seldom fewer than sixty or seventy carriages were seen at Sheldon Church on Sunday evening. Stephen Bull, the brother of Governor

Miniature reproduction of the drawing room in Captain Stuart's home where, in May, 1775, the meeting took place in which Governor Bull discussed Indian affairs as they applied to the quarrel between the colonies and Great Britain. In the room are Governor Bull (seated),

William Bull II, lived at near-by Sheldon Plantation, and it was his custom to invite as his guests on Sunday the more important part of the congregation, while the more humble were sent to the home of his overseer and entertained there at the expense of Stephen Bull. One or two hundred guests each Sunday was stretching the noted Southern hospitality to the limit.

Upon the death of his father, William Bull II inherited the lovely plantation, Ashley Hall, where he had been born. Today that plantation is known as Kennerty Farms.

Bull had been an important person in the colony from his very earliest days. He had ability, wealth, and social position, and he used all of them to the best interests of South

Oucconastotah, a powerful Cherokee chief, Alexander Cameron dressed in his Scottish clan costume, and Captain John Stuart, agent and superintendent of his Majesty's Indian affairs for the Southern district.

Carolina. Even after the beginning of the Revolution and after his decision to remain loyal to the King, Bull held the love, respect, and admiration of Carolinians. They would go far not to hurt him. On January 16, 1775, the public powder and arms were seized by the people of Charles Town. Everyone knew who was taking these supplies. In fact, it was done with the approval of the Revolutionary leaders in the dark of night so that it would not cause any unnecessary distress to William Bull. That gentleman informed the Assembly of "the very extraordinary and alarming disappearance of about 800 guns, 200 cutlasses, and 1,600 pounds of powder and minor stores." The Commons solemnly informed him that their diligent inquiry had failed to bring forth a single person who knew what had happened to them. To their credit, the witnesses did not even smile while they were saying it. They did, however, give a little extra jab, intended for the Lords of Trade, by reporting to the acting governor that there was every reason to suppose that some of the inhabitants of the colony might have taken so remarkable a step because of the very alarming accounts of the doings of the government in Great Britain.

It must have been a real relief to Bull when Lord William Campbell came to take over his office. No longer need he be officially torn between two loyalties which meant so much to him.

During the Revolutionary War, Bull was ill, but he did not spare himself on that account. When Isaac Hayne had been sentenced to death, Bull, who knew that such a sentence was unjust, unfair, and cruel, had himself carried on a litter to Lord Rawdon. He actually begged that the life of the American patriot should be saved, but his pleas were not heeded.

At the end of the war the estates of the men who had been loyal to Britain became the property of South Carolina. Bull's property was among those taken by the state. In 1782 Governor and Mrs. Bull had gone to England to live. From there he requested that he be allowed to lay his old bones down in the land of his birth. His age and illness made a return to Carolina impossible, but he, along with many other loyalists, was excused from all penalties and was allowed to send his slaves back to take care of his lands. In his will we have further evidence that, in spite of the fortunes of war and his sense of duty to his King, William Bull's devotion to the land of his birth was unbroken.

The last nine years of Bull's life were spent in London. His death occurred on July 4, 1791, and he was buried in the Graveyard of St. Andrew's, Holborn, England. In 1792 his widow erected a monument to his memory at the place of his birth, Ashley Hall. On one side is a raised carved portrait of this great South Carolinian, the man who under incredible difficulties five times served his province as acting governor. He was a wise man, just and intelligent. He could see all sides of a question, and he did not go to extremes. Everyone knew that he was completely fair, and everyone loved and respected him for his efforts toward peace. He did much to avoid bloodshed during the ten years when excitement in Carolina was running high and people's feelings were trigger quick. A great man, of a great family, he gave to his province the best in him. He was "noble by birth, yet nobler by great deeds."

Henry Laurens
1 7 2 4 – 1 7 9 2

WHEN, ON October 6, 1780, Henry Laurens was thrown into the Tower of London, he must have thought with sympathy of all those men and women who had been there before him. Surely his mind turned to brave, gallant Sir Walter Raleigh, whose life had been taken in the Tower by James I. Here poor Lady Jane Grey had shrunk from the sight of her husband's headless body, while from the corner of her eye she could catch sight of the executioner with his ax and knew that her head would be the next. Oh, there were sad ghosts who came to Henry Laurens in his dreams, asking if he, too, was going to lose his life here and join their tragic company. In the excitement of the Revolutionary War in America, Henry Laurens did not know what his fate would be. He could not look into the future and tell that he was not to join this historic crowd in death.

Henry Laurens.

From a portrait painted while he was in the Tower of London.

Henry Laurens was the son of a French Huguenot who had fled from France, by way of England, Ireland, and New York, to Charles Town, South Carolina. These French Huguenots, who had left their own country because they were not allowed to worship God in their own way, were a great help in building South Carolina. Many of its finest leaders came from them, but none was of more importance to South Carolina than the Laurens family. Henry Laurens was the eldest son, the third of the six children of Jean (John) Laurens and Hester Gresset. He was born in Charles Town on March 6, 1724.

Very little is known of Henry Laurens' childhood except that he was quiet, well-behaved, and eager to learn. His most intimate friend was his neighbor, Christopher Gadsden. When these two were boys, they formed a "League" in order to keep them out of trouble. They were good boys indeed, if they did all the things they promised:—to stand by each other in every good deed and to rescue each other from anything which might lead to wrong-doing; to leave a group when it was becoming rowdy and always to act together so that no one could consider them "different," or queer. The "Laurens-Gadsden League" had only two members. Unfortunately this close friendship did not always continue. As the two grew older, they took different views of political affairs and finally drifted far apart. But before their friendship ceased, many letters passed between the two young men. For years, it was the home-staying Henry Laurens, who gave news of his wife and children to the much-traveled Christopher Gadsden.

The Laurens family had little money with which to establish themselves in this country. John Laurens set himself up in Charles Town as a saddler, that is, a maker and

The Tower of London as it appeared when Henry Laurens was a prisoner there.

From a rare English print.

mender of saddles and harnesses. Henry Laurens felt great pride that his father was willing to build his fortunes by working at such a plain, respectable business, and he took a little slap at some of his other relatives who were too proud to work. He said, "My father was of different sentiment; he learned a trade." When Henry's father died, he left a great deal of money, most of which went to his eldest son, Henry.

In 1744 Henry Laurens made his first trip to England. Here he was trained to be a great merchant. Unlike most of the Carolinians who were educated in England at that time, he learned no Latin or Greek and never learned to speak French well. He did know enough of that language, however, to speak and write it, though he never felt that he did it well. Even though Laurens' education was mostly that of a business man, in later life he was considered well educated, because he read constantly and was always eager to learn from literature, history, art, and travel. The walls of his library were covered with books. It is said that you could see no wall at all, just books. His friends claimed that Laurens had read and thoroughly understood every one of them. Perhaps his greatest learning lay in his knowledge of the Bible, which he knew from Genesis to Revelation.

While Henry Laurens was in England, he learned not only from books, but also from his London experience. These taught him some very valuable lessons in how to meet men and women of all types. He became the friend of leading English merchants, and many a fine house in London was open to this young man from little Charles Town in Carolina.

Henry Laurens' home-coming was a sad one. Just four days before he left England, his beloved father died. Added to his grief were the cares of his father's estate, which were heavy. Even though he was only twenty-three years old, young Laurens knew his own mind, and he went straight toward the accomplishment of what had to be done. His friends were very much impressed with his sound business judgment, and they saw, too, the quality later to become so marked—he made the best of everything as it came along.

Henry Laurens thought that young men should not have to go to England in order to be educated. He therefore became very much interested in education in South Carolina. He himself had been sent to England, and later he was to take his children there for their education. But Henry Laurens was eager to have a good college in the province and insisted that it should be built on broad religious lines, which would give equal rights to all in their worship of God. It must have been a great joy to him to see both of his sons-in-law, David Ramsay and Charles Pinckney, among the first trustees of the college which arose as an answer to his dreams. In 1785, just seven years before Laurens' death, the College of Charleston was chartered.[1]

He lived just the sort of life you would expect from the descriptions of him. He was very active and sure of himself. He was willing to take the lead, and not much interested in being proved wrong. Religion played an important part in his life and may have helped to keep him happy and satisfied. In 1767 he wrote to a friend, "At home I am always cheerful and never sad, which speaks the general state of my mind." Henry Laurens had one very useful gift—he was able to make good plans, no matter how troubled the times were. He understood human nature; and, though he was a very strict person in business dealings and had no patience with anyone whom he could not trust, he was merciful when he did not think it was the man's own fault. Never in his whole life did he put a man in prison for debt, which was a common custom in that day. In fact, he seldom went to law to collect a debt.

If Laurens had been asked how he explained his great success as a merchant, he might have answered, "Because of my methods, my steady habits, and my hard work. Often before the sun rises I am out of my bed and before my family get up I have written a dozen letters, in fact have done enough work for a whole day."

Every great land-owner in Carolina had slaves in that day. Henry Laurens had a great many, and he was a kind, fatherly master to them. Once he persuaded one of his Negro slaves to be inoculated for smallpox, hoping that a prevention for this horrible disease could be found. The

---

[1] In 1783 Charles Town was incorporated as Charleston.—D. D. Wallace, *The History of South Carolina*, III, 522.

Negro died from the inoculation, but his master had promised him that every member of his family should go free, because he had been willing to take this terrible chance, and so he had felt that the risk of death was well worth while.

Henry Laurens' business career had a number of ups and downs, though usually ups. He did an enormous export business in rice, deer-skins, and indigo, and almost as large an import business in wine, slaves, and indentured servants (white men and women who, in return for being brought to America, agreed to work for a certain number of years, after which they would be free to do as they pleased). His boats touched at all the important ports of the world, with regular calls at London, Liverpool, and Bristol, and occasional calls at Glasgow, Rotterdam, Lisbon, Madrid, and the West Indies. On most of this business Laurens received a 5 per cent commission, but on the "Guinea," or slave, business the commission was exactly doubled. Later in his life Henry Laurens gave up dealing in slaves. His letters about this action are very interesting. He, his brother James, and his son John were among the first Americans to favor freeing the Negroes. All the important people of that day owned slaves. Where could they get them if a merchant did not import them? No one thought any the less of Laurens for this side of his business. Henry Laurens really gave up the buying and selling of slaves because he could not stand it to have human beings so cruelly treated. Instead of frankly saying this, he almost apologized for what he was doing, probably because he did not want others to feel that he was meddling in their business or criticizing his friends.

For a long time Henry Laurens had been buying land.

He wanted to be one of the big plantation owners in Carolina. Finally his land holdings were so great and the operating of his plantations took so much of his time that he retired from the commission business. His entire business life after 1764 was spent in the work of his plantations. It is said that if the Revolutionary War had not come just when it did, Henry Laurens would have received, from his Georgia plantations alone, a sum equal to about $75,000 a year. That means that he was a very rich man.

We are told that it was love at first sight between Eleanor Ball and Henry Laurens. On July 6, 1750, when she was nineteen years old and he was twenty-six, they were married. It would be pleasant to say that they were happy ever after, but unfortunately they had to endure a great deal of sorrow. Although twelve children were born to them, only four lived to grow up, and only three were living at the time of their father's death. Their beloved son John had given his life for his country in the Revolutionary War. It happened when the war was practically over, and John Laurens was killed in an unimportant local fight. This might easily have made Mr. and Mrs. Laurens bitter, but instead they became more sympathetic toward all people who were in trouble.

There was always a great devotion between Henry Laurens and his children. He spent much time with them and followed their education and their social activities with sympathy and interest. When we see some of the handwriting of a young man or young woman of today, we are amused to read Henry Laurens' lecture to his son John on the sin of poor handwriting, which he declared to be an act of great rudeness to the person who had to read the letter.

Elinor Ball Laurens, wife of Henry Laurens.

When Laurens wanted to urge a guest to have a meal at his home, just as would any modern husband he tempted his friend with stories of the splendid mince pies and the famous hams which Mrs. Laurens would be sure to serve him. Would you think it possible that as early as 1764 the Laurenses ate rattlesnake? Wouldn't this letter seem to say that they did? Laurens thanked his friend Andrew Williamson for certain food gifts, saying, "For which I return thanks as I do for the poor unfortunate rattlesnake whose body made an addition to my table today." Rattlesnake was often eaten in frontier days.

In the matter of relations between South Carolina and Great Britain in the days leading up to the American Revolution, Laurens might be said to be a "middle-of-the-road" man. He stood somewhere between the hot-headed men of Christopher Gadsden's type and the "do-nothings," who were perfectly satisfied to let things drift as long as they were not bothered. Laurens did not approve of the British idea of "taxation without representation," which led to the Stamp Act, but he believed that conditions should be changed by lawful means only.[2] Knowing his feelings, a group of hot-heads who were violently opposed to the Stamp Act, took it into their minds that the stamps might be hidden at Laurens' home. A mob of them came one night to his beautiful house, which stood in the center of a large, carefully laid out garden filled with fine trees and shrubs from every part of the world. They demanded that the stamps be turned over to them. Laurens said that he did not

[2] The Stamp Act was passed by the English Parliament in 1765 to raise money in the American colonies by forcing the colonists to buy the stamps and thus pay taxes. The colonists objected so vigorously that the Act was repealed in 1766. However, the Townshend Acts, taxing such things as glass, paper, and tea, were passed the following year.

Henry Laurens' Charles Town home. This is the house which Mrs. Laurens lighted up at the time of the repeal of the Stamp Act.

have the stamps and told them to leave. Perhaps they felt they had to show that they meant business, for they did a little half-hearted searching and then left. They were very careful not to walk on the flower beds and tried very hard to do no harm. With a "God bless you, Colonel, we hope the poor sick lady will do well," they marched away, leaving Mrs. Laurens frightened and ill, but doing little other harm.

Henry Laurens had such large shipping interests that he was much affected by England's attempts to tax the colonies, and when dishonest officials tried to cheat him by compelling him to pay illegal fees, he became very indignant and even twisted the nose of one of them, a certain Collector Moore, who later fled the country to escape punishment for his frauds.

Of course it's not nice to twist the nose of an enemy in public! It's not done, even when the man whose nose is twisted is dishonest. Even if Moore and his friends had written some outrageous pamphlets about Laurens, hadn't that gentleman written some pretty hot ones himself? But his act did bring to a head this quarrel about the rights of the people of Carolina to have fair play in their shipping business, and that is what Laurens had in mind.

Finally the colonists decided not to import anything from England, if they had to pay taxes on it, and they drew up a non-importation agreement. Although Henry Laurens was in favor of the signing of this non-importation agreement and put his name to this paper, which said that he would not buy from or ship to Great Britain, he believed that everybody had a right to his own opinion. He would not allow those who would not sign to be treated as if they were criminals. It was a thrilling speech that Henry Laurens made when he said, "I cheerfully subscribe to this association with my hand, and upon proper occasion I will be ready to seal it with my blood, but I will not declare good men my enemies. The spirit of persecution is hateful to me; it is impossible for me to cherish it." That might well be called the theme of Laurens' life. He was willing to allow other people the right to think and do as they thought right; yet he never gave an inch in his own belief.

If you had lived in pre-revolutionary days and did not believe in fighting duels, would you have refused to take part in a duel and thus be branded a coward, or would you stand and be shot at without returning the fire? Henry Laurens was very much opposed to the whole idea of duels, but several times he was challenged to fight. He accepted the challenges and would stand, facing the fire of the other man but never firing himself. He wrote that more than once he had been brave enough to stand and be shot at, but he was too great a coward to kill a man except when it was absolutely necessary.

In 1770 Henry Laurens suffered the great grief of having his wife die. After her death, he devoted himself entirely to his children, even giving up his business to have more time for them. He took his sons to England and then to Geneva, Switzerland, so that they might complete their education. While he was in England, from the years 1771 to 1774, Laurens made a special point of getting in touch with the leading merchants and the great statesmen of the day. He wanted to give them first-hand information about the grave mistakes they had made in handling the American colonies. He did not want a complete break with Great Britain. He felt that it was a real tragedy that the statesmen who were handling American affairs would not see that they were pushing the colonies further and further away from the mother country.

At last it became clear to Laurens that some sort of war was coming. When it came to a choice, Laurens' love and sympathy were all with America. In 1774 he returned to Charles Town to throw in his lot with the people of his native province. He could easily have remained in England, and the war would have touched him but little. The people saw that their interests meant more to him than his own selfish comfort, and they showed their appreciation, just four weeks after his arrival, by electing him to the first

Henry Laurens. From a portrait in the possession of Mr. Henry Rutledge Laurens, of Charleston. The ring on the little finger of the left hand has been handed down in the family ever since Henry Laurens wore it while in the Tower. The eldest son in each generation uses it as an engagement ring.

Provincial Congress. Very soon he was made president of the Provincial Congress, which had to run the affairs of South Carolina. In June, 1775, he became president of the powerful Council of Safety and a member of the committee which could do anything necessary to take care of the affairs of the province. Under the first constitution, written for the state in 1776, John Rutledge was elected president and Henry Laurens vice-president of the state of South Carolina.

In 1777 he stepped out on the broader stage of national politics. In that year he became a member of the Continental Congress, which met in Philadelphia. Immediately he was put on many of the important committees, and headed several of them. Without a single vote against him, he was elected to succeed John Hancock as the president of the Continental Congress. Laurens said that while he was in Congress he sometimes worked twenty hours a day and that even then he could not finish the heavy duties which were put on him. This was an important time in the life of the new nation, and Henry Laurens could well take credit for a part of its success.

Henry Laurens had a warm friendship for many of the important men of the day. Lafayette became his friend when the young Frenchman was fighting for America in this country. When Laurens was in prison in the Tower of London, both Lafayette and Madame Lafayette worked hard and long for his release. They even offered to pay a large sum of money to win his freedom. John Adams and Henry Lee were also dear friends of Laurens, but his greatest devotion went to George Washington. Laurens felt that no one could take Washington's place.

One of the ways in which the British tried to end the

war was to have Englishmen urge the American leaders to desert the American cause. Of course Henry Laurens, the president of the American Congress, was a very important man, and England tried hard to win him over to its side. One of his dearest friends, Richard Oswald of England, was sent to tempt him. It is needless to say that Laurens did not yield.

We must remember that Laurens had traveled a great deal and knew the Northern as well as the Southern colonies. Therefore he saw the needs of America not only with the eyes of a Carolinian, but with the eyes of an American. He was interested in the welfare of all the colonies. Feeling strongly that it was necessary to protect every part of America, he insisted that the fishing rights off the coast of Newfoundland must be safeguarded. It was a far cry from the waters of Newfoundland to the harbor of Charles Town, and many thought that it was too far for them to worry about. William Henry Drayton bitterly opposed Laurens in this matter. Their political differences became personal ones, and the two South Carolinians were not the best of friends. This unfortunate quarrel ended only when Drayton was dying. Laurens has written of the touching and beautiful renewal of friendship which took place at the deathbed of Drayton.

On December 9, 1778, Laurens resigned as president of the Continental Congress. He did not, however, leave that body until eleven months later. The American colonies were badly in need of funds, and in 1779 Laurens was sent to try to borrow ten million dollars from the Dutch and, if possible, to arrange a treaty of friendship with them. During the more than two years of his stay in Congress, Laurens had refused to receive any pay, for he felt that he could afford the expense better than could the struggling government. He went back to Charles Town for a short time in order to arrange his affairs, little dreaming how long a time he would be absent and how many things would happen before he again saw his home. On August 13, 1789, Henry Laurens set sail from Philadelphia in the little ship *Mercury*.

Three weeks after it sailed, the *Mercury* was captured at sea by the British. Among the papers which Laurens was carrying with him was a rough draft of a possible treaty of friendship between America and Holland. When he realized that the *Mercury* was going to be captured, Laurens put some of his papers in a bag, tied a heavy weight to it, and cast it into the sea, but a quick British sailor fished it out. The British had long wanted an excuse for declaring war against Holland and at last, here in Mr. Laurens' bag, they found it. With the rough draft of the American Dutch treaty as an excuse, Britain declared war on Holland on December 20, 1780.

When Laurens arrived in England he was so ill and so lame from gout, which is a very painful disease usually affecting the feet, that he could not travel to London.

Henry Laurens had not started on this voyage as a spy nor even as a soldier, but as a diplomat. There are certain rights belonging to diplomats. The British, however, completely overlooked the fact that he was a diplomat, not a traitor, and on October 5, 1780, he was sent to the Tower of London. His imprisonment papers stated that he was a state prisoner suspected of high treason against his government. An English writer said then of him, "He is one of the greatest and best men America has ever produced."

Although he was very ill, Laurens was denied the right

of having a doctor until the prison authorities could arrange to have one who would also spy upon him. Pen and ink were denied him, but finally a woman who came in and out of the prison on business managed to smuggle a pencil and some paper in to him. With these he wrote constantly to his friends and relatives and to newspapers which were sympathetic with the American cause. In fact, he carried on publicity for America right under the noses of his enemies. One of the most trying parts of his imprisonment was that he was not allowed to see his family and friends except under very unpleasant conditions. His prison was a set of small dark rooms, and for these he had to pay rent. Every single morsel of food he ate was charged against him. When the first bill for his room rent was presented to him, Laurens made this comment: "Whenever I caught a bird in America I found a cage and vittles for it."

Imagine his astonishment when, after his funds were gone and his gout had become very painful, a bill was presented to him for the two jailers who kept him in sight day and night! " 'Tis enough to provoke me to change my lodgings!" he said. We can well imagine that for this service Laurens refused to pay, for, as he said, if he had as many dollars as would fill his room he'd still refuse to pay his jailers. He had not employed them and he certainly would be glad to get rid of them. He took this opportunity to point out that the stupid demands made on him at this time were quite in line with the bigger stupidities of the British government in dealing with America. "Attempts, sir, to tax men without their consent have involved this kingdom in a bloody seven years' war. I thought she had long since promised to give up such an idea."

The British did everything they could to break Laurens'

spirit. He was shown every account of American defeat. He was offered release from prison, and even high honors, if he would but point out anything for the benefit of Great Britain in the dispute with the colonies. The most heart-breaking effort came when his son John was sent to Paris as a special messenger for the Continental Congress. Henry Laurens was told that the British government was very much displeased at this effort of the son of their prisoner to get aid from France. It was suggested that Henry Laurens should write to John asking that, in order to make things easier for his father, John should return to America, leaving his task undone. Henry Laurens' reply was, "I dearly love my son and he loves me. He would gladly give his life for me, but I will not ask him to surrender his honor."

Many people besides Lafayette tried to have Henry Laurens released from the Tower of London, but nothing came of these efforts until Edmund Burke, the great English statesman, took up his case. Laurens refused to accept any favors which might make him seem to admit that he was guilty of any wrong-doing, nor would he do anything which might be said to brand the colonies as rebels or make him accept any favors from the King.

Finally he was released from the Tower, on bail, December 31, 1781. Unable to stand without crutches, he was taken into court for a hearing. When the court was opened and he was asked to sign a paper which began, "Our sovereign Lord, the King,—" Laurens interrupted to declare in no uncertain terms, "not my sovereign Lord." He was never actually brought to trial. An exchange was arranged by which he was released in England and Lord Cornwallis was released in America. Strangely enough, Cornwallis, while a prisoner of war in America, had been put in the care of Henry Laurens' son John. He had been treated with every courtesy and kindness, which was certainly not true of Laurens while a prisoner in England.

From October 6, 1780, to December 31, 1781, Laurens was a prisoner in the Tower of London. As soon as he was able to travel, he was ordered by the American Congress to join the other peace commissioners in Paris. He reached there only two days before the Articles of Peace were signed and found that Franklin, Adams, and Jay had about finished their work. Laurens had little to do with drawing up the treaty; but he did insist that American fishing rights must be protected and that the British could not carry away from America any American property, including Negroes.

Laurens' name does not appear on the final treaty, for by the time it was signed he had returned to England for service in behalf of his country. In fact, for the next year and a half he was practically an unofficial minister to England and has sometimes been called the first American Minister to Great Britain.

On August 3, 1784, just four years after leaving America, he returned home. After reporting to Congress, where he was mentioned for another term as president, he traveled to Charles Town. He arrived early in 1785. His health had been broken by his terrible experiences and his heart had been broken by the death of his beloved son John. He had lost a great share of his wealth during the war, and he felt that he had earned the right to live the remaining years of his life quietly at his beautiful plantation, "Mepkin." However, his state continued to shower political honors on him.

On December 8, 1792, he died at "Mepkin." In his will he ordered that he should be cremated, that is, his body should be burned, which order was faithfully carried out

The Twisted Oak, one of an avenue of oaks at "Mepkin," the plantation of Henry Laurens

by his son Henry. The ashes were buried beside his son John.

Thus quietly surrounded by those he loved, the life of Henry Laurens came to an end. This son of a saddler played a conspicuous part on the stage of his day. His voice was heard in the councils of his province and his state. His good sense kept the new government out of many troubles. Merchant, planter, legislator, president of Congress, minister to a foreign country, peace commissioner, this South Carolinian, for whom a county in his native state was named, whose name honors a street in the great city of New York as it does in the capital city of South Carolina, was, in the truest sense of the word, one of the "founding fathers" of this nation.

"Lookeing Glass Nob" portraying Henry Laurens. These knobs were also used as cloak pins or curtain tie-backs. They were a form of honoring the heroes of that day. Some of them were unintentionally funny likenesses of our Revolutionary heroes and statesmen.

Christopher Gadsden
1724–1805

H E COULD fight with words or with guns. He could rouse the people to demand liberty, and he could lead them to the charge. Well did he earn his nickname, "the Flame of Liberty." Truly did Christopher Gadsden become "the firebrand of the Revolution."

Christopher Gadsden's father, Thomas, was for many years in the English navy. Later he was appointed to the position of collector of the Port of Charles Town, where his son was born. He filled this position for a period of almost twenty years until his death in 1741.

In those days gentlemen were expected to take part in a little polite gaming. On one occasion Lord Anson, a visiting nobleman from England, was being entertained in Charles Town. It is said that Thomas Gadsden lost so much to Lord Anson that he had to pay his debts by giving to that gentleman a large section of Charles Town, then

Christopher Gadsden.

From a portrait said to be by REYNOLDS.

owned by him and later known as Ansonborough. Christopher Gadsden was about five or six years old at that time. The sequel to this story is that young Christopher, who was about sixteen when his father died, determined that he would buy back every foot of the land his father had lost— and finally he did.

Christopher Gadsden's education was begun in Charles Town; but when he was sixteen, he was sent to England to a famous school near Bristol, where he could be thoroughly educated in Latin and Greek. Young Gadsden doubtless enjoyed his school life, for he could spend his holidays with the very important people who were the relatives of his father, the Gascoigns, Halls, and Gadsdens.

We are told that when Christopher was returning from England, the purser, or paymaster, of the boat on which he was traveling died, and Christopher was pressed into service as purser. In this way he started on a life at sea. It would seem perfectly natural that the son should follow in his father's footsteps and become a seaman. Perhaps the only reason he had not done so earlier was his respect for his father's wish, once expressed in a letter. Thomas Gadsden had written that though it was natural for Christopher to want to go to sea he hoped, "that my son Kit will not." About two years of service at sea was enough for Christopher Gadsden, and he returned to America to begin on his life's work.

Early Carolina had a number of rich and important merchants. Perhaps the most famous were Henry Laurens, the Wragges, Robert Pringle, the Manigaults, and Christopher Gadsden. If there had been no Revolutionary War, and if there had been no need for Christopher Gadsden to use his fiery tongue to rouse the mechanics assembled under the Liberty Tree, he would probably have gone down in the history of Carolina as a great and successful merchant.

In March, 1746, Christopher Gadsden returned to Charles Town and entered business there. By 1761 he had so enlarged his business that he had two stores in town, two in the country, and a large plantation; and he was considered one of the most promising young business men in the province. The great mercantile monument which still bears his name is the huge wharf, a thousand feet in length, which he built about 1770. *The South-Carolina Gazette* described this wharf as "the stupendous work . . . which is reckoned as the most extensive of its kind ever undertaken by any one man in America." Reclaiming the marsh lands on the Cooper River and laying out a subdivision known as "Middlesex" were only two of the business activities of Christopher Gadsden.

It was just the thing to be expected of Christopher Gadsden that, the minute he got into politics, wild excitement would begin. In 1757 he was elected to the Assembly, where he served for nearly thirty years. But at first Governor Boone, who was in a squabble with Carolina regarding the election laws, refused to recognize the election of Christopher Gadsden, although he had been accepted by the Assembly. The governor even refused to let the Assembly meet if Christopher Gadsden was in it. The next Assembly, which was to meet in December, 1762, saw Gadsden again elected. The Assembly protested that the governor had had no right to call their meeting off the time before. The governor would not give an inch, and the Assembly declared that they would have no business dealings with such a man. They did not, and the governmental business of the province was at a standstill until Boone left the colony two years later.

It is probable that Boone had no objection to Gadsden and that he was only using him for what we might today call "a horrible example." On the other hand, it is just like Christopher Gadsden to have turned the searchlight of freedom on the affairs of Carolina. After his experience with Governor Boone, everyone in the colony was talking about the rights of Carolina, the rights and liberties of the people.

Though they may not have known it, this quarrel between Governor Boone, who stood for the rights of the royal government, and Christopher Gadsden, who stood for the rights of the people, was leading to the day when Carolina would listen to the voice of Christopher Gadsden calling out for freedom and independence.

In June, 1765, Massachusetts invited South Carolina to send delegates to a meeting in New York at which all colonies would plan how to fight the unpopular Stamp Act. Gadsden was made chairman of the committee to consider the matter. The committee reported in favor of sending delegates to this congress, South Carolina being the only Southern colony to be represented there. As the delegates of South Carolina to this meeting, the Assembly appointed Christopher Gadsden, John Rutledge, and Thomas Lynch, Sr. An American historian, George Bancroft, gives full credit to South Carolina for the success of this congress when he says that Massachusetts sounded the trumpet, but that South Carolina answered the call. "Had it not been for South Carolina, no Congress would then have happened. When we count up those who, above all others, helped to

An artist's conception of the treatment given to a collector of the Stamp Act money. He has been "tarred and feathered." In the background, men are dumping goods, perhaps tea, into the water rather than pay the Stamp Act tax on it.

bring freedom, we must name the great Massachusetts leader, James Otis, and the great statesman, the gallant, firm, patriotic lover of his country, Christopher Gadsden."

When the hated Stamp Act was repealed, Christopher Gadsden was one of the few men who were not fully satisfied. The reason was that, along with the repeal, went another act saying that Parliament had a right to make any laws for the colonies, and the wisest men of the colonies knew that other laws, as bad as the Stamp Act, would soon be passed. Most people said, "Oh well, let's just let well enough alone." But Gadsden's fear that the people would not realize their danger kept him trying to wake them up. One day he would address a mass meeting; the next day he would write an article for a newspaper. Gadsden was tireless in his efforts to stir the people up toward a final settling of their troubles.

He must have been very much in earnest, for he insisted that rice must be on the list of things affected by the non-importation agreement of 1774. This, as you remember, was an agreement by which the colonists promised not to buy goods imported from England, nor sell to that country. Although as a merchant and planter Gadsden would lose a lot of money by not being able to sell rice to England, he insisted that it should be one of the items on the list. He did not agree with John Rutledge that rice should be left out. It would have been easy for him to have taken Rutledge's viewpoint and thereby to have saved many thousands of dollars for himself, but that was not the kind of thing that Gadsden would or could do.

An interesting side-light on this importation matter is seen in the description of the funeral of Gadsden's wife. No mourning garments appeared at her funeral, because

C A P. XI.

An Act to repeal an Act made in the laft Seffion of Parliament, intituled, *An Act for*
granting and applying certain Stamp Duties,
and other Duties, in the Britifh *Colonies and*
Plantations in America, *towards further de-*
fraying the Expences of defending, protecting,
and fecuring the fame ; and for amending
fuch Parts of the feveral Acts of Parliament
relating to the Trade and Revenues of the
faid Colonies and Plantations, as direct the
Manner of determining and recovering the
Penalties and Forfeitures therein mentioned.

WHEREAS an Act was paffed Preamble.
in the laft Seffion of Parlia-
ment, intituled, An Act for
granting and applying certain
Stamp Duties, and other Duties,
in the *Britifh* Colonies and Plantations in *America,* towards further defraying the Expences of
defending, protecting, and fecuring the fame ; and for amending
fuch Parts of the feveral Acts of
Parliament relating to the Trade
and Revenues of the faid Colonies and Plantations, as direct the Manner of determining and recovering the Penalties and Forfeitures therein mentioned : And whereas the
Continuance of the faid Act would be attended with many
b   Ppp 2   Inconve-

Facsimile of first page of Act to Repeal the Stamp Act.

all of the mourning veils and clothes had to be imported from England. Perhaps this does not strike you as being so remarkable; for today whether one wears mourning or not is more or less a matter of personal feeling. But in those days things were very different. How much mourning each member of the family should wear, the length of the veil, and the width of the crepe border—all were carefully outlined. To appear at a funeral of a member of the family without black gloves was considered an insult to the memory of the dear departed one. In no way could the Gadsdens have shown their devotion to the cause and their willingness to sacrifice for the non-importation agreement more than by not wearing mourning.

When the Assembly chose delegates to represent South Carolina in the first Continental Congress in 1774, they elected Christopher Gadsden, Thomas Lynch, Sr., Edward Rutledge, Henry Middleton, and John Rutledge. These delegates really formed two groups. Christopher Gadsden, Thomas Lynch and Edward Rutledge were the three men who, two years later, took the extreme view that the only way out of their troubles was the complete separation from Great Britain; while Middleton and John Rutledge were the moderates, who hoped to find a common ground on which England and her colonies could stand. Gadsden was the leader of the first group, and John Rutledge the leader of the second group.

In the Continental Congress Gadsden was always with those who were urging toward the Revolution. On February 10, 1776, Christopher Gadsden threw a bombshell into the quiet of the South Carolina Provincial Congress. Friend and foe alike were startled when he presented to them a copy of Thomas Paine's *Common Sense*, which recommended American independence. This pamphlet was considered so wild that the conservative gentlemen of that day were very much upset by it.

Not only did Gadsden shock them with this pamphlet, but he himself came out in favor of complete independence for America, declaring that he could not see any possibility that the colonies could be properly governed, while the government was three thousand miles away, with the Atlantic Ocean between America and England.

Christopher Gadsden was not a particularly good speaker. Certainly he would not have been compared, as was John Rutledge, with the great orator Patrick Henry; but he was forceful, determined, and unselfish. It happens that Mr. Josiah Quincy, of Boston, visited Charles Town in the year 1773. One of the sights which he was interested in seeing was the Commons House in session. About his visit he wrote, "Thomas Lynch, Esq., spoke like a man of sense and a patriot, with dignity and fire. Mr. Gadsden was plain, blunt, hot, and incorrect, though very sensible. In the course of the debate he used these very singular expressions for a member of Parliament: 'And, Mr. Speaker, if the governor and council don't see fit to fall in with us I say let the general duty, law, and all, go to the devil, sir, and we go about our business.'"

Perhaps as time passed, and as their revolutionary activities developed, no two men ever worked in closer harmony than did Christopher Gadsden and William Henry Drayton. They have been described as the two hotheads who led Carolina into the Revolution. It therefore becomes very amusing to realize that at one time they were on entirely different sides of the fence. That was before Drayton became such an ardent revolutionist.

In those days if you did not agree with a man politically or socially, you aired your views in the newspaper, and many amusing squabbles can be traced in the files of those old newspapers. *The South-Carolina Gazette* published Drayton's famous *Letters of a Freeman*. Gadsden did not agree with Drayton, and so very shortly the paper carried this letter: "What a pity it is that the Momma of that pretty child [Drayton] which transmitted to you the paper, signed, 'Freeman' published in your last *Gazette* had not now and then whipped it for lying."

But Drayton did not intend to let Gadsden have the last word; so the next issue of the paper carried a letter which began: "I cannot in point of good manners avoid congratulating the Hen-Huffy Kitty . . . on the birth of a son who wrote the letter appearing in the last copy of the *Gazette* signed 'C. G.'" And so the correspondence continued, with Drayton and Gadsden writing letters back and forth like two little boys calling each other names. Later they forgot their differences and worked together in a common cause, the independence of the United States.

The next time you visit Charleston, go to the site of the famous Liberty Tree on Alexander Street. A bronze marker will tell you that "near this spot once stood the Liberty Tree where colonial independence was first advocated by Christopher Gadsden, A.D. 1766, and where ten years later the Declaration of Independence was first heard and applauded by Carolinians." Under this famous tree the Sons of Liberty would meet to be spurred on by their leader, Christopher Gadsden. Here the flame of independence burned high. Here the undying courage and the unwillingness to admit that American Independence was impossible made Christopher Gadsden the revolutionary hero of his day.

That it was a recognized place of meeting is shown by the advertisement which appeared in *The South-Carolina Gazette* of February 14, 1774: "Every inhabitant of the town or country that can attend the said general meeting on Thursday the 3rd of March is desired to do so by nine o'clock in the morning at Liberty Tree."

The old tree no longer stands in Charleston, but the record of its usefulness as a meeting place for the Sons of Liberty will always stand. We shall always remember, too, the part played by the leader of this band, Christopher Gadsden, in making America and Carolina free.

It has been said that in the Cherokee war Great Britain did not know that she was training soldiers to fight against her in the Revolution. But in the campaign against the Indians many of the best Revolutionary leaders received their training. Christopher Gadsden was one of these men. In 1760, he had served as a captain in the war against the Cherokees; and in the same year he organized one of the most interesting military companies in South Carolina. Finding that there was no field artillery in Charles Town, he raised a company, which was later known as the "Ancient Battalion of Artillery," and trained them himself in the use of cannon. So successful was this company that it lasted for many years.

This training helped Gadsden when, in 1776, he was made colonel of the first regiment of foot of South Carolina. His commission arrived at the same time as Moultrie's appointment as colonel of the second regiment. Gadsden was ranked as the senior colonel. It is interesting to note

William Moultrie, famous Revolutionary soldier.
From an engraving after a painting by TRUMBULL

that because Gadsden had returned to South Carolina to take command of his troops, he, like John Rutledge, could not sign the Declaration of Independence. This piece of paper, perhaps the most important in all American history, marked the end of one part of Gadsden's life. His country-men had declared that they were independent and free men. But it was a constant source of sorrow to Christopher Gadsden that his name did not appear among the signers of the Declaration.

In the defense of Sullivan's Island against the British, Moultrie commanded the fort which now bears his name. Gadsden was stationed at Fort Johnson opposite Moultrie's position on Sullivan's Island. An interesting bit of military history tells us that in 1776 General Lee insisted that a bridge be built from Sullivan's Island to Haddrell's Point so that Moultrie's troops might escape in case the battle went against them. Colonel Gadsden, who was in command at Fort Johnson, undertook to build the bridge. In a few days, through money and materials supplied by him, the bridge was completed. Gadsden was a man who undertook to do things and did them quickly and without fuss. After the success of Moultrie and Gadsden in defending Sullivan's Island against the British, both these gentlemen were made brigadier generals in the Continental Army.

On August 23, 1775, Christopher Gadsden resigned his commission in the army because of a quarrel between him and General Howe about the commanding of troops in South Carolina and Georgia. This resignation, which was accepted by the Congress, brought a great deal of bitterness into the friendship between Gadsden and Henry Laurens. These two men, who had begun their lives in the closest friendship, now became enemies. Henry Laurens was, at the time Gadsden resigned, president of the Continental Congress. Gadsden felt that Laurens should have known he was resigning only to call attention to the need for some improvements in army control. But Laurens took Gadsden at his word and allowed his resignation to be accepted.

The Gadsden-Howe duel. "General Howe said with a smile, 'Why don't you fire, General Gadsden?'"

From an old print.

Perhaps you will remember that Gadsden and Laurens had early had an agreement that neither one of them would get into mischief. Probably Gadsden felt that the man who had been his intimate friend all through childhood and young manhood would understand him thoroughly. On September 11, 1746, Gadsden had written to his friend, Henry Laurens, "Dear Harry: I am out of your class for I was married a few days before I left Carolina to Miss Jennie Godfrey." On December 28, 1747, Henry Laurens had written to his friend giving news of Mrs. Gadsden and the new baby daughter, "your own stamp, exactly." But political disagreement between the hot-headed Gadsden and the conservative Laurens put too great a strain on this very close friendship. In his old age, nothing so angered

Gadsden as the fact that Laurens' new home interfered with his view of the steeple of St. Philip's Church.

Another outcome of Gadsden's resignation from the army was a duel between him and General Howe, who was offended by Gadsden's criticisms and challenged him to a duel. You must have read the story of Major John André, the charming young Englishman who was caught spying for his country and regretfully shot by the Americans. Can't you imagine this delightful young Britisher chuckling over the poem he wrote about the bloodless duel between the two American generals, Howe and Gadsden? The actual fact was that, when they met, a ball from Howe's pistol grazed Gadsden's ear. Gadsden fired into the air. Blood had been drawn and honor was satisfied. Major André saw the funny part of it, as these quotations will show:

> "Such honor did they both display,
> They highly were commended;
> And thus in short this gallant fray
> Without mischance was ended.
>
> "No fresh dispute, we may suppose,
> Will e'er by them be started;
> And now the chiefs, no longer foes,
> Shook hands, and so they parted."

Every woodsman fears the deadly poison of the rattlesnake. It is said that some people have died of fright at the very sight of a coiled rattlesnake about to strike. If this is true, Gadsden chose well when he put a coiled rattlesnake in the center of the flag which he presented to Commodore Hopkins as the service flag for the commander-in-chief of the fleet. This flag of yellow shows a coiled rattlesnake with thirteen full-grown rattles and bears the warning "Don't tread on me." It was first hoisted at the main mast of the *Alfred* on December 3, 1775. John Paul Jones hoisted the Union striped flag at the stern of his boat at the same time. Jones's flag and the "jack" of the navy, with Gadsden's rattlesnake emblem, were the three most historic flags in the United States Army before the official adoption of the Stars and Stripes. The rattlesnake was evidently a popular sign for the colonies.

The year 1778 saw the climax of Gadsden's career, for in March of that year, South Carolina adopted the constitution for which he and William Henry Drayton had fought so long and so hard. The constitution made law of many of his ideas.

After Rutledge's resignation at the time that he refused to sign the new constitution, Rawlins Lowndes was elected

DON'T TREAD ON ME

The Gadsden flag, showing the snake coiled ready to spring, which symbolized the attitude of the colonies toward Great Britain.

to the high office of governor, with Christopher Gadsden serving as lieutenant-governor. In March, 1778, the legislature had passed a law requiring that the oath of allegiance to the new government be signed within a certain time. Punishment for failure to sign was to be severe. Lowndes was ill, and Gadsden, acting as the governor, issued a proclamation allowing more time for the signers. A mob formed and resisted the publication of Gadsden's statement, which resulted in a squabble in the legislature. A great many people probably felt that Gadsden was not consistent. He had been the most active of all the leaders for the Revolution, and yet here he was asking that people be given more time in which to sign the oath of allegiance to the new country! They did not understand that Gadsden always, from the very earliest days until his death, opposed mobs and believed that everything should be done by legal and proper means. They also did not understand that a man who had given everything in the fight for freedom could also have a great enough heart to fight to save the property of those people who had been his enemies in the war, those Americans who had stayed loyal to the King.

Gadsden felt that it was so necessary for the heads of governments to show their displeasure at rioting and mobs that he resigned his office. He thought that, if he resigned, people would understand how serious the matter was.

In 1779 John Rutledge was elected governor of South Carolina. About 1780 Christopher Gadsden again served as lieutenant-governor. He was holding this position when Charles Town fell to the British. John Rutledge had been urged to flee, but had declined to do so for fear people would think he was a coward. It was finally agreed that the vice-president, Christopher Gadsden, and five of the council should stay in Charles Town, and Governor Rutledge should leave.

When the British captured Charles Town, Gadsden was made a prisoner. He signed his parole, or word of honor, not to attempt escape, upon condition that the British would treat him as a gentleman and a prisoner of war. But the British did not keep their side of the agreement. On the twenty-seventh of August, 1780, Gadsden and other well-known leaders were taken from their beds in the night and, between files of soldiers, were marched to a guard-ship. A few days later, they were landed in St. Augustine, Florida. Gadsden was told that he could have the freedom of the town if he would sign another parole. This he indignantly refused to do. "I gave my parole once, and it has been shamefully violated by the British Government. I shall not give another to people on whom no faith can be reposed." He was told that the dungeon would be his home unless he would sign a parole. We can see the grim old man as he declared: "Be it so, I give no more paroles to British officers."

For forty-two weeks he lived in the dungeon of San Marco. This dungeon had been built by the Spaniards according to the cruel prison plans of that day. Gadsden was allowed almost no light, only that which crept into his cell when the sun was high. A common soldier, who admired the spirit of the General, once offered to supply him with a light; but Gadsden, realizing that if the soldier were caught, he would get into trouble, refused this favor.

The British made it a point to allow reading materials to their prisoners and took particular trouble to see that they were supplied with papers which told of the victories of the British. Taking advantage of this allowance, Gadsden spent the long, dragging, weary hours in a most remarkable way. He learned the Hebrew language and came out of the dungeon a more learned man than he went in. Finally, in an exchange of prisoners, Gadsden was freed. He was taken to Philadelphia, and from there, learning of the conditions at home, he rushed back to take his seat in the legislature.

In 1782 the Assembly offered Gadsden the honor of being made governor of South Carolina, but he refused because he felt that his age and ill health, brought on by his confinement in St. Augustine, made it wiser to put the guidance of the state into younger hands. Although he withdrew almost entirely from public life, he did have the great pleasure of sitting in the state convention of 1788 and of voting in favor of the ratification of the Constitution of the United States. This gave him unspeakable delight. It was the crown of everything he had wanted for his country. His voice had been one of the first to speak for the formation of a new, free country; and now he was allowed to help set up the machinery by which this country should govern itself and take its place in the councils of nations.

In 1790 he sat in the convention which met in Columbia to frame a state constitution. Today, in the capital city of Columbia there is a street named for Christopher Gadsden.

We know what Christopher Gadsden did, but do we know what sort of man he was? His fame is based not so much upon what he actually accomplished as upon his virtues and the tremendous influence which he had over his fellow South Carolinians. Sometimes he wanted to "rush in where angels fear to tread." His rashness was well balanced by John Rutledge's calm judgment. He had a temper

St. Philip's Church, Charleston, intimately connected with the lives of many great South Carolinians.

Photo by Bayard Wootten

which he controlled with great difficulty and to which he applied the religion which meant a great deal in his life. There is no instance on record of Gadsden's allowing his private personal interest to interfere with his public duty. A man of great personal courage and endless energy, he could never see failure. He had a high standard of political service and he spared neither himself nor anyone else in living up to that standard. He was an enthusiastic fighter, and he had a loyal following among those highly skilled workmen who were known as the "mechanics." He was willing to be the leader or to serve in the ranks, if only he could accomplish his purpose. "He made no memorable orations, signed no renowned documents, won no distinguished battles; but no citizen of America ever engaged more zealously and unselfishly for so long a time in the service of the Union."

Gadsden admired General Washington so much that he had a portrait of the great American painted by Charles Peale as a present for his own daughter. This portrait now hangs in the Academy of Fine Arts in Philadelphia and is listed as the Peale portrait of General Washington.

Christopher Gadsden was married three times. A number of children were born of these marriages, but not many lived to manhood or womanhood. Christopher Gadsden was a grandfather of at least two distinguished men, Bishop Gadsden, and General James Gadsden, the ambassador to Mexico who made the "Gadsden Purchase."

An accidental fall finally brought death to Christopher Gadsden in his eighty-first year. He died on August 28, 1805, and was buried in his family plot in the west corner of St. Philip's churchyard. At his request the grave was leveled and no marker was erected to show his last resting place. The newspapers of that day give us an idea of how universal and sincere was the mourning for the passing of this grand old revolutionist. The colors at Fort Johnson hung in mourning. A gun fired a salute every ten minutes, from the time of his death until that of the funeral. All the vessels in Charleston harbor had their colors at half mast. At eleven o'clock on the day of the funeral the artillery, which he had founded, paraded to his home and there were joined by officers and men of the infantry of Charleston. All the judges, federal and state officers, clergymen, and friends were escorted by the military forces to St. Philip's churchyard.

The *Gazette* of August 30, 1805, carried an announcement from the governor and commander-in-chief of South Carolina regarding the mourning for this venerable and beloved "sage and patriot," General Christopher Gadsden. Civil officers were told to wear crepe around the left arm; military officers were to appear in uniform, also with crepe around the left arm and with their swords shrouded to the hilt. This was to be worn every Sunday for four Sundays, after Gadsden's death. The actual funeral was conducted with great state by the Sons of the Revolution and the Society of the Cincinnati, which was formed by the surviving officers of the Revolutionary army and is composed of their oldest living male descendants.

In his will Christopher Gadsden provided that his estate should be divided into nineteen equal parts, "being the exact number of grandchildren I now have." To one group of grandchildren he left all of his Hebrew, Greek, and Latin books. All of these men were Yale students and were to add still further luster to the name of Gadsden. To another group of grandsons he left his English books, and to all, equal shares in his estate.

There are three famous portraits of Christopher Gadsden. On the walls of old Independence Hall in Philadelphia there hangs a portrait by Peale. Among the decorations of Constitution Hall in Washington is a painting showing some of the great characters of the American Revolution in South Carolina, and Gadsden is among them. Proudly the newspapers declared that at the Charleston Exposition a portrait of Gadsden would be exhibited in the Hall of History. All of these are the portraits of a great South Carolinian, of a man who saw an ideal of freedom and independence, and who let neither public nor personal hardships stand in the way of realizing that ideal. These are the portraits of a man who was willing to slip into the background, eager to let others get credit for what he did if only his idea came nearer to being a fact. He was a man whom we "delight to honor"—the great American, Christopher Gadsden.

John Rutledge
1739–1800

I T WAS a worried young
mother who gathered her
seven children around her just
after the death of her husband,
Dr. John Rutledge, in 1750.
She was only twenty-six years old, and naturally she was
very much distressed to think that she would have to rear
these children without a father. She now had the task of
educating them and raising them to be the fine men and
women her husband had intended them to be. A little spark
of joy glowed in her heart when she looked at her big eldest
son John, not quite eleven, who was but a few years
younger than she had been when, at the age of fourteen,
she had changed her name from Sarah Hext to that of Mrs.
John Rutledge.

She would have been a very happy mother if she could
have looked into the future and known that her three sons

John Rutledge.
The bust of John Rutledge in the Supreme Court Room,
Washington, D. C.

were to become famous South Carolinians, even famous Americans. Hugh was to be the speaker of the House of Representatives of South Carolina and chancellor of his state. Edward was to set his name on the Declaration of Independence and was to become governor of South Carolina; and John, her eldest, was to be one of the greatest men this country has produced—president and governor of South Carolina, chief justice of his state, associate justice and chief justice of the United States Supreme Court.

John's father was one of two brothers, Andrew and John Rutledge, who came to South Carolina from Ireland about 1735. They established their homes in Charles Town and in the near-by Christ Church Parish. Dr. John Rutledge, one of these brothers, married, in March, 1738, a very remarkable young woman named Sarah Hext; and, just as Mrs. Rutledge celebrated her fifteenth birthday, their son John Rutledge was born. John's education was begun under the loving care of his father and later was continued under a well-known teacher, the Reverend Mr. Andrews, and, still later, in the law office of James Parsons.

In his nineteenth year John Rutledge set sail for London, there to study law. While he was living in London, he met different sorts of men and women. He studied not only law, but also life, and learned how people in big cities thought and lived. His experiences had been those of a young man reared by a remarkable mother who made him develop discipline and self-control, but who could show him only the life of a young, small, provincial city. In London, however, he was able to compare various ways of living and to choose for himself the best of each.

Some years later John wrote some excellent advice to his brother Edward, who also studied law in London. From

The Siege of Charleston during the Revolution.

this letter we are able to learn the things which John Rutledge considered most important in his education. Perhaps you will be surprised to know that he began his letter with this advice: "The very first thing with which you should be thoroughly acquainted is the writing of short-hand, which you will find of infinite advantage in your profession and will give you the means of great superiority over others who do not write it." He also suggested to Edward that he should attend church regularly, listen to the debates in the House of Commons, and pay particular attention to his languages. "If you stick close to French, and converse generally in that language, you will soon be master of it, and I would not have you attempt it unless you are resolved to speak it well and as fluently as you do English . . . whatever you attempt make yourself completely master of."

Although Edward, like his brother John, was in London

to study law, the elder brother warns him, "Don't neglect to learn surveying; that is the principal branch of mathematics which you will have occasion for." Perhaps he was afraid that his brother might not make a good social impression, for he advises, "Let your dress be plain always in the city; and elsewhere, except where it is necessary it should be otherwise; and your behaviour rather grave. Remember the old man's advice to his son: think *twice* before you speak *once*."

John Rutledge was admitted to the bar in England in 1761 at the age of twenty-one, and he at once returned to Charles Town to practice his profession. He had the rare good fortune to establish himself as a good lawyer with his very first case. Perhaps he had arranged his life according to the plan which he later suggested to his brother: "You must either establish it [your reputation] when young or it will be very difficult to acquire it." Certainly John Rutledge took his own advice and became a successful lawyer. It was not long before he had more business than he could conveniently attend to.

In a few years—that is, in 1764—he was given the position of attorney-general pro tem, which he held until June 5, 1765. In the meanwhile, he had gone into politics, his first election being to the Commons House of the Provincial Assembly. While in the Commons House, he became well known for the part he took in the argument between Governor Boone and Christopher Gadsden. You will remember that Governor Boone had claimed wrongly that Gadsden had not been properly elected. Rutledge made a brilliant speech in Gadsden's behalf. He also gave strong arguments against the royal governor's taking away any of the rights which belonged to the people.

Reraising the flag of South Carolina over the Fort on Sullivan's Island.

In 1765, John Rutledge was one of the South Carolina delegates to the congress in New York which met to consider the Stamp Act. There he had the great honor of serving on the committee to prepare a petition to the House of Lords in England, a high honor for so young a man. His calm good sense and ability caused everyone to admire him. Christopher Gadsden attended this congress also. The Northern members of the congress were surprised at the brilliance and eloquence of the members from South Carolina, and were quite charmed with their wit and wisdom. It was said that "the dignity, courage, candor, and noble character of Gadsden; the gentlemanly demeanor, polish and good sense of Lynch; with the eloquence of Rutledge . . .

did more for the reputation of South Carolina than could be imagined."

When the Stamp Act was repealed, Rutledge withdrew from public life for a few years. In 1774 he served as one of the five delegates from South Carolina to the Continental Congress. There were two factions, or parties, in Charles Town. One was made up of the cautious, careful merchants; and the other, of the less patient mechanics. Christopher Gadsden, although he belonged to the merchant group, was considered more or less the leader of the mechanics, and it was this group which selected him as a delegate to the Continental Congress. John Rutledge and his brother Edward proved to be popular with both groups, so that they, with Henry Middleton, Thomas Lynch, Sr., and Christopher Gadsden, formed South Carolina's representation.

In all the quarrel over the rights of the colonies and the rights of Great Britain, John Rutledge was a moderate. That is, he hoped and worked for a plan by which the people living in America could have all the rights which belonged to them and still remain part of Great Britain. Feeling, as did many of the leaders, that life in the provinces of Great Britain offered many advantages and could be safe and pleasant, he worked long and hard for such an arrangement. It was not until he realized that this was utterly impossible that he turned his entire attention to making a success of the Revolutionary War.

In 1774, when the Continental Congress adjourned, the South Carolina delegates had to account to the people at home for what they had done. It was at this Congress that the agreement was entered into by which the colonies promised not to import or export goods which would benefit Great Britain. Rice, one of the major crops of South

Carolina, had been excepted, largely through the influence of Rutledge. He explained that he did not consider it fair to penalize one colony more than another, that the Northern and Southern colonies must bear the burden equally, and that it was not a just division to prohibit the export of rice and allow the Northern colonies to continue their trade, which would bring to them prosperity and wealth. His reasons were so clearly given and his ideas so fair that the majority of the people finally agreed with him. But you will recall that Christopher Gadsden did not agree that rice should be left off the list.

Upon his return to South Carolina Rutledge was made a member of the Council of Safety, which was to guide the province through its days of danger. He thought that he was more needed in South Carolina than in the Continental Congress. It was because he was doing his duty in South Carolina that he was not in Philadelphia to sign the famous Declaration of Independence, but the family was well represented by his younger brother Edward.

After the signing of the Declaration of Independence, the province of South Carolina was no longer officially connected with Great Britain, and a new constitution was therefore needed. With the new constitution, the state of South Carolina was born, and John Rutledge became its first president and commander-in-chief.

It was surprising that so young a man should be entrusted with such a very important job, but he made a success of these first trying years. His courage, tact, hard work, and his ability as a leader helped greatly to build up the state of South Carolina. He served his state as chief executive, or president, as the office was then called, from 1776 through 1778. In March, 1778, a new state constitution was adopted.

It made so many changes in the government of South Carolina that Rutledge resigned his office rather than sign it.

In 1779 when South Carolina was undergoing the terrific experience of being invaded by the British, and when her citizens were in a desperate fix, John Rutledge was again made the chief executive of the state, this time with the title of governor. It was during this very trying period in the history of South Carolina that Rutledge was given the nickname of "Dictator Rutledge." Actually, he never had the powers of a dictator, for though the legislature gave him privileges to conduct the affairs of the state with or without the advice of his Council, they were very particular to limit those powers so that he could not have supreme authority. Perhaps it is safe to say that he had more power than any other governor of the state has ever been given, and it is true that he used this power so fairly that there was no complaint.

At the time of the Battle of Fort Moultrie, when General William Moultrie was putting up a brave defense, it was suggested that it might be wiser if the Americans should give up their position. Rutledge said, "You will not do so without an order from me, and I would sooner cut off my hand than write one."

When Charles Town was besieged, four years later, May 12, 1780, the city fell into the hands of the British. Early in the siege, General Lincoln begged Governor Rutledge and the Council to leave the city. Lincoln thought that if they were free to move about in the state, it would help more to keep up the spirit of the people than any good they could possibly do by staying in Charles Town. Rutledge objected, because the people might think he had deserted them in time of danger. Finally, on April 12, 1780, with the British

South Carolina.

Articles of Capitulation between their Excellencies Sir Henry Clinton Knight of the Bath, General & Commander in Chief of His Majestys Forces in the several Provinces and Colonies on the Atlantick from Nova Scotia to West Florida inclusive; Mariot Arbuthnot Esquire; Vice Admiral of the Blue and Commander in Chief of all His Majesty's Ships and Vessels North America; and Major General Benjamin Lincoln, Commanding in Chief in the Town & Harbour of Charles Town.

Article 1st

That all Acts of Hostility & Work shall cease between the Besiegers and Besieged until the Articles of Capitulation shall be agreed on, signed & executed, or collectively rejected.

Article 1st

All Acts of Hostility & Work shall cease until the Articles of Capitulation are finally agreed to, or rejected.

Article 2d

The Town & Fortifications shall be surrendered to the Commander in Chief of the British Forces, such as they now Stand.

Article 2d

The Town & Fortifications, with the Shipping at the Wharves, Artillery, and all public Stores whatsoever, shall be surrendered in their present State, to the Commander of the investing Forces. Prior to marching on the city, he and three of his Council left Charles Town in order to save the state government.

It was indeed fortunate for South Carolina that her governor was not made a prisoner in Charles Town. The very fact of his being free and able to go from place to place greatly encouraged the people. He not only kept up the spirits of the people by his example and energy, but he also helped the generals, Sumter, Marion, and Pickens. By letter, he made constant demands upon Congress and the Continental Army for aid to South Carolina. Today, when messages are sent before we can bat an eyelash, it is hard to realize how long it took to get news. On October 12, 1780, from Hillsborough, North Carolina, Rutledge wrote to Congress,

"Cannot you get the Board of War to send off an express on the particular day every week, and oftener, if anything material should occur. We would do the same from here, for it is really distressing to be without any regular channel of Intelligence. The General complains that he can never hear from Congress, and when it is considered that his last letter from them is upward of a month ago the complaint will appear to be well founded."

His letters, written from the field while he was with the militia forces or was rushing around trying to get aid, tell of the doings of Marion, Sumter, Pickens, and the British officers, of burnings and hangings—in fact everything happening in South Carolina. He carried with him a private printing press, upon which he printed his proclamations and other state papers.

Facsimile of "Articles of Capitulation" by which Charles Town was surrendered to the British.

"The Constitution of the United States." From a mural painting in the National Archives Building in Washington. John Rutledge, on the left, is the man with the open book. George Washington is in the center. Half-way between Rutledge and Washington, is Charles Pinckney,

Although the British still held Charles Town, on January 8, 1782, Governor Rutledge called the legislature to meet in Jacksonborough on the Edisto. Here he received the enthusiastic thanks of the people and resigned the office of governor. A great compliment was paid to him when the legislature made into law all of Rutledge's suggested plans. Thus he was able to keep the people from passing even harsher laws against those who had sympathized with Great Britain. It was his hope that everything would ·be done to

the man with the cane. Charles Cotesworth Pinckney is the man standing in front of the pillar on the right. He is in uniform.

heal the breach between American sympathizers and British loyalists and to make the building of South Carolina easier and quicker.

John Rutledge had held the highest offices the state of South Carolina could give to him; but a few days after his term as governor expired, he took his seat in the House of Representatives as a member from St. Andrew's Parish. This was only another sign that he was willing to serve in any way needed.

In 1782 he was again elected to the United States Congress, where he served from May 2, 1782, until June 17 1783. Congress was at this time without money, and the army was without pay, provisions, or clothing. It was thought that if members of Congress could go to the states and explain the needs of the new nation, each state would be more willing to help. Rutledge was one of the two men sent by Congress on this mission to the Southern states, and we still may read the splendid talk he made to the Virginia Assembly.

When the convention to frame a constitution for the United States was called, John Rutledge, Charles Cotesworth Pinckney, Charles Pinckney, and Pierce Butler represented South Carolina. Charles Pinckney played the most important part, but John Rutledge's influence was strong. Perhaps he was too afraid of letting the government get out of the hands of a few highly trained statesmen, but when the constitution was actually passed and was brought back to South Carolina, Rutledge argued convincingly that it be ratified by his state.

It would seem that almost every honor had been bestowed upon John Rutledge, but a new field was to open up for him. He had already been in the legislative branch of the government; he had served as the chief executive, and now he was about to enter the third branch of government, the judiciary.

When the United States Supreme Court was formed, John Rutledge was appointed an associate justice in that important group. In 1791, he was elected chief justice of South Carolina, and resigned as associate justice of the United States Supreme Court to assume the duties of this high office in his native state. Again honors had been heaped upon this man who was so well prepared to receive them.

After the ratification of the Constitution of the United States, when South Carolina cast her first electoral vote, this vote was for George Washington for president and John Rutledge for vice-president, a compliment which not only pleased Rutledge, but also strengthened the friendship between him and the great Virginian.

In 1795 President Washington appointed John Rutledge of South Carolina chief justice of the United States Supreme Court, but, as we shall see later, he never held this office.

Two tragedies now entered Rutledge's life. In 1765, he had married Miss Elizabeth Grimké, and their life together had been like one of the romantic novels, which end, "and they were married and lived happily ever after." Ten children were born to them. Mrs. Rutledge's death in 1792 was a terrible experience for her devoted husband. He had already begun to show some signs of the mental illness which completely clouded the last years of his life, and his grieving over her death hastened his sickness.

His mind was further affected by another incident. John Rutledge had been one of the last to give up the idea that the colonies could remain under English rule, but during the Revolution he grew to hate Britain bitterly and to feel a warm friendship for France, who helped America win its independence. When news reached Charles Town of the treaty made by John Jay, in which Great Britain had been favored and France slighted, a meeting of protest was held in St. Michael's church. Here Rutledge made a savage speech attacking the treaty. With his mental disorder as an excuse and his opposition to the Jay treaty as the reason, the United States Senate refused to confirm his appointment as chief justice, and this action completed the wreckage begun

The spire of St. Michael's Church rises superbly above the grave of John Rutledge.

by the disease. His mind was completely clouded and so remained until his death on January 23, 1800.

Thus, after more than thirty years of service to South Carolina, John Rutledge died. He was buried in St. Michael's churchyard. The most gifted and perhaps the hardest working leader of all those splendid men who led South Carolina into and through the Revolutionary War, John Rutledge combined within himself the ideals of that Southern aristocracy which began with the success of hard work, native ability, and devotion to a cause.

John Rutledge was known particularly for his excellent judgment, his knowledge of human nature, and his will to accomplish what he believed was right. He was not a person who made friends with everyone he saw; but whenever he did gain a friend, it was for life. The story has come down to us that Patrick Henry, the famous orator from Virginia, was asked who was the greatest man in Congress, and he answered, "If you speak of eloquence, Mr. Rutledge of South Carolina is by far the greatest orator; but if you speak of solid information and sound judgment Colonel Washington is unquestionably the greatest man on that floor." In this judgment others agreed. The great South Carolina writer and historian, William Gilmore Simms, has said of John Rutledge, "Mr. Rutledge was the Patrick Henry of South Carolina and a statesman, orator, and patriot quite worthy to take rank not only with the great Virginian to whom he has been frequently compared, but with any of the statesmen which the American Revolution produced."

There are several portraits of Rutledge. A fine bust of him is in the Supreme Court room of the United States in Washington. He was tall, grave, and very dignified. He is described as usually patient, fair, and impartial, but capable of getting very angry. His tall, well-knit frame, his broad forehead, dark piercing eyes, and firm mouth made him a commanding figure whenever he rose to speak. In the style of the day, he wore his hair long, combed back, and powdered. As would be expected after having read his letter to his brother Edward, he dressed always in quiet good taste.

Although in the early years of his law practice John Rutledge became a wealthy man, his money and lands were lost during the Revolutionary War; even the books in his library were burned. When he died, he was not able to will much in the way of worldly goods to his children, of whom six sons and two daughters survived, but he certainly left to them a name and a reputation which they could carry with pride.

Perhaps some day you may walk down Rutledge Avenue in Charleston, or visit Rutledge College at the University of South Carolina, or read something from the pen of South Carolina's poet laureate, Archibald Rutledge. If you do, it may bring to your mind this little story of one of South Carolina's greatest men, John Rutledge, "a fascinating companion, a striking orator, an honest man, a fearless patriot, a wise statesman, a pure, just, and well informed judge."

William Henry Drayton

1742 - 1779

BY ORDER of Congress to Colonel William Moultrie . . . Sir: You are hereby commanded, with the troops under your orders . . . to oppose the passage of any British naval armament that may attempt to pass Fort Johnson . . . I have the honor to be yours, William H. Drayton, President, Charles Town, November 9, 1775." Perhaps that sounds like a very mild and unexciting order. It becomes very thrilling, however, when we realize that by this order William Henry Drayton told Colonel William Moultrie to fire Carolina's first shot upon the British.

Had we been in Charles Town at that time, cold chills might have run up and down our spines. Had we been among the hot-heads led by Christopher Gadsden and William Henry Drayton, we might have rushed to join Colonel Moultrie's brave troops. On the other hand, we might well have been among those who mournfully shook

William Henry Drayton.

From an engraving in Drayton's Memoirs of the Revolutionary War their heads with a "Tut, tut, now they *have* done something! The King will never forgive *this*. I'm afraid we shall just have to fight." We might not have realized that this was exactly the impression the smart, energetic, aristocratic young Drayton wanted to create.

William Henry Drayton was the great-great-grandson of that Thomas Drayton who had come with Sir John Yeamans from Barbados in 1671. William Henry's father was John Drayton, a gentleman who had married four times. One wife was the sister of Governor James Glen, and another, Charlotte, who was the mother of William Henry, was the sister of Lieutenant-Governor William Bull II. On both sides of the family, governors and public officers were the usual thing. Into this famous family was born in September, 1742, a son, William Henry Drayton. His birth took place at the family home, Drayton Hall, which had been named by Thomas Drayton, Esquire, for their beautiful home place in Northampshire, England.

Drayton Hall, one of the beautiful plantations on the Ashley River, is still occupied by a Drayton. It is not so well known as the neighboring Magnolia Gardens, which is also the property of the Draytons. There is a record that the house, built before the Revolution, cost $90,000. It was so famous that in later years boats coming up the river stopped there so that returning tourists might visit this well-known estate. One such visitor remarked that in order to reach Drayton Hall it was necessary to pass through Magnolia Gardens. So gloriously beautiful were these gardens that when the whistle was blown as a warning for "all aboard," few visitors had been able to tear themselves away from Magnolia. Usually Drayton Hall remained unseen.

Even today we may view an amusing memento at Drayton Hall—the letters K. W. carved on a tree. During the Revolutionary War the British General Cornwallis used Drayton Hall as his headquarters, the owner, William Henry Drayton, being then in Philadelphia attending the Continental Congress. Be it said to the credit of the British general that he treated the ladies of the Drayton family with the greatest courtesy, although he did put them on exceedingly short rations. Under Cornwallis' command were a great many German Hessians. One of these German soldiers, in his idle moments, carved the initials K. W., which was his idea of a compliment to the English general, whose name he spelled "Korn Wallis."

As was the custom of the day, after being taught the three "R's"—readin', 'ritin', and 'rithmetic—at home, William Henry Drayton was sent, at the age of eleven, to school in England. He was entered, with a number of other distinguished South Carolinians, in the fashionable Westminster School. If you ever visit Westminster Abbey in London, you will surely be shown the famous wooden chair in which every King of England sits to be crowned. Certainly you will be surprised to see this chair, which is perhaps the most famous in all the world, carved here and there with initials. This was done by the pupils of Westminster School, and it is very likely that William Henry Drayton, like the other boys, used his penknife, too. Some of us may some day find a W. H. D. on this "Chair of Kings."

Not only was it expensive to go to this famous school (the cost being about $3,000 a year), but the young students certainly had to work very hard. Charles Cotesworth Pinckney also attended this school, and many years later he wrote a long letter telling something of the life of a little boy at Westminster. He began with Latin grammar, and

Latin went with him until he was graduated. School met every day except on Saints' days. On these days the boys went to church and wrote a special exercise. The hours in the summer were from six in the morning until twelve at noon, with a few minutes off for breakfast. The afternoon session lasted from two until five. In winter school could not begin until seven, on account of the darkness, and each boy had to carry a wax candle in order to study. Religious teaching and Greek were also a part of the plan, so that upon graduation a student was expected to be a Latin and Greek scholar and to know about the Christian religion. Perhaps we will not grumble about our pleasant school days if we compare them to those of the old Westminster School.

For eight years, William Henry Drayton stayed at Westminster, and then he went to Oxford University, not far from London. After three years there he returned to his home in South Carolina. Of course he had to tell his friends that he had some sort of occupation, so he decided to become a planter, though actually the family was so wealthy that it was not necessary for young Drayton to work.

He did, however, read law and was admitted to the bar in Charles Town. As we would expect of a man with such a family background, young Drayton soon became interested in public life. In fact, while still a student in England, he had specialized in history, the laws of nations, and particularly the English constitution and the rights of the English colonies. When he was twenty-two years old, he married Miss Dorothy Golightly, an accomplished young heiress, who was beautiful enough to be a fit mate for the handsome young South Carolinian.

The next year, in 1765, Drayton was elected a member of the South Carolina Assembly. There was beginning to

Drayton Hall.

From an old print.

be much talk against British rule, talk which Drayton did not like. He expressed his opinions very freely. In fact, he wrote a number of articles which showed his loyalty to the British government—articles, by the way, which the Prime Minister and other officials in England read with delight. Finally, in 1769, Drayton had a serious political quarrel with Christopher Gadsden. This quarrel now seems very strange to us, for in later life Gadsden and Drayton were both on the same side—both wished to have a complete break between South Carolina and England.

Drayton's loyalty to England made him so unpopular that finally he left South Carolina and went to England. Here he was received with many attentions. This good-looking, rich young South Carolinian was the man who had spoken and written in favor of the good King George. He was very much the "lion" of the moment and was finally received at Court. Upon his return to South Carolina, he took his seat with his father and his Uncle Thomas as a member of the Royal Council, in which he served from 1772 to 1775. His uncle, Lieutenant-Governor William Bull, appointed him as assistant judge during this period.

And then a curious thing happened. William Henry Drayton, the man who had written and spoken for the British government, suddenly burst forth with speeches and letters showing how wrong Great Britain was in her treatment of the colonies. He indignantly attacked the practice by which excellent, well-trained South Carolinians were discharged from positions of trust and English friends of the King were put in their places. He showed, point by point, why the English Parliament had no right to make laws for America. He suggested a plan for the American colonies to work together. He planned for North America an assembly,

Magnolia Gardens, which rivaled Drayton Hall in loveliness and interest.

or congress, which should have the right to tax the colonies for the King and pass laws which affected all the colonies. Each colony, or province, however, was to be left free to arrange its own affairs. These letters were published and signed, *a Freeman*.

All this made Charles Town buzz with excitement. The visitors at the coffee houses had plenty to discuss. Ladies suddenly became very frequent callers at each other's houses, for certainly they had a great deal to gossip about: "What has come over William Henry Drayton? Why, just a few years ago he was writing articles in favor of Great Britain."

"And imagine the feeling of the King when he hears this news, after he has been kind enough to receive Drayton at Court."

"What does Dorothy think of all this? Is she in sympathy with her husband's radical ideas?"

But perhaps more of them talked about what effect it would have on their beloved acting governor, William Bull. He would be dreadfully embarrassed and might even have to suspend his nephew. Excitement rose to a high pitch. All of Charles Town took sides, and in the midst of all this, bitter as it was for him to do so, on March 1, 1775, Governor Bull suspended William Henry Drayton from the Royal Council.[1]

And thus began the career of the South Carolinian who, next to Christopher Gadsden, was the most ardent worker for an early and complete break with Great Britain, the South Carolinian who, with Gadsden, first raised the cry for complete independence.

In the spring of 1775 Drayton was particularly active in

[1] See p. 57, above.

getting South Carolina ready to keep out the British. He
was largely responsible for the seizing and holding of arms
and ammunition for the American soldiers. Naturally, he

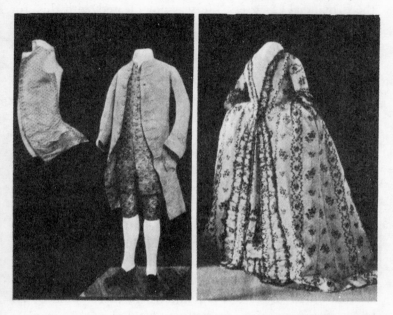

Left, suit formerly owned by Arthur Middleton, who
designed the reverse of the Great Seal of South Carolina.
Right, dress which belonged to Mrs. Arthur Middleton,
worn at the court of Louis XVI and at the Continental
Congress ball in Philadelphia.

wanted to fight as a soldier himself, but the leaders thought
that he could do more good by dealing with other states and
with the Indians. In the summer of 1775 he and the Reverend Mr. Tennent were sent into the up-country to explain
to the backwoodsmen what the quarrel between South
Carolina and Great Britain was about. Later he was sent to

Georgia to invite that colony to become a part of South Carolina, an invitation which, as you know, they declined. On November 1, 1775, Drayton was elected president of the Provincial Congress. He was not pleased with this, for he thought that it had been done "in order to gag him." Little did they know their man if they thought that plan would work! A president might be supposed to do nothing but keep order and call for the roll, but not Drayton. Every debate ended with a speech by the president in which he used the full force of his splendid oratory to present the views of the independence group. This he did so well that he became far more important than he had ever been before.

Drayton felt that the leaders in Carolina were suffering from some strange paralysis. Many of them wanted to wait and see how things went. Carolina had always been a favored province of Great Britain and had fared well, and many Carolinians were still hoping that a compromise could be reached. That was not the attitude of Drayton. He wanted things to get to the point where there could be no hope of compromise. And under his bold leadership, as president of the Provincial Congress, just that thing happened.

All summer two English men-of-war, the *Tamar* and the *Cherokee*, had been patrolling Charles Town harbor. Drayton had the idea that those ships were going to hasten a war between the colony and Great Britain. Although, as William Moultrie said, " he [Drayton] was no sailor, and did not know any one rope in the ship from another," Drayton knew what he wanted to do. He fitted up a little schooner called the *Defense;* manned it, put Captain Scott of Moultrie's regiment over the men, and had Captain

Simon Tufts to sail it. He, the president of the Congress, personally took command. No one could have been more astonished and amazed than the commander of the *Tamar* when the little *Defense* opened fire on her. The *Cherokee* joined in; and, just to be in the excitement, because they were out of range, the American guns at Fort Johnson, fired their heavy shots.

All this time Captain Blake, upon order of Drayton, was sinking hulks in the channel, in the vain hope that this deep passageway could be blocked to British ships. Everybody in Charles Town rushed to the docks. Finally the *Defense* came in, amid the cheers and congratulations of Drayton's friends. Nobody had been hurt, none of the ships had been seriously affected, and Drayton had done what he had set out to do—he had made it difficult for South Carolina to avoid a war. He had fired the people with enthusiasm and helped to start them on the way to independence.

In order to have an orderly government, it became necessary that South Carolina have a state constitution. As president of the Provincial Congress, William Henry Drayton in the morning of March 26, 1776, signed the new constitution. In the afternoon, the same body met as the General Assembly. John Rutledge was elected president, Henry Laurens vice-president, and William Henry Drayton chief justice.

One of the most brilliant and important speeches of his career was Drayton's charge to the grand jury in Charles Town on April 23, 1776. In this speech he gave the reason why America must be free and independent. In fiery words he pointed out the stupid mistakes which had been made by the British. He showed why South Carolinians should, from now on, think of independence, and not of reconciliation.

The Seal of the State of South Carolina, designed by William Henry Drayton and Arthur Middleton. The arms, or side showing the Palmetto tree, is the work of Drayton, and the other side that of Middleton.

He ended with a boastful statement of what South Carolina had already done to win her independence from Great Britain.

In December, 1777, when President John Rutledge and Vice-President Henry Laurens were both forced to leave the state temporarily, Rutledge appointed Drayton acting president until his return.

The Great Seal of South Carolina should be a spur to our memories. The Provincial seal had been taken by Lord William Campbell when he fled from Charles Town. The arms of the new Great Seal were prepared by William

Henry Drayton, and the reverse of it was designed by his friend, Arthur Middleton. Both sides honor the great battle of Fort Moultrie, which was fought on June 28, 1776. The original Great Seal is never used today, because of its inconvenience.

More honors were to come to Drayton. On March 30,

John Drayton, Governor of South Carolina, son of William Henry Drayton.

1778, while still chief justice of South Carolina, he was elected to the Continental Congress, where he served until his death in September, 1779. Except for Gouverneur Morris of New York, no other man in the Congress was appointed to so many committees. He was also sent on some important missions. When the Congress wanted a messenger to go to George Washington at Valley Forge, it selected young Drayton. When a committee was appointed to greet, with proper ceremony, the first minister plenipotentiary to be sent to the United States from her ally, France, Drayton was on the committee. Even the fact that the war was at its height did not dim the elegance of this reception. Gold-trimmed uniforms were the order of the day, and every rule of etiquette was followed in elaborate detail.

While he was in the Continental Congress William Henry Drayton kept a detailed record of its doings. He had copies of all the important state papers as well as of all the debates. What a wonderful store of information we should have today, if these papers had not been destroyed by his friends! But these friends felt that the papers were too secret to be published. Fortunately, however, the papers regarding the affairs of South Carolina, from the beginning of the Revolution to 1779, were not burned. Many years later these were edited and published by Drayton's son, Governor John Drayton, under the title *Drayton's Memoirs*.

Henry Laurens, the president of the Continental Congress, sometimes found his fellow townsman, William Henry Drayton, a little hard to get along with. Frequently they didn't see things the same way, and these political differences affected their personal friendship. But when the news arrived that Drayton had typhus fever, Laurens forgot what he called "Drayton's schoolboy jarrings" and went immediately to ask if there were anything he could do. In a letter Laurens tells of Drayton's desire that Mrs. Drayton have the news of his illness broken to her gently, and of his hope that Drayton will recover.

However, on September 3, 1779, one of the most brilliant, bold, fine characters of the Revolutionary period died. His funeral, which took place in Philadelphia, showed that he was held in high honor. The Continental Congress attended in a body. All the members of Congress were asked to appear with crepe around the left arm and to continue in mourning for the period of one month. It was impossible to send Drayton's body back to South Carolina for burial; so his grave is located in Christ Church cemetery, Philadelphia.

In the death of Drayton at the early age of thirty-seven, South Carolina lost perhaps her most brilliant, and by some people considered her most erratic leader in the Revolution. He was an eloquent and graceful speaker. His manner was courtly and gracious. His son has described him as a man "whose virtues were many and faults few." His death was a great blow to the two children who survived him, Mary, who later married Thomas Parker, and John, later to become governor of South Carolina, the state which his father had done so much to create.

Revolutionary cloak pin honoring William Henry Drayton.

Thomas Sumter
1734–1832

LET'S TURN back the clock and pretend that we are boys and girls in Charles Town on an October day in 1762. "Come on, Mary, you might be able to catch sight of those Indian warriors who have just come back from London."

"Jamie, why *are* you so slow? You are going to miss seeing them, and they are so dressed up in their blue and red clothes! Their faces are all painted with stripes of various colors. Will you look at the medals they have on their breasts!"

"But who on earth is that man who seems to have them in charge? You notice he doesn't let them out of his sight. He certainly is strutting down the streets of Charles Town!"

That young man in the uniform of a Virginia sergeant was Thomas Sumter. This was his very first sight of Charles Town, indeed his first sight of South Carolina, where he

Thomas Sumter in his later years.
Reproduced from a rare contemporary likeness of about 1830.

was to play such an important part. He did not dream that some day a fort bearing his name would protect the very harbor through which he had entered, and that from this fort in 1860 would be fired a shot heard around the world.

This landing in Charles Town was but a stop on the way home. A few years earlier, after his service in the French and Indian War, Sumter had been in the Cherokee country. While he was there, the chief had decided that he wanted to see the Great White Father, the King of England. Sergeant Thomas Sumter had been selected to accompany the Indians to England.

The two months' stay in England was a tremendous success. They were shown all over the country, and everyone made a big fuss over them. Sumter was by no means forgotten, either. Even the royal family had shown him their appreciation. The trip had been financially successful also, for it is said that Sumter collected his share of the gold which was thrown to the Indians. As he stepped forth in the little city of Charles Town, he was an elegant and somewhat bored young man, dressed in scarlet and gold lace.

After all the thrills of London Town, it could not be expected that this young Virginian would find much excitement in the little South Carolina seaport. He had heard that a man named Christopher Gadsden was going to make a speech to the people under the Liberty Tree; and as Sumter had nothing else to do, he decided to hear it. That meeting under the Liberty Tree was his first sight of a well-planned political campaign. It gave him his first patriotic thrill. Perhaps that speech of Christopher Gadsden's was the flame that lit the fire of Sumter's patriotism.

Thomas Sumter had been born near Charlottesville, Virginia, on August 14, 1734. His family did not keep records, and so we are not sure that his father had come to Virginia from England, by way of Wales, as has been said. In fact we are not entirely sure that his father was named Thomas rather than William. But we do know that while Thomas was a very young boy, his father died, leaving a number of sons and daughters to be reared by his wife, Patience, who lived to be one hundred and eleven years old.

There was little schooling for the Sumter children, for it was hard work making a living. Thomas helped his father in running a mill near their home, and later he tended his mother's sheep. Sometimes he was fortunate enough to get a few days' work plowing in the fields of a neighbor, Benjamin Cave. None of the frontier boys could boast of closets full of clothes, and certainly Thomas Sumter could not. An interesting story has come down to us of Sumter and his friend Lucas. They had only one shirt each, which they washed in Cave's branch, meanwhile playing marbles while the shirts dried on the near-by bushes. Unfortunately, we have not been told what happened to Thomas' laundry when the weather was cold and the water was frozen.

Young Thomas was not too busy to enjoy his favorite sport of cockfighting, nor could anything keep him from enlisting, with other young men in his neighborhood, for service in the French and Indian war. It was after this service in the war that he escorted the Cherokee braves to London.

After his return from England, he decided to accept the invitation of the Indian, Outacite, to visit the Cherokee towns before going back to Virginia. He enjoyed his stay among the Indians, and he was particularly delighted with their games. It is said that he could out-run, out-jump, and out-swim all but one of the Indians, a man named Saucy

Outacite, a Cherokee chief who invited Sumter to visit
the Cherokee towns.

From an engraving in Drake's Book of the Indians of
North America (Biography and History of the Indians
of North America).

Jack. He had some exciting moments during this visit into the Cherokee land, particularly in his single-handed fight with, and capture of, the Baron de Jonnes, a French-Canadian who could speak seven Indian languages, and was using all seven of them to stir up the Indians against the English. Sumter, at great personal risk from the Baron and his Indian friends, took him prisoner and dragged him to the nearest English fort.

He now decided that it was time to return to his home, but his home-coming was not exactly happy. No sooner had he reached Virginia than he was put into jail for debt. But few jails could hold this powerful, quick, alert young traveler. Certainly the jail in Staunton, Virginia, was not to be the one to hold him. Soon he escaped, and next we hear of him back in South Carolina, where he stayed until his death some seventy years later.

In 1763 Thomas Sumter became a land-owner in South Carolina. His land was on the south banks of the Santee River near the beautiful Eutaw Springs, about sixty miles above Charles Town. Here at the crossroads he opened a country store. This little country store was the first of a long line of business ventures—ferries over the Santee, mills, and more stores. He bought more land, too, and was made a justice of the peace, a position which carried with it dignity and respect.

In 1767 Thomas Sumter married Mrs. Mary Cantey Jameson, the widow of William Jameson. "Miss Polly," as she was called, came from a fine Southern family. Her home was filled with beautiful mahogany, china and glass, silver and fine linen. Mr. Jameson had left her a rich planta-tion, stocked with fifty-eight slaves. When she married Thomas Sumter, he was thirty-three, and she was some-

what more than forty. Shortly after their marriage, the
Sumters crossed over the Santee to make their home in St.
Mark's Parish, where they shared in the growing prosperity
of South Carolina.

Two children were born to Thomas and Miss Polly, a
daughter, Mary, who died as an infant, and their only son,
Thomas, whose birthday was August 30, 1768.

In the life of Thomas Sumter, we again might play our
fascinating game of "historical if." After the fall of Charles
Town, in 1780, Clinton, the British general, sent his forces
into different parts of the state to be sure that they really
controlled affairs. The cruel British Colonel Tarleton was
sent into the section around Sumter's home, and he ordered
Captain Charles Campbell to search Sumter's house. Sumter, having heard that the British were on their way, had
disappeared, and Mrs. Sumter bravely refused to tell where
he had gone. Campbell put her in chains and insultingly
dragged her into the yard. A young girl, Nancy Davis, who
lived with them and helped with the housekeeping because
Mrs. Sumter was an invalid, locked everything and threw
the keys in the grass. In spite of this brave effort of
Nancy's, the British plundered the house and then burned
it. If they had not done this, perhaps Sumter would not
have become the fierce fighter that he was in the years that
followed.

Buford's Brigade had been cut down by Tarleton, and
the British had boastfully declared that they had "completed the destruction of everything in arms." The affairs
of the American patriots did look black. Several hundred
men of South Carolina, however, refused to admit defeat.
They gathered in small groups throughout the state. They
brought along their old saws, iron tools, old muskets—

A group of Revolutionary heroes. Thomas Sumter is here shown at the height of his powers.

anything to be made into weapons—and the long-treasured pewter of their households was sent by their wives to be melted into bullets. One such group met at Tuckaseegee Ford. They sent for Colonel Sumter, whose earlier war experience had led them to believe that he would be a good commanding officer: "If we choose you as a leader, will you direct our operations?"

"I am under the same promise with you. Our interests and fates are and must be the same. With me as with you— it is liberty or death!"

These small groups of men had at first no real legal standing. They rose all over the state under the leadership of such men as Sumter, Marion, and Pickens. We now call them the partisan bands and their generals, partisan generals. A partisan leader is the commander of a body of independent, quick-moving troops, who are used, not in set battles but in quick, unexpected attacks.

On June 15, Sumter was made a general and became the most important of the partisan fighters. So annoying was he to the British that Lord Rawdon is said to have offered five hundred guineas (about $2,600) as a reward for anyone who would betray him.

Sumter's marches were long and hard, and there was seldom enough food. In fact, the men thought they were lucky if they had one filling meal a day. Their fights were sudden and fierce. Victory or defeat came in a hurry. Sumter risked his own life and that of his men bravely and often. True, there were many defeats, but that did not stop the "Gamecock's" men. After a defeat, they pulled themselves together and went on to a victory. Sumter, in the up-country, vexed the British whenever and however he could. Marion plagued them in the low-country, and, between the two, the English troops under Cornwallis had a miserable time.

Battle followed battle, and finally Sumter was severely wounded. His men begged him to go into hospital. Cornwallis was delighted when he heard the news of the severe wounding of the man who, on October 6, 1780, had been appointed general in command of all the militia in South Carolina. Although unfit for active duty, Sumter acted as intelligence officer for General Nathanael Greene. His scouts would collect information about the British and quickly send the news to Greene's headquarters. In this way the wounded Sumter still proved of tremendous value to the American forces. As soon as his wound had partly healed, he joined his men again.

Sumter was a great patriot, but he was also a man who faced facts. He knew that if he wanted troops and wanted them regularly it would be necessary to pay them. He had a dream of raising six regiments of light-horse, each man to be enlisted for ten months. He worked out a plan by which the recruits were to be paid in slaves and in plunder taken from the loyalists. Governor Rutledge gave it his approval only because conditions were desperate and desperate measures had to be taken.

The location of Sumter's home was a good one in peace times, but he could hardly have selected a more unfortunate place during the war. It was directly on the road of British march. When Lord Rawdon's soldiers were quartered on Sumter's plantation, the men, women, and children fled to safety. Mrs. Sumter, in spite of being paralyzed (she did not walk for thirty years), made her escape on a feather bed which was tied to a horse's back. Although a Negro woman rode behind her to hold her on, she fell so many times that when she arrived at John Barnett's house in the Waxhaws her face and body were black with bruises.

On January 2, 1782, General Sumter had been elected to the legislature, which was to meet in Jacksonborough. He asked General Greene for permission to leave Orangeburg, where his force had been doing police duty, so that he could prepare for the Assembly. This was very important to him, for he had been accused of allowing his troops to take plunder, and he wished to bring the matter up before the legislature.

Clearing his name of the charge of being a plunderer was the most important matter in Sumter's life at this time. The matter came up at legislative meetings and caused a great deal of argument. Two days after taking his seat in the legislature, Sumter asked that a committee be appointed to investigate and report. No formal action was taken, but the legislature expressed its thanks to General Marion for his great service to the state and added also thanks to Generals Sumter, Huger, and Pickens. Sumter was satisfied with this, for it showed that the legislature did not think he had done anything wrong under the circumstances.

Immediately after this, Sumter resigned his position in the militia, never again to appear in the fighting forces of his state. For two years he had been in service, a large part of that time ill from a severe wound. He had allowed himself very little rest. So fierce had been the war in South Carolina that General Moultrie had declared that "even the squirrels and birds of every kind were totally destroyed." That the partisan troops did more than their share in this fighting is recorded by General Cornwallis, who wrote,

"The difficulties I have had to struggle with have not been occasioned by the opposite army. I will not say much in praise of the militia of the Southern colonies, but the list of British officers and soldiers killed and wounded by them . . . proves but too fatally that they are not wholly contemptible."

The British could not hold South Carolina in the face of the nerve-racking strain caused by the partisan troops. These troops were like a shadow enemy, who might jump out at them from every clump of bushes, who destroyed their communications, who, when they seemed to be scattered, mysteriously appeared together again. There weren't enough British soldiers in America to be everywhere at the same time.

After the war was over, Sumter began his long service in the state and national legislatures. He was many times a member of the House of Representatives. He sat in the South Carolina convention which ratified the Constitution of the United States, although he himself was against it, because he thought it gave too much power to the central government. He had declined election to the Continental Congress, but he took his seat in the first Congress of the United States, where his speeches showed his fear of too much power in the national government, a fear which continued until his death.

In 1831, just a year before he died, he wrote a remarkable letter outlining his views and stating that he was entirely in sympathy with another great South Carolina leader of the States' Rights movement, John C. Calhoun. In 1793 he had the shock of being defeated for Congress. It was a real shock, for he had always before been elected without making any special campaign. And now someone was whispering a story that he had been speculating in paper money. In 1796 he was again elected to Congress, where he served in the House of Representatives until appointed to the Senate in December, 1801. In December, 1810, he resigned from the Senate and retired from congressional life.

All through his remarkable legislative career, which might have been enough work for an ordinary man, Thomas Sumter had his finger in every pie in South Carolina. He founded Stateburg, which is located in the High Hills of the Santee, almost in the middle of the state. He tried to persuade his fellow members that it was the ideal place for the capital which was to be located in the center of South Carolina. At any rate he named it Stateburg.

There is a story that General Sumter and Commodore Alexander Gillon, who was one of the commissioners appointed to lay off the state capital, had high words about the selection of a site. Both men became very angry. Next morning it was seen that each had armed himself with a small-sword, and the members of the Assembly felt that bloodshed would probably end the quarrel. What a dreadful beginning for a new capital that would have been! But Edward Rutledge saved the day. With fine tact, he complimented the bravery and patriotism of both veterans. Speaker Grimké finished the peace move, and the danger passed. Columbia was chosen the capital.

Here at Stateburg Sumter built the "Home House," which he intended as a home for all of his family connections and descendants. Here too he bred his wonderful race horses. In 1785 Sumter's famous horse "Stateburg" won the purse which began a racing record which has not been equaled by any horse of his size in America. Sumter was interested in a store, a hotel, and an academy, and all this might have kept him busy. He also was chairman of the commission to examine the claims of wounded veterans, and was a member of the commission to provide for the Catawba Indians. But these were only a few of Sumter's activities. He served as executor for practically everybody who died in his community. He was a charter member of the Santee Canal Company and of the Catawba Company. He had grants for more than one hundred and fifty thousand acres of land. On his plantations he conducted experiments with tobacco and cotton, in an effort to find a southern crop to replace indigo, which was no longer profitable after the Revolution, when England stopped paying a bounty on it.

No one human being could successfully do all these things, especially if he had no money except what he could borrow. Sumter was involved in so many law suits, that the courts had time for little else. "Finally he became, like Robert Morris, Thomas Jefferson and other great figures of the time, one of the most notorious debtors." He owed a great deal of money to the Bank of the State, and finally the legislature said that during his lifetime the old General should be excused from paying his debt to the state bank. But this did not help very much, and for many years, the Sumter family felt the effects of his large debts.

Throughout his life of ninety-eight years Sumter had an amazing amount of strength and agility. He rode horseback until the very day of his death. In fact, just a short time before his death he mounted his horse in his usual manner, by springing from the ground without the aid of stirrups.

Thomas Sumter lived almost a century. His latter years were spent in "South Mount," which he had built for him-

Letter written by Thomas Sumter when he was ninety-eight years old, two months before he died.

self in 1821. Here he turned over the entire lower floor to trade, and here people would come to buy or sell everything—a coonskin, a bale of cotton, or a plantation. The old General felt that it was his responsibility to scold and take care of every vagrant Indian or old soldier who came his way. Squatters were allowed to stay.

It was the popular thing to make General Sumter the toast of South Carolina, and every Fourth of July celebration centered around the old Gamecock, as he had been called for many years. When he traveled among his old Revolutionary comrades, he was welcomed and honored.

While he was still alive, he had become a great tradition.

The old gentleman loved gossip, and a very funny story is told about a young lady whose home was in Stateburg. It seems that she had been away at school for about three years. Early the morning after her return, before the household was up, she was called to the door to speak to General Sumter. He had ridden over on horseback, from "Sumter's Mount" to question and inspect her. After having satisfied himself he rode away, as delighted as any old woman that he could be the first to report to the neighborhood on how she looked and what she had learned. This was not really idle curiosity, nor was it entirely a love of gossip. Sumter had a real feeling of kindliness and love for his neighbors. His thoughtfulness and affection for his lame and silent wife also showed this side of his character.

No one ever thought of Thomas Sumter as a weakling. He was the perfect example of the American pioneer. His exciting career always showed him as a man of force. Whether he was a border adventurer among savage Indians, a soldier, or a lawmaker, he stood out as a strong man. His business ventures came to grief because they were too ambitious for his time. He was the sort of man who could have run one of the great businesses of today—say an automobile factory—but the means and the credit for running such a big business had not yet been worked out.

It is said that he never refused to put his name on a friend's bond, a practice which kept him in hot water. He had a sarcastic tongue, which was sharpened by a keen sense of humor. Naturally he liked to be appreciated, and so it was a real satisfaction to him that in 1783 the South Carolina legislature voted its thanks and a medal, and on

January 13, 1781, Congress expressed its appreciation of his services. In 1798 he had the great honor of having Sumter District named for him.

Perhaps no greater pleasure ever came to Thomas Sumter than the appointment by President Thomas Jefferson of his son, Thomas, to an important position in the American Legation in Paris, unless it was his appointment as minister to Brazil. Some day a great novel may be written about young Thomas Sumter's love affair with the beautiful French refugee, Natalie de Lage, the intimate friend of Theodosia Burr.

Ninety-eight years after he was born, death overtook General Thomas Sumter. Funeral services were conducted by Mr. Furman, and the General was buried by the side of his wife on their plantation at Stateburg. The following Monday the citizens of Columbia arranged elaborate ceremonies to honor his memory. A thrilling parade of volunteer companies led to the speaking, where glowing biographical sketches were presented. A committee was appointed to receive subscriptions for a monument; but somehow, as the years passed, the monument was forgotten. After seventy years, South Carolina pride demanded that a permanent marker be erected. It was to be more appropriate to the brave deeds of this Revolutionary general than the oak tree which then marked his grave. The legislature appropriated sufficient money for a handsome marker of native granite. The inscription closes with the words: "Tanto nomini nullum par elogium." ("Eulogy can add nothing to so great a name.")

Perhaps you may visit this burial place one day. There you will find not only this monument, erected by a grateful state, but on it you will see a bronze tablet, put there after the World War by the Countess de Fontenay. Very fittingly it tells something of the bravery of Thomas Sumter's grandsons:

"To General Thomas Sumter, who fought so
gloriously for the
Liberty of the United States
In remembrance of his two grandsons
Charles and Etienne de Fontenay,
Who fought so heroically and who died so nobly
For the liberty of France in 1916. Hommage
du Vicomte de Fontenay.
Ambassadeur de France."

DOES YOUR heart beat a little faster when you read of the daring rescues made by Robin Hood? Do you sit up half the night finishing the stories of King Arthur and his brave Knights? Francis Marion, the "Swamp Fox" of the American Revolution, was a combination of these heroes of old. With a few ragged men, he made life miserable for the British. He was here, there, and everywhere, but never where the British generals could lay a finger upon him. He and his men did their work so well that the great American poet, Bryant, wrote of him:

> "Our band is few, but true and tried,
>   Our leader frank and bold;
> The British soldier trembles
>   When Marion's name is told.
> Our fortress is the good greenwood,
>   Our tent the cypress-tree;
> We know the forest round us,
>   As seamen know the sea.
> We know its walls of thorny vines,
>   Its glades of reedy grass;
> Its safe and silent islands
>   Within the dark morass.

· · · ·

"Well knows the fair and friendly moon
   The band that MARION leads—
The glitter of their rifles,
   The scampering of their steeds.
'Tis life to guide the fiery barb
   Across the moonlit plain;
'Tis life to feel the night wind
   That lifts his tossing mane.
A moment in the British camp—
   A moment—and away
Back to the pathless forest
   Before the peep of day.

"Grave men there are by broad Santee;
   Grave men with hoary hairs,
Their hearts are all with Marion,
   For Marion are their prayers.
And lovely ladies greet our band
   With kindliest welcoming,
With smiles like those of summer,
   And tears like those of spring.
For them we wear these trusty arms,
   And lay them down no more,
Till we have driven the Briton
   Forever from our shore."

Francis Marion's grandfather, Benjamin Marion, had fled from France because he, a Protestant, was being forbidden the right to worship God as he chose. He was one of a group of French Protestants who escaped and came to South Carolina. These French Huguenots, as they were called, played an important part in our history. About 1690 some seventy families of them settled on the Santee River, forty miles above Charles Town. Benjamin Marion's son Gabriel married another French Huguenot, Esther Cordes. Six children were born to Gabriel and Esther, quite enough

Francis Marion leading a raid through the swamps.

From an engraving after a painting by CHAPPEL

to fill their small cottage on the banks of Winyah Bay, near Georgetown.

In the year 1732 the last of those six children was born and was named Francis. Francis Marion shared with George Washington some of the glory of the winning of the Revolution. They shared another thing, the year of their birth. Marion's birth probably took place in St. John's Parish, Berkeley, but very early in life he was brought to the Winyah home. For a year this baby was so tiny that all the neighbors were surprised that he lived. "He was not larger than a New England lobster, and might easily enough have been put into a quart pot." The lad was tiny, puny, and frail until his twelfth year, when he strengthened and grew fast.

The family had returned to St. John's Parish about 1735, and here young Francis had a little schooling. Here he helped in the work around the farm, and always he dreamed of going to sea. This dream of being a great sailor, of seeing the far ports of the world, would not let him rest. One day his great wish became a reality. He embarked in a small vessel bound for the West Indies. It is said that a huge thorn-back whale destroyed, by a single blow, the frail vessel, which sank so suddenly that the crew of six barely escaped in the lifeboat, without food and without water.

Marion was one of the four who survived this horrible experience, the other two dying of starvation before they were picked up by a passing vessel. Marion was cured. The sea had no more power over him. He no longer heard its wild call, but was satisfied to settle down into a plodding farmer, fishing, hunting, paying devoted attention to his mother, and sharing with his brothers and sisters the tasks of a South Carolina colonial plantation. His home in St. John's Parish was within cannon shot of Eutaw Springs Place, at which one of the most famous battles of the Revolution was to be fought.

As did many young men of that day, Francis Marion received his early training in the fight against the Cherokees. In 1760 he was with Montgomery in that famous campaign. This campaign against the Indians was the baptism of fire for many of the most important men in the Revolutionary field. Among Marion's companions in arms were William Moultrie, Henry Laurens, Isaac Huger, and Andrew Pickens. At this time he served as a lieutenant under William Moultrie, later to become the famous defender of the fort on Sullivan's Island which now bears his name. During this campaign one side of Marion's nature was clearly shown in his sympathy and mercy in caring for the children of his savage enemies.

After the Cherokee campaign, Marion returned to his farming for about fifteen years. During this time the feeling against the British was growing stronger and stronger, and was spreading into the far corners of the low-country. In 1775, when South Carolina called its first Provincial Congress, Francis Marion was sent to it to represent the Parish of St. John's, but his way of serving his country was by deeds, not words. On June 1, 1775, he was commissioned captain in one of the two regiments of infantry which had been provided by South Carolina. Early in the year 1776, Marion was made a major, and because of his strict discipline and constant drilling of his troops, he was said to be a "military architect." During the first years of the war he served at Fort Johnson, Fort Dorchester, and Sullivan's Island, where he assisted General Moultrie. For five years he served in and near Charles Town and was in command of the Second South Carolina Regiment when the Americans tried to take Savannah in October, 1779.

Can you imagine that a broken ankle might be a blessing? A broken ankle was certainly a blessing to Francis Marion, to South Carolina, and to the American forces, for because of it Marion was not captured when Charles Town fell. The story of that famous broken ankle is this: While Marion was dining at the home of friends in Charles Town shortly before the British took the city, the door to the dining room was locked in a joking effort to force the guests to drink themselves drunk. Marion, who never drank much, jumped out of the window and broke his ankle. When the order came that all soldiers who were too ill to fight should get out of the city, Marion left. He traveled by horseback, in great pain, to the Black River swamps, which lie between the Santee and the Great Peedee rivers.

As soon as his ankle had healed, Marion set off to join the Continental army in North Carolina. General Gates was then in command. He immediately gave to Marion the important task of keeping the British soldiers from crossing the Santee River. For this Marion collected a small group of militia men, armed with whatever weapons they could find. They were so ragged, their costumes were so ridiculous, and their weapons so strange that it was hard to keep the regulars from laughing at them.

After the fall of Charles Town and Gates' defeat at the Battle of Camden, military affairs in South Carolina seemed hopeless. The only chance for the Americans lay with the partisan bands under Marion, Sumter, and Pickens. Their shrill whistles or hoots like an owl or cries like a wildcat warned of danger. When their bugles sounded, on they went toward the rescue of their state.

The people of Williamsburg had formed a fighting force of their own,.and they wanted a smart leader. An invitation was sent to General Marion, who had just been commissioned by Governor Rutledge. At this time the famous Marion's Brigade was formed. It was composed of men who had no fear, who were powerful and brave. They were good marksmen—they had to be, for there were no bullets to be wasted. Above all, they were clever in the ways of the wild. They earned the right to be called "men of the Swamp Fox." The bogs and heavy forests of the swamp country held no terrors for them. Like silent Indians, they could slide in and out, under the leadership of Marion, whom they loved with a great affection. They became one of the best and most feared groups of partisan fighters.

During his campaigns, Marion would march long distances in one day. There were no carefully planned, well balanced meals for him or his men; no army kitchen followed to provide food at the end of the day. Instead, these men made their marches with little more than cold potatoes and a drink of cold water. Their rough homespun uniforms gave little warmth, and fortunate was the man who had a blanket to cover him when he slept out of doors. On rare occasions they had the good fortune to eat beef. There was no complaint, no murmur of dissatisfaction. They were fighting for their homes, their freedom, and they could do what their leader did. But if they could only have some salt! There was little to be had, and what they did find, cost ten silver dollars a bushel, which today would amount to about a hundred dollars. Marion collected some salt and distributed a bushel to each patriot family in his neighborhood and yet had some for his own men. By this action he became the dearly beloved hero of all the people who ate his salt.

The British generals, Cornwallis and Tarleton, were exceedingly eager to get their hands on the Swamp Fox. Trap after trap was set for him. British troops scoured the country. Marion would strike Tarleton in the rear, and the Englishmen would think that he had fallen into their trap.

"Ah, at last, we've caught the Old Fox."

"Perhaps you think you have, Mr. Tarleton, but when you get there, I am gone."

In order to understand Marion's success, we must realize that he commanded no well-organized regiment or brigade. His men came and went as their families needed them. He could never plan in advance exactly how many men he could count on, and those he had were so poorly equipped that frequently they went into battle with only three or four rounds of ammunition. Sometimes there were several hundred in his camp, and at other times he could almost count them on his fingers.

However, he did know that if he ever sent a really urgent message to them, they would come. He understood their difficulties, and by patience and tact he made this ragged, untrained group of men into one of the most effective bodies of troops in the war. If things went right, the British found themselves opposed by a strong force; but if things went wrong, the British found that they were chasing not men, but shadows. The work of Marion's men in breaking up the communications of the British, in keeping the loyal-

Marion crossing the Peedee.

From an engraving in the possession of the author. The engraving was made from a painting by W. RANNEY

ists from joining the British army, did much to bring victory to the South. The battles of King's Mountain and Cowpens, the constant harrying of the enemy by Marion and Pickens, turned defeat into victory.

Three times Marion tried to capture the well-fortified city of Georgetown and finally he was successful. However, in one attempt he suffered a great personal tragedy. His nephew Gabriel, who was very dear to him, was taken by the British and put to death as soon as it became known that his name was Marion. War had never been a glorious thing to Francis Marion. And now it became even more horrible. From the close of the year 1780 until the end of the fighting, war in South Carolina was a terrible thing for everyone. Marion's gentle spirit was hurt every day by the suffering, the hatred, and the terrible loss of life. The glory of war was completely lost for him in the horror of war. It was necessary that he fight to free his state, and that is the only reason he endured it.

After one of his defeats at Georgetown, Marion retired to a camp which he set up on Swan Island, where Lynches Creek and the Peedee River come together. This island is in the midst of one of the large South Carolina swamps. Because of its dense vegetation it was a good hiding place. Here the injured could get well, and those who were on the way to health could grow a little corn to add to the diet of the marching troops. Marion took over all the boats in the neighborhood. He fortified the island and was so successful in hiding that not even his own men could find him. Scouting parties went out regularly, and when they reported that it was the right time, the force would strike and then speedily disappear on their island.

There is a famous story about a young British officer who came to this camp to ask for an exchange of prisoners. He was blindfolded and led in and out among trees until he was completely lost. The story goes that when he was presented to General Marion, that gentleman invited him to dine and then served what was to him and to his men a grand dinner of nothing but sweet potatoes. When the young British officer spoke of this very monotonous meal, General Marion is said to have explained that they were fortunate to have enough potatoes to go around. The young Britisher was so impressed by the bravery and cheerful suffering of these Americans that he asked to be excused from fighting against them, for, said he, "You can't defeat men like that."

When General Greene came into South Carolina as the commander of the regular troops, he found Marion very willing to coöperate. Once in a while they did not agree, but most of the time they worked well together. Marion was particularly useful to Greene in giving him full and accurate information about the whereabouts and the doings of the British.

Probably the greatest reason for Marion's success was that he always did the unexpected. He never followed the beaten track. He never had to wait for bridges. He swam the deepest and widest rivers on his horse Ball, with the horses of his men close behind. Toward the end of the campaign, powder and shot were very scarce indeed, and many rifles had become useless. Marion realized that now cavalry might succeed where anything else would fail. The blacksmiths of Kingstree were given a busy time. Saws, farm implements, in fact everything they could get their hands on, were made into broad-swords. Four companies of men were put on horses and sent out on the road to use their swords for cutting down the British.

A rather amusing story has come down to us concerning Marion's swift movements. Once when the General and his little

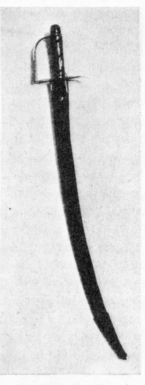

A home-made Revolutionary sword worn by Sergeant Ezekiel Crawford of Marion's Brigade. It was made from a plantation whipsaw by a blacksmith named Potter.

force had to make one of their quick flights into North Carolina, they had two cannon with them. These heavy pieces of artillery slowed their progress entirely too much. Marion decided that they should be hidden in the swamp, and never again did he carry around such heavy equipment.

Just before the war ended, Marion turned over his command to General Peter Horry and went to serve in the Jacksonborough legislature. It was hard for him to say farewell to his men. To them he was the grandest man in America, and to him they were the men who had obeyed his every command, and had made it possible for him to help free his beloved state. In the legislature, his voice was raised for mercy for the Tories, those men who had been loyal to the British. When a law was proposed by which the partisan generals should be excused from any legal demands upon them because they had destroyed or seized private property, Marion agreed that such a law was wise but demanded that his name be omitted. "If I have done any man personal harm, I will make personal payment," he said. It was indeed a tribute to him that he was never asked to make such payment. In 1790 he served in the convention which wrote a constitution for the state of South Carolina and in 1791 he was in the state Senate.

After the war, Marion returned to his plantation to find that little but the soil was left. Ten slaves remained to help him begin life again. He was penniless and tired. An effort was made, however, to make things easier for him; and in 1784 he was appointed commander of Fort Johnson. The year before, the Senate had given him a vote of thanks and had ordered a gold medal presented him for "his great, glorious and meritorious conduct." The medal, by the way, was never made. The appointment as commander of Fort John-

MANDEMENT

DE MONSEIGNEUR

L'ÉVÊQUE DE NANCY,

PRIMAT DE LORRAINE,

QUI ordonne que le TE DEUM sera chanté dans toutes les Eglises de son Diocese, en Actions de graces de la prospérité des Armées du Roi en Amérique.

OUIS-APOLLINAIRE DE LA TOUR-DUPIN-MONTAUBAN, par la grace de Dieu & l'Autorité du St. Siege Apostolique, premier Evêque de Nancy, Primat de Lorraine : Au Clergé Séculier & Régulier, aux Communautés soi-disant exemptes & non-exemptes, & à tous les Fideles de notre Diocese, Salut & Bénédiction en notre Seigneur.

Facsimile of an order issued by the Bishop of Lorraine, in France, calling for a special Thanksgiving service because the Americans and their French allies had won a glorious victory at Yorktown.

son, an office created just for him, was a good way of rewarding him for his great service in the past. But even in those days some jealous people did not like to see a great man rewarded. Because of objections, his salary was reduced to $500 a year, which was almost too little for him to live on. His pride was hurt; but, after all, he had no money and he had to keep his job for a while, at least.

There was, however, still a great deal of happiness to come to Francis Marion. Mary Esther Videau, a rich cousin, "a lady of forty summers," became his wife. They liked the same things, were interested in the same people; and their growing affection brought happiness to both of them. Immediately after his marriage, Marion returned to Pond Bluff Plantation and lived there happily the rest of his life. Mrs. Marion opened her hospitable home to the friends of the General, and many an interesting story has come down of their entertaining. It is also amusing to read the comments upon the frequent visits the General made to his old friends and companions-in-arms, when he carried with him his old tent, camp bed, and cooking utensils. In this way he was equipped exactly as he had been when serving with his famous brigade.

Fortunately, a number of letters exchanged between General Moultrie and General Marion have been saved. An old order book of General Marion has also come down to us. From these we are able to get some first-hand information about this gentle, quiet, silent man who loved books, hunting, riding, and cared little for society or festive gatherings. Shortly before his death he exclaimed, "Thank God, I can lay my hand upon my heart and say that since I became a man I have never willfully done wrong to anyone." This tells us almost all we need to know about his character.

You will remember that Marion started life as a baby so tiny it was thought he would not live. As he grew up, he became lean and dark. He was always below normal in height, and his strong body was well set upon awkward legs. His bright blue eye and high well-shaped forehead gave him an intelligent expression but he was never considered a good looking man. At the time he took command of his brigade, he is described as wearing a tight-fitting jacket of coarse, red cloth. Upon his head he wore the same cap with the silver crescent which had been given to him when he became an officer five years earlier.

In spite of his rough life as the Swamp Fox, Marion was always a careful dresser. The disorderly way in which his soldiers wore their hair is said to have upset him very much. From his order book it would seem that this was true. On January 23, 1778, he issued an order from Fort Moultrie which provided that the men must have a hair-cut, a head-dress, and be shaved daily by regular barbers. If they were found on parade with hair uncombed or a beard they would be "dry shaved" and their head was to be dressed on parade before the assembled company. It seems quite reasonable to take for granted that Marion's men were shaved!

Marion would never sit for his portrait. John Blake White of Charles Town, dramatist and artist, painted a portrait of him from which all the others are taken. The story goes that once when the artist was a little boy he sat on Marion's knee and watched his face closely. Years later he produced the well-known portrait from memory.

Death came to General Marion at his home at Pond Bluff on February 27, 1765, when he was sixty-three years of age. He was buried at Belle Isle Plantation and his grave was marked by a plain slab. About 1890 a great storm blew a tree across the gravestone and destroyed it. The legislature of South Carolina unanimously voted to set up a new handsome granite tomb. A bronze panel bears the original epitaph, part of which reads: "History will record his worth, and rising generations embalm his memory, as one of the most distinguished patriots and heroes of the American Revolution." Another panel tells of the opinion of the people a century after his daring deeds had been performed: "Esto perpetua." ("Enduring forever.")

Andrew Pickens

1739–1817

IF YOU were called "Sky-
agunsta," "the Border
Wizard Owl," would you be
insulted or would you be highly complimented? That was
the name the Indians gave to Andrew Pickens, and he considered it high praise. As far as we can tell today, "Skyagunsta" means "Principal Man," and the wizard part
probably shows that the Indians thought Pickens could
make very wonderful magic. They had good reason to
think this.

Andrew Pickens' family came to South Carolina from
Pennsylvania. His parents belonged to a Scotch family
which had settled in Ireland, and so were called Scotch-
Irish. They came to America in search of greater freedom,
"A state without a King; a church without a Bishop." Even
in his very early teens Andrew Pickens had had three
homes, which were far from each other. His father Andrew
and his mother Anne had gone first to Paxton Township,

Andrew Pickens.

From an engraving after a painting by SULLY

Pennsylvania, where Andrew was born. Their next home was in Augusta County, Virginia, and perhaps it was here that Andrew received most of his limited schooling. Word came that there were rich lands in the upper part of South Carolina, and so the Pickens family became a part of that movement which settled the up-country of Carolina with strong, vigorous pioneers. The third home of the family was at the Waxhaws in upper South Carolina.

Although young Andrew had little chance to go to school, he spent a great deal of his time learning from nature. Hunting and the growing of crops were the chief occupations of his younger days. This outdoor life was probably the reason why Andrew Pickens was always strong and healthy.

About 1756 his father died, leaving the homeplace to Andrew and his brother John. About four years later, the two boys sold their property and bought land at Long Canes, in western South Carolina.

In the Cherokee War of 1760–1761, the whole settlement of Long Canes was practically wiped out by the Indians. Those who were fortunate enough to escape fled to the Waxhaws for protection. Truly, in the case of Pickens the old saying, " 'Tis an ill wind which blows nobody good," was true. Among those who fled from the Indians were the family of Ezekiel Calhoun. They were overtaken by the savages and most of them were scalped. One of the members of this party was Rebecca Calhoun, beautiful and gay. It is said that she had the horrible experience of seeing her grandmother scalped. She was forced to watch, helpless, from the bushes into which she had escaped. Later her uncle, Patrick Calhoun, returning to bury his dead, found and rescued his beautiful young niece, and took her to the Waxhaws. Andrew Pickens met and loved Rebecca Calhoun. She was a beautiful girl, healthy and active, in her middle teens, while he was almost twenty-one. It seems probable that this romance began almost immediately, but before the young couple could be married Pickens was to serve in Grant's expedition against the Cherokees. In this he was in good company, for his fellow officers were such men as Colonel Thomas Middleton, Lieutenant-Colonel Henry Laurens, Major John Moultrie, Francis Marion, and Isaac Huger. Perhaps there would have been no Andrew Pickens left after this expedition, if it had not been for Henry Laurens, who, when young Lieutenant Pickens was fiercely attacked by the Indians, came to his rescue.

On March 19, 1765, the home of Ezekiel Calhoun was thrown open for the wedding of his daughter Rebecca, who on the next November 18 would be exactly twenty years old. Ministers were few, and not always at hand when they were wanted; so William Calhoun performed the ceremony. The wedding festivities lasted for three days, without a break, and the great-great-grandchildren of those who attended the wedding still talk about it. It was the largest crowd that had ever gathered for a social occasion in upper South Carolina, and there was much music and dancing. It was with the very good wishes of many friends and relatives that the young couple began their life on Pickens' plantation near the present Abbeville, South Carolina. The grace, charm, and good looks of the new Mrs. Pickens have become so famous that numbers of stories are told about this lady, who herself was a heroine of the Revolutionary War.

We must remember that in the up-country people did

not know as much about the difficulties with Great Britain as did those in the low-country. The people as a whole had no quarrel with England, and a great many of them were loyal to their King. Richard N. Brackett has explained this feeling very well. He said, "All good men loved the King; not to do so was a crime." The King stood for law and order; he was the beginning and the end of government. Every day many prayers were sent toward Heaven asking that the King be rightly guided and protected. Not to drink the King's health was considered a disloyalty. The people had not yet reached the point where they could forget all this and fight against their King. On the other hand, there were many people in the country who were loyal to the American cause. Thus neighbors were on opposite sides; and even members of the same family could not agree. This is always one of the horrors of civil war. Andrew Pickens, long before the beginning of the Revolution, was one of the up-country men who believed that taxation without representation was unfair. No one in the low-country could have been more opposed to the Stamp Act than he was. His attitude made a deep impression on his neighbors, for they had great respect for this tall, quiet, hard-working man who thought much and said little.

Pickens and some of his neighbors began the fight for the freedom of his country at the very beginning of the Revolution. At the bloody battle of Ninety-Six Fort, seven months after the famous Battle of Lexington and Concord and eight months before the Declaration of Independence, Andrew Pickens and his men first raised their swords against Great Britain. Pickens himself thought that his defeat of General Boy'd at Kettle Creek on Valentine's Day of 1779 was the most important blow he struck against the loyalists of South Carolina and Georgia. After the battle Pickens saw that Boyd was dying and asked if he could do anything for him. The British officer, knowing that nothing could save his life, asked Pickens if he would be sure to see that Mrs. Boyd received his watch and other valuables. This of course was done by Pickens. Mrs. Boyd was so grateful for the kindness of her husband's enemy that upon her death she left the watch to General Pickens.

At the beginning of the Revolutionary War the Council of Safety thought it wise to raise two regiments in the up-country. Andrew Pickens fought with these forces. When Charles Town fell, knowing that further resistance was useless, he marched his men out of the fort at Ninety-Six and gave his parole to the British. Feeling that his parole was his word of honor, he later refused to take up arms against the British again, even though others were doing so. It was typical of Andrew Pickens to believe that as long as the British kept their word to protect him and his family, it was his duty not to break his parole. However, the British did not keep their part of the bargain. Dunlap's gang plundered Pickens' home, as Campbell had plundered Sumter's home. Pickens felt that now he was free to take up arms against the British. So strong was his sense of keeping his word that he would not fight without personally going to the British and telling them. We can imagine the surprise of the English captain when this tall American backwoodsman walked into the British post and calmly announced that he withdrew his parole because the British had not kept their word. Captain Kerr begged him not to go back into the army, warning that if he were captured he would surely be put to death as a rebel.

Charles Town was surrendered to the British on May

2, 1780, and by 1781 Pickens had raised a regiment of men
for ten months' service, to be paid as were the men in
Sumter's army, that is, in plunder taken from the loyalists.
When they went forth to fight, they were armed with
whatever their own money could buy. They rode their
own horses and provided their own ammunition. Many
instances of Pickens' bravery and his ability in military
planning have come down to us. At the battle of Stono his
horse was shot from under him, but that did not stop his
fighting.

The battle of Cowpens is said to have been the most
brilliant example of military tactics in the Revolution. Just
before the battle Pickens joined Morgan's forces; in fact
he sent his scouts for sixty miles around gathering the
militia men to fight with Morgan against Tarleton. Between
them, with Morgan on the top of the hill and Pickens down
the slope, these two leaders did great damage to the British.
So brave was the stand made by Pickens and his men that
honors came thick and fast. On March 9, 1781, "for gal-
lantry and bravery at the Battle of The Cowpens, a sword
was voted to Brigadier General Andrew Pickens by Congress," and in his message of January 18, 1782, Governor
Rutledge praised Pickens and his men highly. In 1783 the
South Carolina legislature voted its thanks and a medal to
General Pickens. In 1794 Pickens was given the highest rank
of his career, that of major general. He had served as private, lieutenant, captain, major, colonel, brigadier general,
and finally major general. The last rank he held for only
two years and then resigned.

Pickens also served with General Nathanael Greene, and
both men in after years spoke of each other with admiration. General Greene always made a point of telling what

an excellent commanding officer General Pickens had been.

The battle of the Eutaw Springs was Pickens' last major engagement of the Revolutionary War. Here he was severely wounded in the breast. By the time he got back into the service, there was not much left for him to do except help to settle the Indian problem.

It has often been said that if it had not been for Marion in the low-country, Sumter in the middle-country, and Pickens in the up-country, South Carolina would not have been freed from British rule. Theirs was a long, hard period of fighting.

All during this difficult time, Rebecca Pickens had played a very brave part also. When her husband first marched off to war, he left his wife and several small children unprotected in their frontier home. Later in the war, when Mrs. Pickens and the children joined the many refugees who went with General Greene's army toward safety, Pickens urged her to return home because he knew that all the extra hungry mouths to feed made it very hard for General Greene. He also knew that these wives and children of the soldiers could do a great service to their country by keeping the plantations running and helping in this way to provide food. Mrs. Pickens' bravery in doing as her husband wished, led many other women to do the same.

Pickens' experiences with the Indians were very remarkable. They both feared and loved him, and they had reason for both. In 1782, when he led a force against the Cherokees, ammunition was very scarce. The General had his men mounted on horses, each carrying a short saber which had been made by the local blacksmith. A terrifying sight they must have been as they swept, five hundred strong, against the surprised Indians, whom they defeated so definitely that a lasting peace was made. Two monuments stand in the upper part of the state honoring Pickens' Indian campaigns. One celebrates his famous victory of the Ring Fight near Tamassee, Oconee County, South Carolina. He was surrounded by the yelling, painted savages, who greatly outnumbered his white force. Fearing that all his men would be captured and scalped, he looked around for a last desperate chance, which he saw in the cane brake. He set fire to the cane, so that the burning cane sounded like rifles popping and so frightened the Indians that he was able to win this desperate battle. The other monument tells us about the Treaty of Hopewell. It was signed under a large tree near his home and ended the fighting among the Cherokees, Creeks, Chippewas, and Choctaws and the men from Georgia, Tennessee, and the Carolinas.

Pickens was asked by George Washington to come to Philadelphia to consult with him about the best means of settling the affairs of the Indians of the South. Washington felt that Pickens, who had worked with the Indians and was truly interested in their affairs, would suggest what was best for both the white and the red man. Later Pickens was offered the command of a brigade under General Wayne in a campaign against the Northern Indians, but he declined. He did, however, serve as one of the commissioners of the United States for all treaties with the Indians. The hardest work he did in this respect was during the year 1797, when for six months he was in the field arranging terms and conditions. One of his friends has told an amusing story about this difficult work. It seems that when the treaty of New York was finally signed between the United States and the Creek Indians, this friend excitedly rode over to tell General Pickens the good news. He found the

AUSTENACO, Great Warriour,
Commander in Chief of the Cherokee Nation.

"Austenaco," one of the important Indian chiefs with whom Pickens dealt.

From an engraving after a painting, thought to be by Sir Joshua Reynolds, *made when Austenaco was in England in 1762.*

General and his family much more interested in the fact that their son Ezekiel had just been selected valedictorian of his class at Princeton.

General Pickens served on the Indian commission until his withdrawal from public life. The Indians feared the power of this white soldier, but they also loved him.

After his defeat of the Cherokees, Pickens established his home at Tamassee, "The place of Sunlight." What a thrilling sight it must have been to see the Cherokee chiefs in their brightest finery, with their faces painted, coming to bring to "Skyagunsta," their Wizard, the first fruit of their crops, the best of their labor. Many years after the General's death, when his children traveled in the Indian country, they were urged to be the guests of the Indian chiefs, for the children of "Skyagunsta," the red man's friend, were more than welcome in the cabins of the Indians.

After the Revolutionary War there was much building up to be done in the new nation, and thoughtful men knew that they had a great deal of hard work ahead of them. Andrew Pickens was one of these men, and he threw himself into the rebuilding of the Ninety-Six District, in which he then lived. Records have shown that the war had left, in that district alone, 1,400 war orphans and widows. The people needed lawyers, courts, and other means of justice. Andrew Pickens was one of the justices of the peace to hold the first court after the Revolutionary War in what is now Abbeville County. His son, Andrew Pickens, Jr., who was to be governor of the state of South Carolina from 1816 to 1818, was then five years old, and he drew the names of the first jurors.

Andrew Pickens served in the South Carolina legislature

The Old Stone Church, in the graveyard of which Andrew Pickens is buried.

Photo by Carl Julien

from 1781 to 1794. On December 2, 1793, he was elected to the United States Congress. A very old friend has left a record of what a fine military figure Pickens made as he rode off to Congress, on his milk-white Spanish horse. "From his holsters a brace of silver mounted pistols glittered in the sunlight. Under a tri-cornered hat his hair, now showing a silver that was greying the darker strands, was pushed smoothly back and tied in a cue. His ruffled shirt he wore with an undress military coat and on his top boots he wore a pair of silver spurs. Ten paces behind came Pompey, on a stout draft horse. He wore a livery of blue with scarlet facings and bore the portmanteau [satchel] with the dignified pride of a servant to a revered master."

Pickens was a member of the convention which wrote the 1790 constitution for South Carolina. He declined a second term in the United States Congress, but was re-elected to the state legislature in 1800. He also served as one of the commissioners to settle the boundary line between South Carolina and Georgia.

In the councils of his country Pickens played an important part. He was retiring by nature and kept himself very much in the background until some important matter came up. He did not speak often, but when he did, he won people by his common sense, his wise judgment, and his calm way of presenting the matter. At last, feeling that his long years of service were over, he retired to his sixth and final home, "The Red House," at Tamassee. Here the hospitality of the General and his charming wife to their many relatives and friends made a delightful life of rest and peace after years of fighting and planning.

The War of 1812 broke harshly into this peaceful life. Without his knowledge, his neighbors again elected him to the legislature. That body unanimously offered him the nomination of governor; but he wisely declined, feeling that the government should be in younger hands. It is sometimes mistakenly stated that General Andrew Pickens was governor of South Carolina. He was not. His son Andrew Pickens, one of the eight children who survived the General, was the chief executive of the state from 1816 to 1818, and his grandson, Francis W. Pickens, served as governor from 1860 to 1862.

This man Andrew Pickens was a rather remarkable character. He was tall and thin, with strong, well-marked features. His far-seeing, powerful eye was that of a woodsman, a frontiersman. His well-developed muscles made it possible for him to spend many hours in the saddle without weariness and without sleep. His active life, strong phy-

sique, and superb health were a great advantage in the work
he had to do. One of the most remarkable things about him
was that he never seemed to sleep.

For himself, he was not particularly ambitious, but for
his country, his ambition
knew no end. He was never
particularly interested in
money, although he had
some very valuable lands,
which he left to his children.
The opportunity to serve his
country and his people he
thought of as a gift from
heaven, and for it he never
sought, or wanted, public
applause. In fact, after the
service was given, he seemed
never to think of it again.
He was a simple man, far
more interested in the care
and education of his family
than he was in the honors
bestowed upon him. His habits gave no hint of his tremendous energy.

Governor Francis W. Pickens,
grandson of Andrew Pickens.

One of the strongest forces in his life was religion. He
was an ardent Presbyterian, who demanded that his family
live by the strict rules of his church. He was one of the
group who financed and published the *American Family
Bible,* and into his copy of this book he personally wrote
the records of his family life. It is said that Andrew Pickens
seldom smiled and never laughed. That he did not talk
much is evident from the description given by a friend,

William Martin, who said, "He would first take the words out of his mouth between his fingers, and examine them before he uttered them."

In summing up his services, Pickens himself wrote to Charles Lee that he would leave it to his country to decide whether he had been of any service. Whatever the public should decide, he had, within himself, the knowledge that, in everything he had done, he had been guided solely by his interest for the welfare and happiness of his beloved country. Certainly his country then was not as extensive as it is now, but he knew it thoroughly; Pennslyvania, Georgia, Virginia, Florida, New York, the Indian country, and the lands beyond the Mississippi, all of them he knew and loved. Though Andrew Pickens himself probably never visited New England, his sons were educated there.

The romance, which began so long before, when little Rebecca Calhoun escaped from the Indians, ended only when Rebecca "departed this life" in December, 1814. The old General's health was still good, and each sunny day he would have his chair taken out in the yard at Tamassee, where he would think over all the thrilling events of a long life. On just such a day, when he was almost seventy-eight years old, Andrew Pickens, on August 11, 1817, died. There was no hearse, no elaborate funeral ceremony. His body was put in the gig, which had so often carried him and Becky to church, and was taken to the Old Stone Church, of which he was a founder and an elder, and here his body was put next to that of his beloved wife. Perhaps no hero ever had simpler words on his tombstone: "He was a Christian, a patriot and a soldier." South Carolina appreciated this hero of the Revolution. She gave his name to a county and to one of the streets in her capital city.

Charles Cotesworth Pinckney

1746–1825

MILLIONS FOR defense, but not one cent for tribute." These rousing words went around the world. Charles Cotesworth Pinckney was a hero of the day, for in these words, it was said, he had defied the French government. Parties were given to honor the man who had made this strong statement. It became as familiar to American patriots as the immortal, "Give me liberty or give me death," of Patrick Henry. But Charles Cotesworth Pinckney never really said it. What he did say was, "No! No! Not a sixpence!" which, under the circumstances, meant about the same thing.

Charles Cotesworth Pinckney was a very remarkable man. This is not surprising, for both his father and his mother were remarkable people. He was the eldest son of Chief Justice Charles Pinckney and the famous Eliza Lucas. Eliza Lucas was a young lady of charm, beauty, and wit. She was so delightful and had so many good qualities, that

---

Charles Cotesworth Pinckney.

From an engraving after a painting by TRUMBULL.

Eliza Lucas Pinckney's dress, worn by Mrs. E. Milby
Burton, née Sally Pinckney, a direct descendant of Eliza
Lucas Pinckney. The silk from which the dress is made
was grown by Mrs. Pinckney on her own plantation.

when the first wife of Mr. Pinckney realized that she was going to die, she called her husband to the bedside and asked that he marry her dear friend, the young Eliza Lucas, and he did. At the time of their wedding, Mr. Pinckney was about forty-six, and is said to have been charming, gay, well-mannered, good-looking, and well-educated. He was a rich lawyer-planter, speaker of the House of Assembly and a member of the Royal Council of the province.

Charles Cotesworth Pinckney was born in his father's house in Charles Town on February 24, 1746. His education was a matter of great concern to his beautiful young mother. When he was only four months old, Mrs. Pinckney wrote to a friend in London, asking that she send to her some toys which would teach young Charles Cotesworth to "play himself into learning." When this baby grew up, he did not approve of his mother's attempt to teach him when he was so young. Many years later he said that this early teaching was "sad stuff," and "that by haste to make him a clever fellow he had nearly become a stupid one." He never allowed his own children to be taught until they had arrived at a reasonable age.

You will remember that gentlemen of early Carolina thought that their children should be educated in Europe. Therefore, when Chief Justice Pinckney was offered a place in London as an agent of Carolina, he and his family were glad to accept. In this way they were able to educate their children, and still keep the family together. After a "quick passage" of twenty-five days, the Pinckney family arrived in London, to find England filled with the dreaded smallpox. Before she would allow the children to go out in public, Mrs. Pinckney took a small house "for the inoculation," which protected people from smallpox as vaccination does today. The inoculation was successful, and the children were soon well enough to pay their respects to the royal family. At this time Charles' sister Harriott described to the Crown Princess the beauties of her province of Carolina.

After five years in a lower school, Charles entered the famous Westminster School. After finishing there, he entered Oxford, where he studied law.

When he had completed his legal studies in England, he went to France to study botany. He also finished a course in chemistry and another in military science. He thus had an exceedingly varied education.

Meantime his father and mother had left England for their home in Charleston. It was understood that the boys would follow in a short time, but actually they were both grown men before their mother saw either of them again, and their father never set eyes on them after he left England, for he died before they returned to America.

He believed the education of his boys to be so important that in his will he demanded that, even if it were necessary to sell their real estate, the children should be given a full, well-rounded, and complete education.

In 1769, at the age of twenty-three, Charles Cotesworth Pinckney returned to his home in Charles Town, after extensive travel in France and Germany. His mother wrote to him advising him to take a good ship, but asking him not to tell her when he was to sail, for she did not believe that she could stand the anxiety of awaiting his arrival—such were the dangers of travel in that day. As soon as he landed in Charles Town, he took up his business activities, which were naturally extensive, for his father had left a large property to be managed. He also began the practice of law.

Not long after his return, the young man was appointed acting attorney-general for the province. Throughout his long and varied career, he always returned to his profession of law. Men who lived at the time have described him as a learned lawyer, with remarkably good common sense, and successful both in the court room and out. He was not particularly brilliant in his practice of law, but he did get results, and he had an immense practice, up to the time of his death. He was more interested in making the law simpler and in helping young and inexperienced lawyers than he was in making money for himself. He paid special attention to the needs of widows and orphans, even when he could expect no pay.

President Washington paid Charles Cotesworth Pinckney a great honor as a lawyer. In a remarkable letter, sent to him and Edward Rutledge, Washington offered to either of these gentlemen the seat in the Supreme Court which John Rutledge had just resigned. They were to decide between themselves which one should have it. Both men declined because of the press of private business. This matter of declining great honors became a habit with Charles Cotesworth Pinckney, for in August, 1795, he declined the position of secretary of state in Washington's cabinet, feeling that he could be of more service in South Carolina. Just a year earlier, Washington had asked him to serve as secretary of war. The President had written that what he wanted was a man who would be bigger than his party loyalties, a man who knew military science and who would have the best interests of the country at heart. Such

LITTLE MISS PINCKNEY

By ROSE MILLS POWERS

LITTLE Miss Pinckney, seven years old,
Very much scared, if the truth be told,
Journeying down in a coach to Kew,
The Princess Royal to interview;
In silk brocade and a feathered hat,
Her dear little heart going pit-a-pat,
And bearing a gift, if Her Highness please,
     From Carolina, far overseas.

Little Miss Pinckney begs to say,
By Her Highness' leave, that she bore
     away
From her native land, with fond intent,
Three birds to Her Highness to present:
"An indigo bird and a nonpareil
And a yellow bird that singeth well."
She ends her speech, poor little dear,
With a muffled sob and a furtive tear

"JOURNEYING DOWN IN A COACH TO KEW."

"Little Miss Pinckney."

Facsimile of a poem in St. Nicholas, *November, 1918.*

"PRATTLES ABOUT THE PRETTY BIRDS."

Little Miss Pinckney, scared to death,
All in a tremble and out of breath,
Finds herself on the princess' knee,
Cuddled and kissed by royalty;
And, soothed by Her Highness' kindly
      words,
Prattles about the pretty birds,
Red and yellow and green and blue,
In the rice plantations of Ashapoo.

Little Miss Pinckney, bless her heart!—
"Was n't London, so gay and smart,
Better by far than the strange wild west?"—
Answered she loved her own land best.
A loyal little colonial maid,
She spoke up bravely and unafraid,
Kissed royalty's hand, and courtesying low,
Little Miss Pinckney turned to go.

"Little Miss Pinckney" was Harriott, sister of C. C. Pinck-
ney.

a man could be found, he felt, in Charles Cotesworth Pinckney. But Pinckney declined this high honor also.

While they were still in England, the young Pinckneys had been active against the Stamp Act. Sixteen years away from their beloved Carolina had still left them ardent Americans. Just before returning home Charles Cotesworth Pinckney had a portrait painted as a gift for one of his classmates. In it he is represented in the very act of making a speech against the Stamp Act.

When the Revolutionary War came, naturally Pinckney took a prominent part. Immediately upon his return from England, he put to good use the knowledge which he had gained in the military school in France. Soon he was made a lieutenant of militia. When the first regiment of South Carolina was reorganized in 1775, he was made the ranking captain. By quick promotion he became a major, and in September, 1776, a colonel. When the war broke out, Pinckney was assigned to the defense of the fort on Sullivan's Island. He also served on a number of important committees.

After the failure of the British in their first attempt on Charles Town, the war in South Carolina was more or less at a standstill. Charles Cotesworth Pinckney received leave of absence from his regiment and joined General Washington, as one of his aides. He was with Washington at the famous battles of Brandywine and Germantown. Then he rejoined his regiment and in 1778 was with them when they fought in Florida and at the siege in Savannah.

During the second attack on Charles Town, Pinckney was associated with General Moultrie. When the fall of Charles Town did take place, Pinckney was made a prisoner.

At first he was treated with great courtesy. The British

tried, by friendliness and flattery, to win him from his American loyalty. Little did they know the kind of man he was! In describing the efforts made by the British to win him, Pinckney wrote: "The freedom and independence of my country are the gods of my idolatry. If I had a vein that did not beat with the love of my country, I myself would open it. If I had a drop of blood that could flow dishonorably I myself would let it out."

Finding that kindness would not make Pinckney desert the American cause, the British tried to break his spirit by their harshness. There is on record a petition which Pinckney and his fellow prisoners at Haddrell's Point, near Charles Town, sent to Congress, telling of their hardships and saying that they had no money with which to buy supplies. During the thirteen months of their captivity they were allowed only nine days' pay. Once Pinckney was allowed to visit in Charles Town because he was ill. While he was there, his son died. Although he was torn with grief and the little boy was still unburied, the British demanded that Pinckney return to his prison. Relief came finally, when in February, 1782, he was exchanged as a prisoner of war. Pinckney rejoined the army and just before his discharge was made a brigadier general.

After the end of the Revolutionary War, General Pinckney continued his active interest in military affairs. Between the period of 1795 and 1798 he was major general of the state militia.

In 1787 Charles Cotesworth Pinckney served in the Constitutional Convention in Philadelphia as one of the delegates from South Carolina to frame the United States Constitution. In this convention he took a very prominent part. To him goes a large part of the credit for the provision by which no religious test should ever be made before a man could hold office. In addition, he suggested that 1808 should be set as the date at which Congress would take over the control of the foreign slave trade. He argued strongly that the Senate should have power to agree to treaties in order to put a check on the power of the president. Perhaps the most amazing of all his ideas was that senators should serve without pay, as a public duty to their country.

No one was surprised at Charles Cotesworth Pinckney's religious attitude, for he had shown his idea in his own state. Although he was a strong believer in, and an active member of, the Church of England, no man in South Carolina put up a harder fight to give equal rights to all religious groups. His church and religious activities occupied a large part of his time. In 1810 he became the first president of the Charles Town Bible Society, an office which he held until the time of his death.

After his work in helping to frame the Constitution, he was made a member of the South Carolina convention which had to decide whether to accept it or not, and he was one of the leaders in having South Carolina ratify the new Constitution.

In 1790, he helped to draw up a new state constitution for South Carolina. The committee which was appointed to frame that constitution was composed of such distinguished men as Charles Cotesworth and Charles Pinckney, John Rutledge, Henry Laurens, Christopher Gadsden, Rawlins Lowndes, Arthur Middleton, Thomas Bee, Thomas Lynch, Jr., and Thomas Heyward, Jr. Most of these names are those of old friends, for they are the men who helped to make the history of South Carolina.

Adoption of the Constitution.

From a painting by J. B. STEARNS.

Charles Cotesworth Pinckney did not have a very high opinion of the up-country. He was one of the men who most strongly urged that the capital be kept in Charleston, and he really was largely responsible for the fact that, from 1790 to 1865, South Carolina had practically two seats of government, one in Charleston and one in Columbia.

Although Pinckney had declined all of the honors which President Washington had urged upon him, there was one honor which he did accept. In July, 1796, President Washington wrote from Mount Vernon, offering him the position of minister to France. Doubtless he accepted the position in hope that he could do something to settle the troubles then threatening to cause war between France and the United States. He arrived in Paris in December, 1796, and ran straight into trouble. The government of France flatly declined to recognize Pinckney's official standing.

That was bad enough, but worse was to come. Hoping against hope that he could do something for his country, Pinckney stayed in Paris until February, when he was insulted by the police, who told him that if he did not receive a visitor's permit to stay in France, he would be arrested. You can well imagine that this made Pinckney furious, not only for himself but because it was an insult to the representative of the United States of America.

He immediately left for Amsterdam, where he was shortly joined by John Marshall and Elbridge Gerry. The three men returned to Paris, hoping to put through the work for which they had been sent. The Directors, as the heads of the French government were called, let it be known that if the United States would slip to them a bribe of about a quarter of a million dollars, France would sign the agreement with the United States. To this outrageous demand, Pinckney said, "No, no, not a sixpence." He refused to have anything to do with bribery.

Everybody thought that the United States was sure to be forced into a war with France. Upon his return to Charleston, a brilliant dinner was given in Pinckney's honor. As he entered the city hall, the band played "Pinckney's March," an elegant new piece, composed for the occasion.

In preparation for the war with France which might come, Washington made Pinckney a general, and put him in command of all posts and forces south of Maryland, including Kentucky and Tennessee. Later he was given charge of all the cavalry. That General Pinckney was truly a great man is shown by the way he felt about his own position in the army. General Knox, who had about the same rank as Pinckney, declined to serve under Hamilton, feeling that the higher rank should have been given to him.

Pinckney offered his slightly higher place to Knox, saying, "Let us first dispose of our enemies. We shall then have time to settle the matter of precedence." It was typical of General Pinckney that he would not allow himself to get involved in little squabbles about personal honors. Fortu-

Plate from a thousand-piece set of china purchased in France by Charles Cotesworth Pinckney at the time he was nominated for the presidency of the United States.

nately, all these preparations proved to be unnecessary, and the trouble with France was settled without fighting.

Still more honors came to Pinckney. In 1800 he was the candidate of the Federalists for vice-president of the United States, and in 1804 and again in 1808 he was named as his party's candidate for president of the United States.

We wonder how Charles Cotesworth Pinckney found time to engage in all the activities that interested him, and at the same time to manage his business so well that he became one of the rich men of South Carolina. He believed strongly in education and supported the movement which led to the organizing of the South Carolina College, which we know today as the University of South Carolina. His name was the first to appear as an elected member of the Board of Trustees, and for fifteen years he served as the president of the Board. For many years he was president of the Charleston Library Society, which is also in existence today. As the owner of a big plantation, "Belmont," he was interested in agriculture and was an active member of the South Carolina Agricultural Society.

In 1805, Charles Cotesworth Pinckney became the third president general of the Society of the Cincinnati, an organization formed by the survivors of the officers of Washington's army and composed of their oldest living male descendants. He held this position until his death.

Dueling was a common means of settling personal quarrels in Pinckney's day. He never believed in it, and when his great friend Alexander Hamilton was killed in a duel, Pinckney wrote a remarkable letter of protest, in which he pleaded that dueling should be done away with. This letter is still in existence.

A man of imposing and handsome figure, Charles Cotesworth Pinckney was full of fun and humor. Few men of his day were more trusted and admired. His liberal and independent thought, coupled with his excellent judgment, made it possible for him to size up men and movements accurately. He was constantly busy with public affairs. Once he had occasion to write to his friend Ralph Izard about how much he despised men who were idle. He felt that riches were no excuse for a man's not working, even if he did not need the work for himself. There was plenty of work to be done for his nation or for his community.

A great South Carolina writer has said of the two brothers, Charles Cotesworth and Thomas Pinckney, that

P. J. Redouté Del.   *Plee. Se*

PINCKNEYA *pubens.*

"Pinckneya pubens," or Georgia bark, named in honor of Charles Cotesworth Pinckney by the famous French scientist, André Michaux.

they were cultured, simple gentlemen, who had been placed by fortune in such a position that they could offer hospitality daily to their friends. Though they assumed high duties, they were brave and gentle, never snobbish, and never craving honors. Both of them were given high honors, but they had devoted their lives to what they thought was their duty to their state or nation without hope or expectation of receiving money for it.

In his eightieth year, on August 16, 1825, Charles Cotesworth Pinckney died in his beloved Charleston. The Charleston artist, Charles Fraser, designed the memorial tablet which is in St. Michael's church in Charleston.

Charles Fraser also wrote the words on the memorial to this great South Carolinian. Perhaps he can sum up for us the place Charles Cotesworth Pinckney should have in our hearts: "General Charles Cotesworth Pinckney, one of the founders of the American Republic. In war he was a companion in arms and friend of Washington. In peace he enjoyed his unchanging confidence. . . . He bequeathed to his country the sentiment, 'Millions for defense, not a cent for tribute.' . . . His name is recorded in the history of his country . . . and cherished in the affections of her citizens."

America cherishes the name of Charles Cotesworth Pinckney. We of his native state hope and pray that always our country will be true to the sentiments held by him, "Millions for defense but not one cent for tribute."

Charles Pinckney
1 7 5 7 — 1 8 2 4

I SN'T HE wonderful? He's almost like an angel."

"An angel, huh! The only angel he's like is Satan."

How can a man be both an angel and a devil? How can he be compared to the saints of old, and at the same time be called the curse of his country, a traitor to his class? That has been the fate of many politicians, and certainly it was the fate of Charles Pinckney.

No statesman in South Carolina ever held so many high offices in both state and nation as did Charles Pinckney. Four times he was governor of South Carolina. He was a member of the United States Congress in both the Senate and the House of Representatives. He was United States minister to Spain. He was the father of the Democratic Party in South Carolina. But perhaps his greatest claim to fame was the important work he did in framing the Constitution of the United States. One would think that his

Charles Pinckney.

From an engraving after a photograph.

name would be on the lips of every loyal Democratic South Carolinian. Perhaps the story of his life will explain why some people thought him anything but an angel.

By family background, Charles Pinckney was an aristocrat, in any way we might measure him. He was the son of Colonel Charles Pinckney, an important man in early Charles Town, and of Frances Brewton Pinckney, who was herself a member of one of the oldest English-American families. Charles Pinckney the elder had been a wealthy planter and a distinguished lawyer. In the early days of the Revolutionary War he was on the side of Great Britain, but later he accepted the American cause and worked hard for it. After the fall of Charles Town in 1780, the father, Charles Pinckney, again became a loyal subject of the King, and two years later his estates were taken from him by the newly-formed state of South Carolina. This is very different from what happened to his son; for after the fall of Charles Town, Charles Pinckney, the son of Charles Pinckney, was captured by the British and was sent to prison in St. Augustine, at the same time that Christopher Gadsden went.

Although it has been said that Charles Pinckney was educated in England, as were his cousins Charles Cotesworth Pinckney and Thomas Pinckney, that seems to be a mistake. Most, and probably all, of Charles' education was received in Charles Town. Dr. Oliphant, who was a professor of Greek, Latin, French, Spanish, and Italian, listed Charles Pinckney as one of his star pupils. It was quite natural that young Charles should learn law under his father, who was one of the best lawyers of his day. Perhaps young Pinckney never attended college; but after his service in helping to frame the Constitution of the United States, Princeton University gave to him an honorary degree, Doctor of Laws, as a mark of appreciation for the important part he played in framing this greatest of American papers.

Although Charles Pinckney was admitted to the bar in Charles Town, he did not practice law to any great extent. Instead, he soon became interested in politics, where his knowledge of the law was useful.

Charles Pinckney was a very young man at the time of the Revolutionary War, but he served in the American forces. He was a lieutenant at the Siege of Savannah and was on duty in Charles Town when that city fell to the British. Refusing to accept the protection of the British, he remained a prisoner until June, 1781, when he was exchanged for a British prisoner of war. His suffering and his service for his country might easily have made him one of the bitter leaders after the war. Instead, he was among the hardest workers for mercy and kindness to the defeated British and the loyalists. It was his idea that the triumph had been for the country, not for the men who did the fighting, and that, if the people wanted to show that they were worthy of their independence, they would not make things any harder than they had to for their late enemies. Today we would say, "He is a good sport."

After he was released from prison in St. Augustine, he returned to Charles Town; and on November 1, 1784, he was sent as a delegate to the national congress in Philadelphia. He served there until February 21, 1787.

Many important matters had to be considered during the sessions of this Congress. In 1786 a plan was suggested to have the United States give up all claim to the right to use the Mississippi River below the mouth of the Yazoo for twenty-five years. In return for this, Spain would give to the United States special trade privileges. To Charles Pinckney

The Signing of the Constitution. Charles Pinckney is the man opposite Washington, looking over the shoulder of Hamilton, the man who is signing.

From a painting, "We the People," by HOWARD CHANDLER CHRISTY.

this seemed a very poor swap, and he fought against it. Finally he and his friends had the bill defeated.

Pinckney was strongly in favor of a government of all the states. He knew that it took someone at the head of such a government to run it, and he knew that it took money to run any government. At this time the United States had no constitution. It had only the "Articles of Confederation," which the thirteen colonies had drawn up so that they could work together in fighting Great Britain. These Articles of Confederation did not provide any way of raising money to run the new government.

Charles Pinckney was one of the first men to see that something would have to be done about this. Therefore he joined a group of men who, on February 15, 1786, begged that some laws be passed by which the national, or federal, government could get money regularly and without a squabble each time a payment was due. At that time the federal government could only ask the states to send money to meet the government needs. It had no way to make them do so. In March of that year Pinckney was sent to talk to the New Jersey legislature and to ask them to change their action. They had refused to pay the amount of money which the federal government had asked of them. So clear was Pinckney's explanation of the needs, and so earnest was his request, that New Jersey decided to send the money.

But Charles Pinckney well knew that men could not go to all the different state legislatures forever, asking them to do the things necessary to make a united government work. He realized that changes in the Articles of Confederation were necessary. Finding that even this was not enough, Charles Pinckney was one of the first statesmen in America to urge that the Articles of Confederation be thrown away and a new constitution be adopted which would make of the states, not thirteen little nations, but one great nation.

Surely all of us have read the Constitution of the United States. If we are true American patriots, we have thrilled at the care with which those early leaders protected our rights and made life in the United States safe and pleasant, even glorious. And we can safely say that few men did so much in forming the Constitution as did Charles Pinckney of South Carolina. He had had a great deal of experience in trying to make the federal government work under the Articles of Confederation, and he knew its weaknesses. His trips to other states of the Union had shown him what they needed. From his experience under the Articles of Confederation and from his knowledge of the needs of governments, he decided to prepare a plan for a constitution for the United States.

As soon as South Carolina selected Charles Pinckney, with John Rutledge, Charles Cotesworth Pinckney, and Pierce Butler, to serve as delegates to the Constitutional Convention, which was to meet in 1787, Pinckney began the outline of a complete constitution. This plan he took with him to the meeting in Philadelphia. We must remember that Pinckney was about twenty-nine years old, and to many of the old, wise statesmen he must have seemed pretty much of an upstart youngster when he handed to the Convention a completely written plan of a constitution. Of course this Pinckney plan was not used as a whole, but it is now believed that at least thirty-one or thirty-two of Pinckney's ideas went into the new Constitution.

Finally the Constitution of the United States was adopted by the Convention in Philadelphia. Then it had to be sent to the individual states, for them to accept or reject, and all the delegates went home to help their states decide. John Rutledge and the Pinckneys put it across in South Carolina. Both in the legislature, and later in the state convention which was called to ratify the Constitution, they explained every point about which there was an argument. The up-country opposed it. So did a group of low-country men, led by Rawlins Lowndes. On May 23, 1788, the South Carolina Convention adopted the Constitution.

In the Constitutional Convention in Philadelphia Charles Pinckney had been a believer in government by men of the upper class, who seemed to have the wealth, the time, and the knowledge to devote to government. Imagine, then, how people felt when Charles Pinckney, the son of one of the wealthiest families in America, a man who had been brought up in the same style as a nobleman of England, became·the leader of democracy as it was preached by Thomas Jefferson.

Charles Pinckney was a Charlestonian, but he supported the constitutional amendment which in 1808 gave the back-country additional representation in the legislature of South Carolina, so that a small group of wealthy low-country men could not keep the unfair representation by which they held the power in the legislature. In 1810 he urged that the vote be given to any white man who was more than twenty-one years of age, whether he owned property or not. You will remember that before that time it was necessary for a voter to be a land-owner or a taxpayer.

It was Charles Pinckney who managed Jefferson's presidential campaign in South Carolina, and for this many members of his own family became his enemies. His cousin, Charles Cotesworth Pinckney, was running for the vice-presidency of the United States on the opposite, or Federal-ist, ticket, and many people thought that the very least Charles Pinckney could do, if he couldn't help his cousin, was to keep quiet. By birth, by education, in fact by every standard which his friends knew, he should have been a Federalist, lined up with the other Pinckneys.

Now perhaps we can answer the question: How can a man be both an angel and a devil? To the common man for whom Pinckney labored, he was an angel; but there were no words bad enough to describe the feeling that the higher classes, his relatives and early friends, had toward him.

Four times Charles Pinckney was elected governor of

South Carolina, a record no other man ever held. One of the most interesting papers in South Carolina history is the message which Governor Charles Pinckney sent to the legislature in 1797, urging that public free schools be established throughout the state and that they be run according to the best educational knowledge. He made the very wise comment that if a government was to be built for the happiness and freedom of its citizens and was to do as those citizens wished, it was absolutely necessary that the people be educated. Then their opinions and desires could be based upon the proper ideas. He might have stated it very simply:—If people are to govern themselves they must have an easy means to educate themselves so that they will know how to govern their nation wisely.

Silhouette of Charles Pinckney owned by Miss Josephine Pinckney.

While Pinckney was governor of South Carolina, the capital was changed from Charleston to Columbia. The governor was not at that time required to live in Columbia. It would be interesting to know how much of his time Governor Pinckney spent in the new little capital city. We do know that he owned a home which he called "Mount Tacitus," located about two or three miles from the heart of

Columbia on the bank of the Congaree River. Edward Hooker, a young visitor to Columbia, wrote on November 15, 1805, that he had gone to the home of Charles Pinckney and had found it a large two-storied building, square, "not very elegant in appearance rather ancient and neglected." Was this the house in which Governor Pinckney lived while he attended the legislative sessions in Columbia? Did he build it for that purpose? We are told that when President Washington visited South Carolina, Governor Pinckney entertained him, not in Columbia, but in his beautiful home in Charleston. Although the President refused to accept any individual hospitality, he did allow the Governor of South Carolina to give a breakfast for him at Fee Farm, a "private dining" at which fifteen or eighteen gentlemen were guests, and also a magnificent reception and ball at the Pinckney home on Meeting Street.

The beautiful home in which Governor Pinckney entertained President Washington was considered one of the finest in America. Nothing, not even the earth upon which it stood, remains of it today. The earth was removed to help form the fortifications on White Point Battery when the Union troops were trying to take Charleston.

In March, 1801, Charles Pinckney began another part of his colorful and varied career. On that date he was appointed by President Jefferson as minister to Spain. While he served in Madrid, Louisiana was sold to the United States by France. Spain was exceedingly angry, for it said that the condition upon which it had sold Louisiana to France was that Louisiana should not fall into the hands of a third nation. There was great excitement, and Spain was making things very uncomfortable for Pinckney. Monroe, who was also in Europe, was ordered to join Pinckney in Madrid. But even he found himself so involved in an ugly situation that he finally packed up and came home. Pinckney had left some little time before Monroe.

Charles Pinckney was always a great admirer of the ladies and was a great favorite with them. For the rest of his life he considered the ladies of Spain the most beautiful, talented, and charming of the many whom he had met in various parts of the world. He may not have been successful diplomatically, but he was socially.

Charles Pinckney married into the family of one of the great leaders of the Revolutionary period. On April 27, 1788, he was married to Mary Eleanor Laurens, the twelfth child of Henry Laurens. The well-known South Carolina politician, Henry Laurens Pinckney, was their son.

Charles Pinckney had inherited wealth and he had made a good deal of money for himself. At one time his income amounted to about $80,000 a year. When he spent all his time in public life, his personal affairs naturally suffered greatly. In his early career, the Pinckneys had lived in the most expensive manner. They were famous for their traveling. Little by little, however, Charles Pinckney's fortune was spent. The people in whose hands he left his business affairs managed them very badly. After his return from Spain, his personal financial affairs were in sad shape indeed.

Many tales have come down to us about the famous Pinckney home. One writer has described it as being filled with the most beautiful works of art, wonderful pictures and statues. There was a library of twenty thousand volumes written in at least six languages, all of which Charles Pinckney read with ease. This wonderful collection of art treasures, practically all of the Pinckney papers, and the house itself were destroyed in the Charleston fire of 1861. A picture of the beautiful Lady Hamilton and a portrait of Charles Pinckney were the only two of his art treasures saved.

From this portrait and from descriptions written by friends at the time, we are able to gain a good impression of how this amazing man looked. He was one of the handsome men of Carolina. Tall, well built, and with a flashing eye, his good-humored companionship and delightful manners made him a welcome guest. No Southern statesman appeared to better advantage. He carried himself like a lord, and his clear musical voice, persuasive manner, ease in conversation, charming social graces, and very decided popularity with the ladies made him a much-talked-of man. When he spoke at a meeting he was sure to win his audience with his fund of knowledge and his sincere and eloquent presentation. Perhaps no American of that period had stauncher friends or more bitter enemies.

Charles Pinckney has been described as a vain man, but against this we must balance his tender devotion to his three young children who so badly needed him after the death of their mother in 1794.

It would seem that by 1818 Pinckney would have felt that he had served his country enough. When it seemed probable that the Federalists would be able to elect a congressman from the Charleston District, Pinckney, rather than have this happen, allowed himself to be selected as the candidate for his party. His term of office lasted from March 4, 1819, to March 3, 1821. But he was not happy in Washington at that time. He found the climate too cold and the work too strenuous for his more than sixty years; so he would not allow his name to be mentioned for reëlection. He did, however, leave his mark upon the Sixteenth Congress by his fiery speech against the dangers of the Missouri Compromise. You will remember that under this Compromise slaves were to be allowed in certain states formed from the Louisiana Purchase and not allowed in other states. Pinckney saw for years into the future and realized that this matter of slave y was bound, sooner or later, to bring tragedy and civil war to America.

When he was sixty-six years old, on October 29, 1824, Charles Pinckney died. It is hard for us to realize that no one is absolutely certain where he is buried. It is generally thought that his grave is in the churchyard of St. Philip's in Charleston, but no stone marks his resting place. Within the last few years memorials have been erected to him in several different places, notably in the state house in Columbia. His real memorial is in the hearts of the Democrats of South Carolina and in the gratitude of the people of this country for the Constitution of the United States. In this great document he put his ideals of a free people, educated and prepared to govern themselves with justice, progressiveness, and understanding. Every time we are reminded of the Constitution under which we live in freedom and independence, we might remember this great South Carolinian who did so much to bring to us this freedom, which we take as a matter of course and which makes of us the most fortunate people in the world.

Stephen Elliott
1771 – 1830

LET'S IMAGINE that we are playing the game which has been popular for so many years. Maybe you know it by the title 'What's My Name?' It has been played ever since people first began to be interested in history. It was very popular when I was young, too. Can you guess who I am? Could you guess if my name were not at the top of this page? 'What's My Name?' I was a very successful banker; in fact, I was the first president of the bank of my state, and my picture appears on a four-dollar bill issued by that bank. My legislative record was excellent, and my name certainly took a lot of space in the reports of the sessions I attended. Perhaps my greatest claim to fame is as a naturalist; or, to be exact, as a botanist. It is not surprising that I had a great deal to do with the beginning of the first museum in America, is it?

"Now don't get me confused with my son, who bears the same name, but who was the first Bishop of Georgia and a

Stephen Elliott.

very great churchman. You might fall into another trap, too, for I am not the man who was a Confederate general. He is my grandson. If it would not be misleading, I might mention that I had quite a reputation for being a good draftsman and a fairly good poet. I could tell you lots more about myself, but perhaps you have guessed already—Yes, STEPHEN ELLIOTT. Now that you have guessed, I shall vanish into the mists of history and let the rest of my story be told by some one else."

Stephen Elliott, who was born in Beaufort, November 11, 1771, was the third son of William and Mary Barnwell Elliott. His father had settled in Beaufort and had bought a great deal of land. In 1760 he married Mary Barnwell, the granddaughter of the famous John Barnwell. Unfortunately, William Elliott died when Stephen was very young, but the boy was fortunate in being under the care of his elder brother, who saw that he was given the best education possible.

One of his early teachers was the Reverend Abeil Holmes, of Beaufort, who later moved to New Haven, Connecticut. That may have been one reason why it was decided to send young Stephen to Yale University, in New Haven. At any rate, he left Beaufort for New Haven in the fall of 1787. After he reached there, it was decided that he was not quite ready for Yale; so he spent that winter in the school of a Mr. Baldwin. He knew no Greek, and had not been told that it was expected of him. He was an excellent student in Latin and French, but Yale required that he be able to read the New Testament in the original Greek before he could enter. In November he began his study under Mr. Baldwin, and at Christmas time he went to pay a holiday visit to Dr.

Stiles, the president of Yale. Dr. Stiles put him through a complete examination without his knowing it and then told him that he had done so well that he could enter the college after the vacation period.

At sixteen, Stephen Elliott was entered at Yale University. When he was graduated, he was chosen to give the only oration in English. The title of it was the almost overwhelming one, "On the Supposed Degeneracy of Animated Nature in America." Surely he could not have learned enough to write on such a subject just from his classwork! We are not surprised to learn what Mr. Hezekiah Howe wrote about him. He said that Elliott would come every day into the book-shop in which Howe worked and spend hours looking over the best books on the shelves. He was so interesting and well-mannered that Mr. Howe liked to have him, and in that way Elliott could read books which he could not then afford to own.

After his graduation from Yale, Stephen Elliott returned to his home in Beaufort. He immediately began the management of his farm lands there and in Georgia. He spent the winters attending to his business affairs in Georgia, and the summers in Beaufort, where he could see that things went right and yet enjoy the cool breezes of the coast country.

It was in Georgia that Stephen Elliott's romance began. In 1796 he was married to Esther Habersham, daughter of the Honorable James Habersham. At least two of the children of Mr. and Mrs. Stephen Elliott became famous. These were James Habersham and Stephen. Stephen went into the church and became the greatly beloved first Bishop of the Episcopal Church of Georgia.

At about the time of his marriage, Elliott was elected from the Parish of St. Helena to represent it in the legislature. Almost as soon as he arrived in Columbia to attend the legislature, Elliott took the place of leadership for which he had been trained. He served several terms in the House of Representatives; and his name appears on nearly every page

Left, Bishop Stephen Elliott, son of Stephen Elliott.

Right, William Elliott, author of *Carolina Sports by Land and Water.*

of the records. Sometimes he is mentioned as a member or chairman of an important committee; at other times he is named as the man who suggested some necessary law. In 1808 he was elected to the state Senate, to fill the place of his dead brother, William, who had formerly represented his Parish.

Stephen Elliott's legislative career was a fine one, and he had a part in the making of many of the important laws of his day. His two most important legislative acts had to do with the Free School Act of 1811 and the Bill for Establishing the Bank of the State of South Carolina in 1812. Elliott has been called the "Father of the Free School System of South Carolina," because on December 3, he had the honor of presenting a bill, which he had helped to prepare: "To establish Free Schools Throughout the State." This bill was passed, with various changes and improvements.

In 1812 the legislature realized that some better plan of banking and finance would have to be worked out for the state. Stephen Elliott was appointed on the committee to supply a better system of bank notes, or paper money. As a result of the bill introduced by Elliott, the Bank of the State of South Carolina was organized. Stephen Elliott was made the first president of the bank, an honor which he had earned by his knowledge of banking.

When he became president of the Bank, which had its headquarters in Charleston, it was necessary for Elliott to move to that city. In 1812, the Elliott family became residents of Charleston, and here they lived until the end of Stephen Elliott's life. The change in his plans, his heavy duties as president of the bank, and his absence from his plantations made Elliott want to sell his Georgia lands. His own reasons were, as he said, that "I have never been successful as a rice planter and on account of the health of my Negroes, which becomes more important to me when I cannot attend to them myself." It might have been good business to sell these plantations, but Elliott also felt it was best for his Negroes to have someone near to look after them properly.

One of the best mementos we have of Elliott as a banker is a little pamphlet which he sent to the legislature in 1819. It has the title, "The Nature of Currency." Currency, as you know, is the name of the coins or paper money used by people in their business dealings. Elliott's pamphlet is an interesting discussion of the question: Which is better for every-day use, coins or paper money? He also sent a very interesting paper to Congress on the tariff.

As a banker Elliott was a great success. Most of the banks of the various states had a good deal of trouble. Times were hard, and the managing of a state bank (which of course was "in politics") was not easy, but Elliott did it well. Are you wondering why you never hear of this bank today? It is no longer in existence; it was closed by the legislature in July, 1868. The troubled days of the war and the years following the war were too much for the bank.

While Stephen Elliott was serving as president of the Bank, he was elected as president of the South Carolina College to succeed Dr. Jonathan Maxcy, its first president. Elliott was naturally flattered and pleased and immediately accepted the position. Some of the people who were fighting the bank started a story that Elliott was only too glad to get out of the bank and that he was "deserting a sinking ship." Although he was eager to become president of the college, Elliott resigned before he ever took office. He could not endanger the future of the bank, and he certainly could not allow people to say that he would desert it when he was needed. To the end of his life Stephen Elliott was the president of the Bank of the State of South Carolina. But Elliott was yet to have part in the college life of his state.

In 1822 that remarkable man, Dr. Thomas Cooper, who became president of the South Carolina College instead of Elliott, wrote to Dr. John Wagner of Charleston. He suggested that the medical boards of Columbia and Charleston should join to establish a medical college for the state of

South Carolina. The opening of the college came on November 8, 1824. Sessions were held in a building on Queen Street in Charleston.

The new educational institution prospered until a rival school was opened in 1831. This new-comer was called the Medical College of the State of South Carolina, which was just near enough to the old title to be very confusing. In 1839 the two merged, both continuing in the Queen Street building. In 1913 the college moved to its present splendid quarters on Lucas Street. At that time the entire system was taken over by the state of South Carolina and is now truly the Medical College of South Carolina.

In Elliott's day, some very famous men served on the faculty of the medical school. Among them was Louis Agassiz, professor of anatomy, who went from Charleston to Harvard University and world fame. Stephen Elliott had a great part in the beginnings of this school. Before 1822, he

Devil-fishing as vividly described by William Elliott in
Carolina Sports by Land and Water.

had begun his popular free lectures on botany, which were attended by large crowds of men and women. Later he lectured on minerals and on the nature of the earth's surface, a science which is called geology. The next step in his teaching was his election as the first professor of botany and natural history in the Medical College.

On November 13, Stephen Elliott gave the address at the opening of the Medical College in Charleston. This address is a most interesting summary of the reasons why South Carolina needed a Medical College. In it Elliott showed how stupidly wrong the old idea was that people had to leave South Carolina in order to gain an education. He made all manner of fun of the idea that it was too hot in South Carolina for people to study and learn. Elliott feared that doctors might think that medicine was all they would need to know, and so he pointed out that it was necessary for a good doctor to have a well-rounded education. Today all medical schools follow this plan of Elliott's; for before a student can enter a good medical school, he must be a graduate of a college and hold either a Bachelor of Arts or a Bachelor of Science degree.

Right in line with Elliott's scientific interest was the part he played in the founding of the Literary and Philosophical Society of South Carolina. On May 28, 1813, a society with the fascinating name of the "Antiquarian Society of Charleston" was organized. Shortly afterwards the society changed its name to the far more commonplace "Literary and Philosophical Society of South Carolina." Stephen Elliott was elected its first president, and served in that position until his death.

In 1850 the Charleston Library Society turned over to the newly-organized Society the very large scientific collection which the library had been making for a great many years. This, with the collections made by members of the Literary and Philosophical Society, became the foundation upon which the Charleston Museum was reorganized. This museum, which is still in existence, was the earliest museum of its kind ever to be opened in the United States. Elliott contributed also many of his personal collections. His herbarium, or collection of herbs, is still owned by the Charleston Museum. Elliott was interested in every phase of science and made an excellent collection of insects and shells, which he found on the seacoast of his native South Carolina.

Many people in South Carolina do not remember that Elliott was the president of a bank. Nor do they know that he was one of the founders of the Medical College, but almost everyone knows that he was one of the great naturalists of South Carolina. During the years 1800–1808 Elliott spent much of his time practically alone on his plantations. During that period he collected the information and specimens from which he wrote his now famous book, *Sketch of the Botany of South Carolina and Georgia*, which was published in two volumes between the years 1821 and 1824. In this book he listed more than a thousand flowers, trees, and shrubs which grow in South Carolina and Georgia, and which had never before been recorded.

Wouldn't you think that Stephen Elliott had plenty to do with his various jobs? Evidently he didn't think so, for in 1821 he and Hugh Swinton Legaré began *The Southern Quarterly Review*. This was a magazine like the famous English reviews so popular in that day. In the ten numbers of this magazine, seventeen of the eighty-nine articles are said to have been written by Elliott. They covered such varied subjects as "The Life of Napoleon Bonaparte," "The

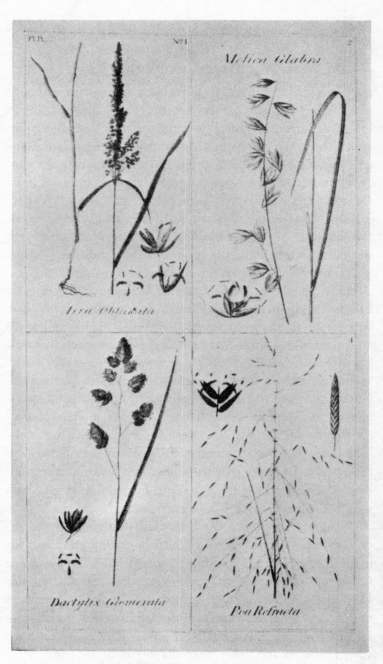

Plate IX, from Elliott's *Botany of South Carolina and Georgia*. No. 1 is known commonly as Hairgrass; No. 2, as Melic grass; No. 3, as Orchard grass; and No. 4, as Meadow grass.

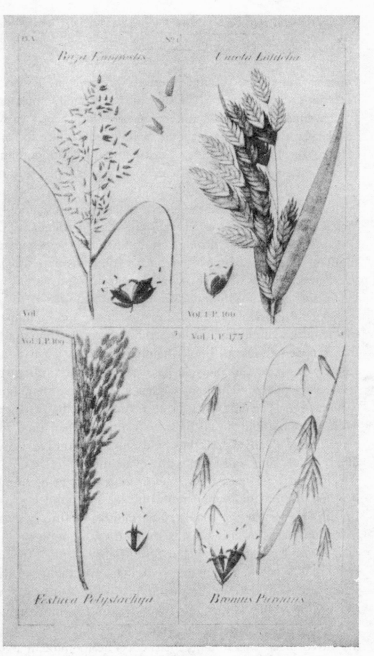

Plate X, from Elliott's *Botany of South Carolina and Georgia*. No. 1 is known commonly as Quaking grass; No. 2, as Spike grass; No. 3, as Fescue grass; and No. 4, as Brome grass. (Common names supplied by Dr. Paul J. Philson of the University of South Carolina.)

Constitution of the United States," "Travels in Russia," "Education in Germany," "The Future of Cuba," "Internal Improvements," "The Manufacture of Sugar," and "How to Classify Plants." Elliott might well have been listed as an author, for his style is easy, clear, and readable, and he turned out more articles than many a professional author of today.

In spite of Elliott's many talents and his enormous amount of information, he was a very mild, modest gentleman. His simple manners, easy disposition, refinement, and understanding of other people's troubles made him very much liked, and it is easy to see how he became as important as he did in the social and literary life of Charleston. In 1816 he was elected president of the Library Society, and he undertook and accomplished the enormous task of cataloguing the fourteen thousand books belonging to the Charleston Library Society. On the side, he was an expert draftsman and wrote poetry which was considered better than fair.

Someone asked him once how in the world he managed to do so much and do all of it well, how he had time for everything. He answered that he ordered his life carefully. There was a time and a place for everything.

Elliott was able to crowd an enormous number of things into his life, but he went beyond his strength and he paid for it. On March 28, 1830, eight months before he was fifty-nine years of age, he was stricken with apoplexy and died. Two days later, the bells of St. Michael's tolled for his funeral. The whole community—perhaps we might say the whole state—grieved at the passing of this great man just at the height of his labors. No man was every more truly mourned, and yet nearly one hundred years passed before his burial place was suitably marked. The monument over his grave was unveiled on February 26, 1933. His relatives arranged for the stone to be set. One of his kinsmen, Huger Elliott, of the Metropolitan Museum of Art, designed the simple memorial which bears the short inscription,

Stephen Elliott, 1771–1830
Son of William Elliott and Mary Barnwell
Elliott
Botanist, Banker, Planter, Legislator,
Teacher

It is a fitting tribute to this great South Carolinian, of whom it was said, "Elliott is dead—his work lives on."

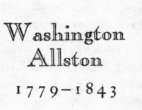

Washington
Allston
1779–1843

LITTLE WASHINGTON
ALLSTON sat by the
fire, listening to the eerie voice
of old Uncle Ned tell about "the Great White Spook"
that haunted the place where buried treasure might be
found.

"Chile," said Uncle Ned, "Dem nigguhs knew that dey
was diggin' fo' buried treasure where the Great White
Spook kept guard. Co'se you know, if you have a preacher
'long, dey scares off the spooks, so dey took the preacher
'long. The white man what was bossin' the job look up in
the sky and Lo'd a mercy there was that great white spook,
jus' a coming closer and closer. Every time he see the spook
he poked the preacher, but the preacher he so interested in
the treasure he ain't never once look up. Co'se the nigguhs
what was diggin', dey was jus' a gruntin' and a diggin', and
dey ain' look up neder. But all of a sudden dey felt sumpin'.
It was cold and clammy and all the countryside was gettin'

Unfinished portrait of Washington Allston by himself
when a young man. From Flagg's *Life and Letters of
Washington Allston*, published by Charles Scribner's Sons.

dark and Lo'd when dey look up dere was that white spook right on top of 'em. Dey was so scared dey never tho't of the preacher or nothin'. Dey just gave one yell and lit out and nobody ain' never seed 'em till yit."

Just as the great climax was reached a voice from the "big house" was heard: "Washington, Washington Allston, come in this minute. Don't you know it's time for you to go to bed? Every evening I have to call you in from the slave quarters. What do you find so fascinating out there?"

Perhaps the little boy, who was to grow up to be one of the famous painters of America, thought, as most children do, that mothers always call at the wrong time. He hated to be taken from the circle of friendly Negroes, who would tell him ghost stories by the hour—and how he did love to hear them! Try as they might, they couldn't find stories too scary for this young South Carolinian. Here he learned the delight of wild, frightening, ghostly stories. Here, too, he learned about bandits and pirates, and for many years he used them as the subjects for his paintings.

Washington Allston was born November 5, 1779, in South Carolina, probably at Brookgreen Plantation, which is now a beautiful museum-garden, given to the state of South Carolina by Mr. Archer Milton Huntington. It seems fitting that the birthplace of one of America's great artists should now be a museum of some of America's finest art.

The first of the Allston family to come from England to America probably landed here in 1685 and settled on the rich rice lands which border the Waccamaw River near Georgetown and Pawley's Island. Here the family became rich and influential. If you should try to study something about the history of Waccamaw Neck, you would find yourselves greatly confused by the number of famous Allstons whose land holdings were scattered up and down the river.

On his mother's side, also, Washington Allston had some famous ancestors. In the family Bible, Washington's birth was recorded by his father, William, "My son, Washington, was born Friday night, half after eleven o'clock, the fifth of November, 1779."

During the Revolutionary War Washington Allston's father served as a captain in Marion's Brigade. Shortly after the battle of Cowpens, Captain Allston returned to his home in Waccamaw and died. Just before his death he asked to have the child Washington brought to him. When he saw his little son, he made this interesting prophecy: "He who lives to see this child grow up will see a great man." Mrs. Allston had a feeling that these words, coming from a dying man, were a sacred trust and that she must give Washington Allston every opportunity to make them come true.

The spring after the death of Captain William Allston, Cornwallis, the head of the British forces, made his head-quarters in the home of the Widow Allston. He and his officers treated her with great respect. One evening while they were dining, someone mentioned to the British officers that there was a son in the family who was named for the great American General Washington. The officers asked to have Washington Allston presented to them, and it is said that the boy behaved in just the way all mothers want their children to behave when being shown off. Because of his perfect behavior, and in spite of the fact that he was named for an enemy general, Cornwallis is said to have kissed the young American.

Some years after the death of her first husband, Mrs. All-

Portrait of Allston's Mother, by Washington Allston.

From Flagg's Life and Letters of Washington Allston

ston said that she was going to marry Dr. Henry C. Flagg, former chief medical officer in Greene's army. Her family objected, mainly because Dr. Flagg was a Yankee. Mrs. Allston, however, said that she had married the first time to please her family; this time she was going to please herself. And marry she did, although by that marriage she was cut off from her share in the family estate. As far as the children were concerned, having Dr. Flagg become their stepfather was one of the best things that could have happened to them, for he was much interested in their education and training. He was particularly eager to see Washington succeed and gave a great deal of time and attention to him.

After having been taught a little at home, Washington Allston was sent to school in Charleston. His first teacher was a Mrs. Colcott. Once when young Washington was naughty, Mrs. Colcott made him sit alone for an hour or so. Having nothing else to do, Allston drew a picture of a boat on the bottom of a chair. This was such a remarkable piece of work for a child that Mrs. Colcott kept the chair carefully locked away from harm, as long as she lived. If you were particularly good, or a very important person, you might be given a look at the famous Washington Allston chair.

All during his school days, Washington Allston was playing at some sort of art. He would dress up sticks so that they would look like real people. He modeled in sand, and amused himself in what seemed to his family very queer ways. During one vacation he painted a picture of the eruption of Mount Vesuvius. When he showed the picture to his family, they thought it was so good that they were afraid he might disgrace them by becoming, of all things in the world, a professional painter. Dr. Flagg particularly felt that this could never be allowed. Of all his step-children, he had chosen Washington to be the one to follow his own profession and become a physician. There was a Mr. Rogers

A Marine in Chalk.

From the original in the Boston Museum of Art, as reproduced in Flagg's Life and Letters of Washington Allston

in Newport, Rhode Island, who ran an excellent school. So young Washington was shipped off to be educated at the Rogers school.

There were good pictures in Newport, lovely colorful prints, and nothing could stop the young painter from copying them. He also formed a friendship, at this time, with the young painter, Malbone, whose miniatures were to become famous. Young Allston moved in the best society, painted to his heart's content, and learned enough to satisfy the high standards of Mr. Rogers.

When he was sixteen, he entered Harvard. His preparation had been so good that, after doing his required work, he still had a few hours each day left over. Perhaps you can imagine how he used them. Of course he painted. First he made a survey of all the good pictures to be found at Harvard, and then he copied, copied, copied them, all the time learning more about mixing colors, handling his brush, and getting the effects which the great artists had put on canvas. Here his friendship with Malbone became even stronger. Allston's admiration for the work of his friend led him to try his hand at painting miniatures, but, as he himself expressed it: "It was no go," and he left the painting of the tiny pictures to his friend. Not all of Allston's painting at this time was of a serious nature. He did one ridiculous series in water colors, called the "Buck's Progress," buck, in this instance, being not an animal, but a drunkard.

In 1800 Allston was graduated from Harvard. Although he had been more interested in art than in his studies, he was always conscientious in whatever he had to do, and so was graduated with honors. He was also made poet of his class, for his classmates knew that he could write as well as paint.

One of his classmates, Leonard Jarvis, has left an interesting description of Washington's life at Harvard. It seems that the class was greatly excited by a report that two South Carolinians had arrived. Everybody was eager to see them, for South Carolinians were an unknown quantity to the class. How would they look? What would they wear?

Jarvis records that the two young South Carolinians were dressed far more fashionably than anybody else in the class. One of them was Washington Allston, who was quite a

The fountain and pool on the site where the house in which Washington Allston was probably born used to stand.

graceful gentleman. His handsome body and beautiful face were in harmony with his gentle, delightful manners. "Those who hated one another most heartily—and there were good haters in our class—and who agreed in nothing else, united in respectful and kindly feelings toward him."

Allston's room was the stopping place for many of his friends who lived in Boston. Jarvis tells an amusing story about a cold night when two friends, Leonard Jarvis and Ned Dana, had happened to stay quite late visiting and both dropped by to spend the night with Allston. Unfortunately the bed would not hold more than two sleepers. Allston very wisely refused to say which one should stay. It was agreed that, as Jarvis said, "He who first undressed and got into bed should stay there. Dana consented to the proposal, and never were garments slipped off more rapidly. Ned beat me by a stocking, so I had to dress myself again and plod my solitary way homeward, of a bitter cold night."

Dr. Flagg had never given up the idea of making a doctor out of Washington Allston. But Allston himself had decided to become a painter. Finally his family consented, and he started his career as an artist. Shortly after his graduation from Harvard, he returned to South Carolina. There he renewed his friendship with Malbone, who was then living in Charleston. He also became intimate with another South Carolina artist, Charles Fraser.

Allston now felt that he had reached the point where he had to visit Europe and study the great paintings of the world. Before he left Charleston, he arranged to have the money which had been left to him by his father turned over to him to pay his expenses in Europe. Many of his friends, who had great faith in him, offered to lend him enough money for his great adventure, but he preferred to be independent and therefore refused help.

In 1801 Washington Allston and Malbone landed in London. Young Allston at once registered at the famous art school, the Royal Academy, of which his fellow countryman, Benjamin West, was president. This was the first formal training in art which the young American had received. It is amazing that in just a year he was ready to exhibit some pictures. Three pictures from his brush created much comment. They were "French Soldier Telling a Story," "Rocky Coast with Banditti," and "A Landscape and Horseman." The first one, which was a comic study, was sold at once and received favorable comment from no less a person than the great English painter Sir Thomas

Lawrence. Evidently Allston had not expected such quick success, for not long after arriving in London he had taken several water-color paintings to an art dealer. The dealer promised that he would sell all that Allston could supply. So Allston, who had a horror of being stranded far from home without money, set to work, with his mind at ease. He had arranged for what he called "a way of escape."

Allston had invested all he had in his great adventure, and he did not intend to let it end in England. Very soon he left London for Paris. With him went another American painter, John Vanderlyne. Perhaps nowhere in the world at that time was there a more complete collection of great art than at the Louvre Art Gallery in Paris. Whenever Napoleon conquered a country, he would bring back to the Louvre the greatest treasures of the conquered land. He himself gloatingly said, "Every victory gives me a *master*." The Louvre was at this time entirely filled with the treasures of the world, many of which were returned to their rightful owners after Napoleon's defeat at the Battle of Waterloo. Allston had the great opportunity of studying at the Louvre at this time. Having viewed its many treasures he wrote, "I am by nature, as it respects the arts, a wide liker." Being a "wide liker" in the arts is a sure way of bringing great pleasure into our lives.

Paris was delightful. But Allston longed to get to Italy, which he considered the home of great art. After several months in France, he left for Italy, stopping for several months at Sienna in order to learn the Italian language. When he thought that he had learned enough to ask questions and understand the answers, he went first to Venice, next, to the great art galleries in Florence, and finally, to Rome, where he was joined by Vanderlyne. The two young

men were, at that time, the only American art students in
Rome.

In his four years in Italy, Allston learned a great deal
about art, but he did more—he began the great friendships
of his life. Here James Fenimore Cooper, who wrote the
famous "Leather-stocking Tales," was visiting. In the world-
famed Cafe Greco, Cooper and Allston met Shelley, Keats,
and Byron, three of the greatest writers of English poetry.
In Rome Allston first knew his friend, Washington Irving,
the man who wrote "The Tale of Rip Van Winkle." The
two Washingtons became the intimate companions of Samuel Taylor Coleridge, the English poet who wrote "The
Ancient Mariner." Washington Irving, who had a slight
talent for painting, became so interested in it, because of his
friendship with Allston, that he decided to become a painter
instead of a writer. Fortunately for American literature, he
found that he could not do as well with the brush as with
the pen, and so he went back to writing.

Let us hope that his enjoyment of painting was made
greater by the advice Allston gave him on how to view a
great picture gallery. Allston said, "Never attempt to enjoy
every picture in a great collection unless you have a year to
bestow upon it. You may as well attempt to enjoy every dish
in a Lord Mayor's feast. . . . Study the choice piece in
each collection; look upon none else, and you will after-
ward find them hanging up in your memory."

During the time that Allston was in Europe, there was a
great political upheaval. Many important changes took
place. One thing that happened was rather unimportant to
the world, but it is very interesting to us. When the poet
Coleridge was on his way back to England, he was told that
Napoleon was trying to capture him. This was to punish

The avenue of oaks in Brookgreen Gardens supposed to have been planted by William Allston, the father of Washington Allston.

him for some criticisms which he had written about Napoleon. The boat on which he was traveling was pursued by a French ship; and when it seemed that Coleridge was going to be captured, he hastily threw overboard all his papers. In the bag was his famous diary, which contained many pages about his American friend, Washington Allston. Down to Davy Jones' locker went the work of years—and (what is far more important to us) Coleridge's description of Allston.

It was this same political upset which caused Allston to decide to return to the United States. In 1809 he landed in Boston, Massachusetts. His reputation had crossed the ocean before him, and he was received with many honors. He wrote to a friend that he had been so honored and had so many engagements and so much excitement that he didn't have a single hour in which to sit down calmly and think. In 1819 he was made an honorary member of the New York Historical Society. His visit to America was a very important one to Miss Anne Channing. This young lady, at the age of thirty-one, finally became Mrs. Washington Allston, ending an engagement which had lasted from the time that Allston was a junior at college.

Few Americans had ever received such good art training as Allston had. He had studied under the finest masters in every department of painting, and he had also studied anatomy so that he knew the structure of the human body. Finding that it was easier to paint his figures if he could work from plaster models, he studied sculpture also. Thus he was prepared in every way to become a great painter.

In 1811 Mr. and Mrs. Allston sailed again to England. This time they took with them a pupil, Samuel F. B. Morse, and were later joined by another famous American artist, Charles F. Leslie. With this return to England, Allston's period of most brilliant work began. Practically all of his finest paintings belong to this time. The picture which won for him the English Academy first prize and a purse of 200 guineas, was "The Dead Man Revived." The art world praised his picture highly and acknowledged that he was a great artist.

The painting of this tremendous work taxed Allston's strength to the limit. Sometimes he would forget to eat and most of the time he neglected to sleep. As a result, in 1813 he became very ill and never entirely recovered. From that time on, he had not one single day in which he was entirely well. Following closely upon his illness, the death of his wife was a great shock to Allston. For weeks he was so distressed that his friends wondered if he would ever be able to paint again; but he did work on for many years.

One of the most interesting things we know about Allston is the way he prepared his palette. A painter's palette is a shield-shaped piece of wood or metal, on which he mixes and tests the colors he is going to use in his painting. This is an important matter for a painter. Allston says, "For the next painting I prepare my palette thus: At the top I put a good lump of white; next to it some yellow (say yellow ochre, raw sienna, or Naples yellow, according to the complexion I am to paint). Then red (vermilion is the best, but I always put by it some Indian red and lake to strengthen the lowest tints if required), lastly, ultramarine blue, and by the side of it a little black. My palette, you perceive, now has white, black, and the three primitive colors."

From this Allston went on to explain how he used the colors to get the effects he wanted. Perhaps he was more famous for his ability to portray light than for any other single quality in his paintings. One of his paintings, "Uriel in the Sun," is especially famous for its sense and feeling of sunlight. An amusing story is told about a little girl who, when she first saw his picture of "The Mysteries of Udolfo," went around the room closing all the window blinds. When asked why she did this, she said, "I'm shutting the light off that picture." Imagine her surprise when she discovered that the light was *in* and not *on* the picture!

To get ideas for his pictures, Allston went either to the Bible or to other famous books. He read as many novels and tales as he could get his hands on. He painted sublime, grandly beautiful subjects. He did not often paint pictures of the ordinary or familiar things of life. Portraits were not popular with him, and he did very few of them. Among the best are one of his mother, whom he loved devotedly, and one of his brother-in-law, Dr. Channing, who was a great friend. Of all his portraits, the most famous is that of Coleridge, a famous portrait of a famous man. It was painted in England, but there was another one, begun in the happy days of their friendship in Rome, which was never finished.

Not a great many of the fine pieces painted by Allston during this period of work in England have found their way to America. Another American painter, Thomas Sully, brought the famous "Cavern Scene from Gil Blas" to America. He considered it so fine that he raised, by public subscription, $3,500 with which to buy it for the Pennsylvania Academy of Fine Arts. Allston was very appreciative of this compliment paid by a fellow artist and considered the price a generous one. Today the picture would bring many times that amount if the Academy were willing to sell it.

Have you ever heard the story of the old man of the sea who climbed upon the back of Sinbad the Sailor and refused to be shaken off? Wherever Sinbad went, he had to lug around the heavy old man of the sea. Finally he made the old man so drunk that he rolled off.

Washington Allston had his "old man of the sea." It was a tremendous picture called "The Feast of Belshazzar." For more than thirty years he worked on this enormous painting, which he based strictly on the Bible story in the Fifth Chapter of Daniel. It tells of the handwriting on the wall, which none of the King's wise men could read, but which Daniel said meant the downfall of Babylon. This picture was the "doom of Allston's art, the gloom of Allston's life."

"The Feast of Belshazzar," by WASHINGTON ALLSTON.

The task of finishing it hung over his head like a heavy weight. Ten friends, who had great faith in this picture, had promised to pay $10,000 when it was finished. In fact, some of the friends paid their $1,000 ahead of time. Each month, each year, Allston expected to finish the picture. To him, it seemed a debt of honor which must be paid.

In 1820 he wrote from England to Leslie, who lived in Charleston, "The finishing of Belshazzar is all I wait for to be once more a happy husband." When he died, twenty-five years later, "Belshazzar" was still unfinished. Allston had declared that no human eye should see it until it was finished, and it was not until after his death that his friends gazed upon it. The picture was to have had two hundred complete, individual figures, and was to be as large as the side of an ordinary room. Even in its unfinished state, it is a magnificent work, and it does not look unfinished to its admirers.

In 1839 Allston was offered a commission to paint two handsome pictures for the rotunda of the new Capitol in Washington. This was, of course, a great honor, but he regretfully refused. He gave as his reason that he was unfamiliar with the painting of war subjects and that he did not know United States history well enough; but his friends knew that the real reason was that he did not think it right to give up his work on "Belshazzar" to begin another big picture.

Honors were being showered upon Allston in England. The art world recognized him as a genius, and he was being spoken of as a possible president of the Royal Academy, to follow Benjamin West. He was elected an associate of the Academy after he left England, a rare honor for an American.

Suddenly he announced that he was returning to the United States. "Why?" asked everyone. Homesickness? An irresistible longing for America? Or was it because his South Carolina agent had been either careless or dishonest and had allowed his property to get into very bad shape? His friends were distressed to have him leave England. West declared that Allston's return to America was a tragedy. But this did not change Allston's plan. In 1818 he returned to the United States and went again to New England.

The English poet Southey wrote of him:

> ". . . he who, returning
> Rich in praise to his native shores, hath
> left a remembrance

Long to be honored and loved on the banks
   of Thames and Tiber:
So may America, prizing in time the worth
   she possesses,
Give to that hand free scope and boast here-
   after of Allston."

It is sad to relate that Allston's return to his native coun-
y brought only disappointment and some unhappiness. Ill
alth, debt, the lack of fellow artists would have been bad
ough, but he had other troubles. His studio was a poorly
ghted barn; he had no models and no means with which to
nploy them. Never again was he able to paint as he had in
ngland.

There was one great happiness in store for him in Amer-
a however. On June 1 he was married to Miss Martha R.
ana, daughter of Chief Justice Dana of Massachusetts and
ter of his friend, Richard Henry Dana. There must have
en great patience in the Channing-Dana family. For this
ife, who was a cousin of the first Mrs. Allston, also waited
n years to marry him.

Perhaps next to his art, Allston showed the greatest en-
usiasm for his friends. His devotion to Coleridge has been
entioned, and a letter from Coleridge shows his friendship
r Allston. He wrote, "Had I not known the Wordsworths
should have esteemed and loved you first and most; and,
it is, next to them I love and honor you." The friendship
ith Washington Irving, which was begun in Rome, became
er dearer as the years passed. Malbone, Fraser, Green-
gh, Morse, and Leslie were devoted friends of Allston.
any years after his period of study in England, Morse
rote that his dearest hope in connection with his new in-

"The Youthful Franklin," by ROBERT TAIT MCKENZIE.

One of the many statues in Brookgreen Gardens, Washington Allston's former home.

ention, the telegraph, was that it might make enough
money for him to relieve Allston of all financial worries.

Allston's main interests were, of course, art and literature,
but he had another very attractive side. He was a great
stickler for good eating; he loved parties, theatre, and the
dance, though he never played cards. His elegant manners
and charm earned for him in college the nickname of
"Count." If he had not been a great artist, he might have
become famous as a brilliant talker. Night after night, his
friends would gather in his home to hear him talk into the
early morning hours. No one was ever known to be bored.
This habit of staying up late at night rather shocked the
quiet neighbors in Cambridge, the little college town where
he made his home after his second marriage. However,
everyone liked him. He was popular with young and old.

His daily routine would certainly justify the old remark,
"Artists are queer people anyhow." In the first place, he
had two rather amusing habits left over from his bachelor
days: He insisted on getting his own breakfast and making
his own bed. Immediately after breakfast he would light a
cigar and read a book on art, to put him in the right mood
for painting. About one o'clock he would take a pitcher of
ice water to his studio, and then begin preparing his palette,
which took about a half an hour. Next he would gaze at
his picture, awaiting the proper inspiration; a few hours of
work would follow; then home to dinner, usually with
friends. Afterwards there would be talk on art, science,
literature, politics, myths, ghost stories—every subject
under the sun. At nine, tea, toast, cake, and preserves would
be served and there would be more of the famous conversation. In spite of all this, it is recorded that he was a very
hard worker.

Religion meant much to Allston. Many times he said in jest that, next to religion, his cigar was the greatest consolation in his life. Soon after his marriage to Martha Dana, he and his wife joined the Congregational Church. When some of his Episcopal friends criticized him for leaving that church, he said, "I am not an Episcopalian nor a Congregationalist. I hope I am a good Christian."

Perhaps it was just a part of being a good Christian that he could never pass a beggar. His friends felt that he often was imposed upon, but when they told him so he smilingly replied, "I would far rather give to one unworthy person than to have someone go in need." He himself, after the first years of his manhood, was always in need of funds. Once he was down to his last sixpence, but as soon as he sold a painting, he shared the small sum he received for it with a fellow artist who, he said, needed it more than he did. At the time of his sister's death he was supposed to inherit something of her estate, but he signed his share over to his brother, William Moore, for, he declared, "William has children, and I have none. I have a profession and he has not."

Perhaps a better nickname than the college one of "Count" was "Father of American Painting." If Allston had done nothing but help young American artists as he did, he would have earned a place in our affection. He knew what struggles the young artist faced. Once a young painter came to him for advice. The young man was rather lukewarm about painting as a profession, and we can well imagine that he was completely discouraged by Allston's answer: "If a man *must* be a painter let him come prepared to bear up a mighty burden." "The love of money never made a painter, but it has ruined many." He knew that

"Reaching Jaguar," by ANNA HYATT HUNTINGTON.

honest criticism was the best gift he could give to a student, and so he mixed his praise with a little needed harshness, as when he told a student, "Your trees do not look as if birds could fly through them."

Allston was never fortunate enough to have children of his own, and so his pictures were his children. Once a friend asked him which of his pictures he liked best. He replied, "I love all my children."

Allston was a very conscientious man and sometimes sacrificed his own good for what he thought was right. For instance, his painting of the "Agony of Judas," which he did while he was discouraged and distressed after his own illness and the death of his wife, was considered the best head he had ever done. He himself was afraid that it might some day cause someone to do a horrible deed, even commit a murder, so terrible had he made the face of Judas. Rather than have this happen, he himself destroyed this fine piece of work. While working on the "Feast of Belshazzar" he decided that it would be more artistic to have a lamp lowered a few inches. This meant that every single line in the picture had to be redrawn in order to fit the change. Allston worked hours upon hours, days upon days, for one solid month, to redraw every line of his tremendous picture, all in order to lower an unimportant lamp a few inches.

Besides being a painter, Allston was a poet. In 1850 it was said that he was one of the chief poets of America. This is perhaps too high praise, but he is generally considered one of the better minor poets of this country. His ability as a writer was recognized in Europe sooner than it was in this country. In fact, all of his art was recognized earlier abroad. One interesting phase of Allston's poems cannot be overlooked—he had a way of writing a poem to accompany a picture. Of course we've all heard of music written for poems, but it is not often that the same man paints a picture and writes a poem about it.

The only long tale written by Allston was "Monaldi," published in 1841 although it had been written twenty years earlier. The scene of this story is Allston's beloved Italy. The hero was an artist who defeated the villain, a discouraged man of letters. Jealousy, envy, and revenge are all to be found in this hair-raising tale.

After the death of Allston his *Lectures on Art* were published by R. H. Dana, Jr. They had been prepared to deliver to a class, but were never used in that way.

Allston's death came very suddenly, on July 9, 1843. Mrs. Allston had invited some of her family to dine and spend the evening. Mr. Allston came in at dinner time, completely exhausted. He had spent the day working on the "Feast of Belshazzar." In order to paint the face of the soothsayer, it was necessary for him to stand on a ladder. All day he had gone up and down, up and down that ladder, and he was worn out. However, after rest and a good dinner he seemed to feel like himself again. After the guests had left, he sat in his chair and "fell asleep," never to waken again. His funeral was held as the rays of the setting sun fell on the many mourners gathered around his grave. Harvard students, bearing lighted torches, formed a guard of honor. The Dana family had been completely dazed by the shock of his sudden death, but they finally realized that perhaps his passing was a joyous one, for "he had escaped that terrible vision—the nightmare, the incubus, the tormentor of his life—his unfinished picture."

Just a few years before his death, an exhibition was held

in Boston at which the public had an opportunity to see all of Allston's American-owned paintings. The exhibition met with great success, and in 1842 his picture "Spalatro" was exhibited in Charleston. Fraser considered it an unforgettable picture, and South Carolina now adds Allston's name to the list of her unforgettable sons.

Robert Mills
1781–1855

ON THAT August day in 1781 when Robert Mills was born in Charles Town, the South Carolina seaport was still in the hands of the British. If the people of Charles Town could have looked years ahead, they would have seen that this little baby, born to the Scottish William Mills and his wife, Ann Taylor, was to become the first real American architect, and that, one hundred and fifty years after his birth, Americans would be praising his work.

Robert's parents had six children to educate, but they were able to send Robert to the College of Charleston, which even then was an excellent school. Robert was a great reader, and he made the best of his opportunities while in school. This, combined with his knowledge of nature, gave him a well-rounded education. He was graduated from the College of Charleston about the year 1800, and very soon began the study of architecture.

Robert Mills.

From a portrait bust made by A. WOLFE DAVIDSON.

Regular training as an architect was something new among Americans. A great deal of the building of that time was done by men whom we would call contractors or builders. Mills is generally considered to have been the first professionally trained American architect. He started his training with the idea that a successful building must have three qualities: beauty, order, and convenience. Can you think of anything more important than these?

There were some fine architects practicing in this country when Mills was a young man. Among them was the British James Hoban, who built the old State House in Columbia. In 1792 he won the contest for the best plans for the president's house in Washington and moved there to supervise the work. About 1800, Mills entered Hoban's office to learn the fundamentals of construction, draftsmanship, and the rules concerning the use of stone, brick, and plaster. In 1802 Mills submitted plans for a new college building at the South Carolina College. Although he was only twenty-one when he submitted these plans in the contest, Mills' work was so good that he received half the prize of $300.

About 1802 Mills had the great good fortune to gain the interest of President Jefferson. A "short visit" to Monticello, Jefferson's home in Virginia, lengthened into a two years' stay. Jefferson was greatly interested in architecture and had spent much time and study on it. He had in his home perhaps the most complete library on architecture to be found anywhere in America. Jefferson's interest and his library were a great help to the young South Carolinian.

While Mills was still a guest at Monticello, Jefferson suggested that he should tour the Northern states and fill his mind with examples of architecture in that part of the coun-

The Circular Church in Charleston. Robert Mills was the architect of the original building, destroyed by fire in 1861.

From a photograph by Bayard Wootten

A portion of the Lansford Locks, built by Robert Mills while engineer for the Board of Public Works of South Carolina.

From a photograph by Carl Julien

A stone arch of the Lansford Locks.

From a photograph by Carl Julien

try. Armed with many letters of introduction from Jefferson, Mills set out on his journey, which increased his interest in architecture and gave him new ideas about it.

President Jefferson was to have still another influence on Mills' life. When he was visiting Jefferson, Mills met Eliza Barnwell Smith, who was to become his wife. Miss Smith came from a very prominent Virginia family, so prominent that Mills thought it necessary to get the president of the United States and the governor of the state of South Carolina to write to Mr. Smith that he came from a fine South Carolina family, and that they thought he would be a suitable husband for Miss Eliza. When Mr. Smith received these letters, he allowed Mills to "pay his addresses to Eliza." Mills spoke of his marriage as his "greatest fortune." This carefully bred young Virginia girl smoothed many of life's rough edges for her husband. When the family needed money, she was not too proud to earn it. Not being a trained business woman, she turned to the things she knew and gave lessons in drawing or music. Once while they were living in Charleston, she taught music on a rented piano. Another time, while they were making their home in Washington, she opened the "Young Ladies Academy," and was quite successful in this attempt to run a school.

For several years, between the years of 1803 and 1808, Mills served in the office of the great architect Latrobe, who is said to have brought back to America much of the beauty of the old Greek architecture, famous for its lovely and stately columns. As draftsman and clerk, Mills learned not only about Greek architecture, but also how to conduct an architect's office and how to combine the work of that profession with the knowledge of a scientific engineer.

About the time of his marriage, Mills left Latrobe's em-

Stairway in the Wickham-Valentine home in Richmond, designed by Robert Mills.

The Fireproof Building in Charleston. Robert Mills, architect.

From a photograph by Bayard Wootten

ploy and began practice for himself. His career was to take him back to South Carolina, to Baltimore, Washington, Philadelphia, Virginia, Tennessee, and New Orleans. Everywhere he was to leave a trail of glorious accomplishment.

One of his very earliest buildings was the circular Congregational Church in Charleston. Here again he "scored a first," for this was the first time in America that the auditorium type of church, now so familiar to all of us, was used in America. Some of the very best of Mills' work was in the designing of churches.

Splendid work followed in quick succession. In 1812 he did a fine job of adding fireproof wings to historic Independence Hall in Philadelphia, and in the same year he built the longest arch span bridge in the world at that time. Two years earlier he had designed the capitol in Harrisburg, Pennsylvania, the same building which, with some modernizing, was used until late in the nineteenth century.

When he was called upon to build the Memorial Church in Richmond, a new interest in architecture came to Mills. This church was to be a memorial to hundreds of people who had been burned alive in a horrible fire in a theatre of that city. The more Mills read of it, the more his sympathies were touched, and from that time until his death, he experimented with fireproof buildings of all kinds. Most of his work, from then on, shows the use of stone slabs, which

Mills Building, South Carolina State Hospital. Robert Mills, architect. Probably the first separate institution in America for the care of the insane.

From a photograph by Carl Julien

would lessen the fire hazard. The earliest completely fire-proof building in the United States is the Record Building in Charleston designed by Mills, which has resisted not only fire but earthquake. It stood squarely through the terrible Charleston earthquake of 1886. This would have pleased Mills very much, for he had made an extensive study of earthquakes and of ways to protect buildings against them.

Among other interesting buildings designed by Mills while he was in Richmond, was the home occupied by the Confederate president, Jefferson Davis. It is known as the White House of the Confederacy and is now a museum.

About the year 1820, South Carolina began a very modern plan of public works. Enormous sums were appropriated by the legislature for roads and canals during the next few years. This was to be no haphazard work but was to be carefully planned. Mills had already published a very remarkable plan for the building of canals upon which boats could sail. These canals were to link up the low-country of South Carolina with the Atlantic Ocean and the Mississippi River.

In 1820 Mills became the engineer and architect for the state in putting up needed buildings. In this work he was doing the very things he had dreamed of all his life. South Carolina needed new jails and new court-houses, and Mills had the opportunity of building them. The court-houses in Kingstree, Newberry, Yorkville, Greenville, and probably others, were built according to the plans of Robert Mills. The jails in Union, Spartanburg, Lancaster, and Yorkville were the result of his planning. Of all the remarkably fine work which Mills accomplished in this state, perhaps none does him more credit than the building at the State Hospital in Columbia, which was erected in 1822. There were only three hospitals for the insane in all of America at that time, and very few in Europe. A novel feature of the State Hospital, which is still in use, is what we would call a roof garden, but which Mills described as "a garden on the roof." Here again Robert Mills recorded a "first."

There seems to be little doubt that at least a part of Mills' stay in South Carolina was in Columbia. The Presbyterian Church of that city records that he was made an elder on June 12, 1824. Certain buildings in Columbia, besides the State Hospital and the now burned Rutledge building, are thought to have been built by Mills. Among them are the center building of the present men's division of the Bible College and the central building of the old Chicora College plant.

If we did nothing but list the buildings for which Robert Mills drew plans, we could use many pages. Most of us do not have the opportunity of seeing these buildings, and so we must content ourselves with naming only a few. A textile mill in Philadelphia, an old Spanish palace in St. Augustine, which he rebuilt; bridges, waterworks, and customhouses were among the great variety designed by this famous South Carolina architect and engineer.

In 1830 South Carolina stopped spending money for public buildings. Mills then became the architect employed by the United States Government. When he received this appointment, he moved to Washington, where he served as the architect of public buildings through the administrations of seven presidents, for the years of 1836 to 1852.

Naturally Mills had been a great admirer of President Jefferson, and he was almost as great an admirer of another Southern president, Andrew Jackson. At the time that Mills published his *Atlas of South Carolina*, of which we

Camden Court House. Robert Mills, architect.

shall speak in detail later, he sent a copy of the map of Lancaster District to President Jackson, who acknowledged the gift in these words, "I have rec'd your favor of the 15th ulto. accompanied with a map of the district of Lancaster within which I was born."

More than fifty great buildings bear witness to the fine work which Mills did when he was the federal architect. Added to this are the many small buildings, bridges, and public works of all kinds. He was the architect of the beautiful Treasury Building, the Patent Office, the old Post Office building, and the Washington Monument. Any one of these would have been enough for the lifetime of an ordinary man.

Mills had still not reached the height of his powers. To

him was given the privilege of building the first three monuments to the Father of his Country. When the city of Baltimore first thought of erecting a monument to George Washington, they called for architects and artists to enter a contest. Mills' design of a great tall column crowned by the figure of Washington was the design finally selected.

The question of the day was, "How were they ever going to get that huge statue on top of that tall shaft?" The architect, however, quietly went ahead, using his skill as an engineer to plan this difficult task. "Mills the engineer was helping Mills the architect." Almost the entire population of Baltimore turned out to see it done, and it is said that many sporting gentlemen lost big bets.

The crowning achievement of Mills' life was the famous Washington Monument in Washington. Mills had already had two useful experiences. In 1825, the Clariosophic Literary Society erected a monument to the memory of Jonathan Maxcy, the first president of the South Carolina College. This monument, which stands in the center of the old part of the University campus, was designed by Mills. He also planned the De Kalb monument in Camden. A great many other famous monuments were the work of Mills, but just now we shall consider the greatest one—the Washington Monument.

Even before the formation of a nation, the people of the United States had thought of erecting a monument which would show their appreciation of their great general, George Washington. In 1836 architects were asked to submit designs. Mills' design was selected. Subscriptions, however, did not come in as quickly as they should, and not until 1848 was the cornerstone laid. Mills himself took a prominent part in the ceremonies, riding in the carriage

The Washington Monument. Designed by the South
Carolina architect, Robert Mills.

From a photograph by Horydczak

with Daniel Webster, Dolly Madison (the wife of President
Madison), and Mrs. Alexander Hamilton.

Mills' design was one of simple grandeur. He always
thought it unfortunate that his entire plan was not carried out. It called for a grand circular building, with columns in front, from which should spring an obelisk (a
square, pointed-topped column) five hundred feet high.
The monument, as it stands today, is without the circular
building or the columns, but it is considered one of the
finest in the world.

A fourteen-year-old Washington school boy, William
Brown Meloney, has best told what it means to us. He said:

"The Washington Monument was built with stones contributed by the nations of the world to honor the founder
of this Republic. In its shadow, it seems the creator's finger
pointing to the stars. From Arlington, where sleep the men
who loved freedom more than life, it looks like a giant's
spike God might have driven into the earth and said:

'Here I stake a claim for the home of liberty.' " [1]

When Mills lay dying in 1855, the shaft had been raised
only to 152 feet, but he had perfect faith that finally it
would some day rival the famous obelisks of Egypt, Greece,
or Rome, and he was not mistaken. Mills planned the
Washington shaft so that it would be perfect by the meas-
urements given as the rule by artists many hundred years
before he was born: "A naked shaft the height of which is
ten times the width of its base, so that with the base of the
shaft fifty feet square, it must be that the height of the
shaft is five hundred feet."

[1] Reprinted from Gallagher: *Robert Mills*. By permission of the Columbia University Press.

First Baptist Church in Charleston. Robert Mills, architect.

Mills continued as a public architect and engineer until he was past seventy. Then he retired, to do the things he had long wanted to do and for which he had not found the time.

One of the things he had found time to do in a busy life was a great deal of writing. His most famous book is his *Atlas of South Carolina*. In 1819 the legislature of South Carolina had authorized the Board of Public Works to prepare maps of the state and of the individual districts. The *Atlas* appeared in 1825.

It is entirely possible that if Mills had not been a famous architect, he would have become famous because of another book, his *Statistics of South Carolina*. This work of more than 700 pages was published in 1826. It is full of facts about the history, the geography, and the plant and animal life of every part of the state. All prominent men came in for attention. It is said, "Not a bird nor a flower escaped his notice." Many men would have considered this book enough for a man's life-work.

Another delightful bit of writing from his pen was the *Guide for the Visiter to the Capitol in Washington*. It tells all about the Capitol building, its works of art, its places of interest, and its history. *The American Pharos, or Lighthouse Guide*, which was published by Mills in 1832, shows the most amazingly detailed knowledge of every phase of the coast line. In it are described more than 160 lighthouses, which dotted the Atlantic seaboard, the coast of Canada, the banks of the St. Lawrence River, and the Gulf of Mexico. Simply to have traveled to all of those places must have taken months, if not years, of Mills' time.

Left, Presbyterian Church, Camden. Robert Mills, architect. Note that the entrance to the church is at the back of the building.

Right, back of the Camden Presbyterian Church, showing the elaborate entrance stairways.

From photographs by Carl Julien

Mills' Scottish ancestry probably showed in a number of different ways. It certainly cropped out in his red hair, which his friends politely called auburn. He was not a good-looking man, though his blunt, regular features immediately created a good impression. His musical laugh and his Scotch-Irish wit made him popular in any company. He had the habit, fashionable at that time, of taking snuff, which he did "with an old time elegance that would have passed the censorship of any court in Europe."

No one was ever more opposed to alcohol than Robert Mills. Many times he expressed the opinion that drunkenness was the worst sin America had. His tender heart led him into all sorts of reform. He was particularly interested in the welfare of the Negro and as early as 1821 proposed that the United States should establish a colony in Africa to which they should send American Negroes, who would be given every opportunity to establish themselves there. Mills was one of the very earliest of prison reformers. He held the opinion that the proper object of prison was not punishment, but the re-forming of the criminal into a good citizen. With this idea in mind, he recommended that prisoners be given the best and most humane treatment possible.

It was impossible for Mills' active brain to rest. In 1831 he published a pamphlet showing the necessity of roads built to carry the traffic of "steam wagons and carriages," which he predicted would some day make traffic a real problem and would cause tremendous wear to the roads. His "steam wagons" bear a strange resemblance to those things which today we call automobiles. A reaping machine interested him tremendously, and he even went so far as to send a plan for one to Thomas Jefferson, asking that the

Lancaster Court House. Robert Mills, architect.

President comment upon it. This Jefferson graciously did, saying that he thought it might be very successful. Although Mills lived in the age of canals and felt that they were very necessary for transportation, he was also planning for railroads long before the first railroad in South Carolina was put into operation. His friends probably thought he was crazy when he suggested a monorail or one-rail road. Today the monorail has been successfully used in many places, notably in Germany. One of his greatest enthusiasms was for draining and making usable the thousands of acres of swamp land in his native state.

Mills was a regular diary keeper. Sometimes he would amaze his friends by the remarkable things that came out of his little black book. One day a friend mentioned that he wished he knew how to tune a piano. With the remark, "Thank heavens for the diary habit," Mills reached into his pocket, pulled out his diary, turned the pages and, presto! gave him a formula for tuning a piano.

Mills' formula for tuning a piano, as demonstrated by Mr. G. S. Sturdevant.

Until the end of his life Mills remained the light-hearted, gay, and gentle artist of his early days. He died on March 3, 1855, and all the newspapers mourned the passing of a man whose life had been "spent with but a single thought, that of serving his country for which he had idolatrous regard." For many years his grave in the Congressional Cemetery in Washington was known only as "Number 111." Finally the Allied Architects of America felt that by marking his grave they would honor themselves, and the Daughters of the American Revolution of South Carolina gave enthusiastic assistance. In 1936 a proper marker, designed by Phil G. Golden of Washington, was unveiled. It tells of a man who, through the simple dignity and beauty of the buildings he designed, brought something fine into American life. The work of Robert Mills is as beautiful today as it was when he was here to enjoy it.

When Robert Mills' name was presented as one worthy to stand in the Hall of Fame, the *New York Evening Post* of June 7, 1920, said: "Who would have believed that the designer of the Washington Monument and the Bunker Hill Monument could keep his name from becoming a household word? To have planned *either* of these monoliths ought to be enough to insure the planner's fame; to have planned *both of them* would be to take a bond of fate." The *Evening Post* went on to say that there were probably few people who could remember having heard the name of Robert Mills, and ended, "We are interested in him not because he is famous, but *because he ought to be famous*."

Robert
Young
Hayne

1 7 9 1 – 1 8 3 8

ALL RIGHT, I'll tell you
a story about a great
South Carolinian, Robert
Young Hayne."

"Oh, Daddy, I know about him. He's the man who had
the famous debate with Daniel Webster," piped up eleven-
year-old Amy, proud of her historical knowledge.

"Sis, you don't know what you are talking about. He
wasn't any such thing. He's the man who, when he was
governor of South Carolina, sent that sassy note to Andrew
Jackson," rudely interrupted big brother John.

"That just shows how much you know. He was the man
who practically started the railroad we took to go to Cincinnati last year. The conductor told me so," contributed
young Tommy, who had already settled in his own mind
that he was going to be a railroad engineer.

"Wait a minute, children. You are all right. Hayne was
every one of the things you say. And he did them all in a

Robert Young Hayne.

From an engraving after an original drawing from life by
J. B. LONGACRE

life of less than fifty years. Why, when he died his children weren't much older than you are now . . ."

The name of Hayne, or Haynes, as it is sometimes spelled, has a way of cropping up all through South Carolina history. As early as 1700 John Hayne had come from his home in Shropshire, England, and had .settled in Colleton District, South Carolina. The coat-of-arms of the family appears in *Burke's Peerage* (the book which explains about the noble families of England), showing that the Haynes were people of importance in their home country. Some of the family fought in the Revolutionary War, on the side of the colonists. In fact, Colonel Isaac Hayne, sometimes known as the "Martyr Hayne," was of the same family. Another notable member of the Hayne family was the gifted South Carolina poet, Paul Hamilton Hayne, who was a younger cousin of Robert Young Hayne.

William Hayne, the father of Robert Young Hayne, married Elizabeth Peronneau. They had fourteen children, two of whom became famous. William Hayne was a fairly successful planter. At twenty-three he had been elected a member of the Convention which framed the new state constitution. At the time of Robert's birth, the Hayne family were living on their plantation, "Pon Pon," in Colleton District, near Charleston. Here, on November 10, 1791, the fourth son of William and Elizabeth Hayne was born. He was named in honor of an uncle by marriage, Doctor Robert Young, whose widow acted as a second mother to the young child until he was ten years old. For nine years he lived in Beaufort and in the near-by country. Friends of his early days said that he showed no unusual traits. He did, however, develop a keen sense of observation and a remarkably fine memory.

About 1800 he returned to his parents in Charleston and entered school. The Haynes were not rich people, and it takes a lot of money to educate fourteen children. Robert had to take his chances with the others, and his schooling went only through the grammar grades. This does not mean that he did not finally become a highly educated man. He gained his education by personal study and reading. He himself said that he had read every line of *Plutarch's Lives*, over and over, and that he knew the plays of Shakespeare almost by heart. He also went to see the many good plays which were presented in Charleston.

Most of Hayne's boyhood was spent in the country. The labors of a farm developed his body, so that he had an unusual amount of strength and vitality, and this helped him later on, when he needed to do vast amounts of work.

As Hayne grew to be a man he felt that it was time to drop the silly fears or superstitions of his childhood days. He thought this so important that he used to test himself to see that there was no sign of such fears left. He would listen to the scariest ghost stories, spend the night in a graveyard, deliberately walk under a ladder, or wait for a black cat to cross his path. Any little "hangover" shivers which might appear were sternly controlled.

It is probable that the Hayne family had too little money even to think of sending young Robert to college. When he was about eighteen, he entered the law office of Langdon Cheves (pronounced Chiv'-es), the most active lawyer in Charleston. Here he was trained to become a lawyer. When his law course was completed, he passed the bar examination with flying colors. He was not yet twenty-one

Charleston in 1850, a few years after Robert Y. Hayne was mayor of the city.

and so he could not practice in the courts. However, he was given his certificate as a member of the bar, upon his promise that he would not use it until his twenty-first birthday. Immediately upon being admitted to the bar, young Hayne went into the office of Langdon Cheves. Then Mr. Cheves was elected a member of Congress and left his enormous practice in the hands of his young friend and assistant, Robert Young Hayne. So it happened that Hayne, at the age of twenty-one, found himself handling one of the most important legal practices in the state. Evidently his clients were satisfied with him, for they did not go to another lawyer.

Not only did Hayne hear legal discussions in the office of Langdon Cheves; he was constantly surrounded by people who thought and talked politics. In just a few years the state of South Carolina was to be under the sway of Langdon Cheves, William Lowndes, and John C. Calhoun, though in the very early days of Hayne's practice, Stephen Elliott probably was the most influential man in the state. The whole town talked politics, and this is not surprising when we remember that in 1800 Charles Cotesworth Pinckney of Charleston had been the Federalist candidate for the president of the United States, and in 1821 the South Carolina legislature nominated another Charlestonian, William Lowndes, for the same high office.

Before he was twenty-one, Hayne was a member of the bar, and at twenty-two he had a wife. On November 3, 1813, he married Miss Frances Henrietta Pinckney, daughter of Governor Charles Pinckney. After her death Hayne was again married, this time to Miss Rebecca Motte Alston. Family ties were very strong to Hayne. He took care of his own immediate family, and he reached out to help more distant relatives.

While he was in the militia, a great honor came to him, an honor which was to prove a training school for his great success. He was invited to make the July Fourth oration before the "Seventy-six Society" and the "Palmetto Society," meeting in St. Philip's Church. To be asked to make this oration was a much-sought-after honor, and before he was twenty-two years of age Hayne had won it. His company of cadet riflemen escorted their captain to his great triumph. His speech was given, and the papers spoke well of it. Perhaps no one was more surprised than Hayne when his speech caused a "paper war" between two people signing themselves, "Veritas" and "Philo." Each one wrote to the newspaper about the success or failure of Hayne's speech. Instead of sulking because of the criticism, young Hayne carefully studied everything that was said and decided to correct his mistakes. As a result of his efforts, sixteen years later he could hold his own with Daniel Webster, the man who was known as the greatest orator and debater in America, if not in the world.

Hayne himself soon stepped into the political arena. In 1814 he went to the legislature as the candidate of the Democratic-Republican party. He had hardly reached Columbia when Governor Alston appointed him quartermaster general, a position which really was an important one. In time of war this officer had to see that the troops were supplied with all that they needed. At this time the coast was threatened by the British and the frontier by the Indians, so that the quartermaster general was kept busy. Certainly Hayne had little time to rest, for he was conducting his own business, taking care of his legislative duties, running the office of quartermaster general, and acting as one of the trustees of the estate of his father-in-law, Charles Pinckney.

In 1818 Robert Young Hayne was elected speaker of the state House of Representatives, which meant that he would have to conduct its meetings. This election was a great surprise to young Hayne. He had been in the legislature for four years, and had observed the proper way to conduct a meeting, but he did not feel that he knew enough to carry on the business of the legislature in the orderly, quiet manner which was best for getting things done. So he borrowed a copy of Jefferson's *Manual of Parliamentary Procedure*, locked himself in his room, and spent the entire night memorizing what he should do in every situation. He learned his lesson so well that his rulings were never overthrown. In fact, they were seldom even questioned.

Immediately after the adjournment of the legislature, Hayne became the attorney general of South Carolina. In this office, he was known for justice, mercy, honesty, and efficiency.

In 1822, although he had barely reached the legal age for a United States senator, he became a candidate for the

"Sailing Car." *From* The History of the First Locomotives in America, *by William H. Brown, 1871.*

From The History of the First Locomotives in America,
by William H. Brown, 1871.

Senate and defeated his opponent. On March 4, 1823, he
entered the United States Senate. When he stood for re-
election in 1828, he had no opposition.

In the Senate Hayne spent most of his effort in trying
to check the ever-rising tariff. A tariff is a tax collected by
a government upon articles which are imported from
foreign countries. We in the United States pay a tax (or a
tariff) on dresses made in France, cheese manufactured in
Holland, and olives grown in Italy. Suppose that a man in
the United States started a cheese factory. He might find
that he could not sell his cheese for as little money as the

man in Holland could sell and ship his cheese to this country. If the United States government put a tax on the cheese which came in from Holland, so that it would have to sell in this country for exactly the same as, or more than, the American-made cheese, the American people would be more likely to buy the cheese made in America instead of the cheese imported from Holland. The American cheese business would thus be protected by a tax or tariff. This is known as a protective tariff. Hayne did not believe in this kind of tariff, which protected manufacturers. Most of these manufacturers lived in the North and the South felt that it was being unjustly taxed to protect the North, while the North did not seem to care what the South wanted.

Hayne's great fear was that the federal government would become too powerful, and that the states would lose some of the rights which had been given to them in the Constitution of the United States.

The climax of Hayne's senatorial career was now approaching. Six great figures stood out on the stage of national politics: Clay, Webster, Hayne, Jackson, Livingston, and Calhoun. Two of them were about to make history. The greatest debating contest which the United States Senate has ever witnessed, was the debate between Robert Y. Hayne, of South Carolina, and Daniel Webster, of Massachusetts. The debate lasted for two weeks. It began as a discussion on the free lands in the West. But before the gentlemen were finished they had covered the tariff, Negro slavery, the Constitution, the writings of Jefferson and Madison, whether Massachusetts or South Carolina had done more to win the Revolutionary War, the purpose and reason of the Hartford Convention (an assembly to protest against the War of 1812), and finally the good and bad points, the rights and wrongs of nullification. The idea of nullification which was held by the South Carolina statesmen was that a state which did not approve of a national law passed by the United States Congress could declare that law "null and void," as far as it applied to that state. In other words, South Carolina could remain a part of the Union and yet pay no attention to a law which was passed for the entire nation but which Carolina did not consider constitutional. Secession meant that if a state did not approve of a national law it could withdraw, or secede, from the Union.

Never had the nation been treated to such a display of grand oratory as during the Webster-Hayne debate. The galleries were packed at every session. The papers were filled with accounts of Webster's or Hayne's speeches. There was a great deal of comment from every side, as this young South Carolinian dared to match his wits with Webster, the greatest orator in American history.

It is hard to say which won the battle. Perhaps we'd better call it a draw. The general feeling was that Webster made the better speeches, considered only as speeches, but that Hayne had actually come nearer to proving his point. Even today the speeches of both Hayne and Webster are given to students as models of good oratory.

When the nullification question became most serious, Calhoun was anxious to take a more active part in the debate. In order to do so, he had to resign his position of vice-president. This was necessary because a presiding officer is not allowed to take part in debate. He wished to become a senator, and Robert Hayne resigned as a member of the Senate, to make room for Calhoun.

Upon his return to South Carolina in 1832, Hayne was elected governor of his state, and was thrown into the very midst of the nullification quarrel. He played an important part in the Convention of 1834 and as governor defended the policy of his state with vigor, and yet with understanding of the views of others. Andrew Jackson was President of the United States at the time, and he sent his famous proclamation telling, in fighting words, what he would do if the people of his native state of South Carolina tried to break up the Union.

But Jackson had found his match in Hayne. The answering proclamation issued by Governor Hayne was written in exactly the same tone as the one he had received from "Old Hickory" Jackson. Hayne also called out ten thousand citizen-soldiers to meet any troops the President might send to South Carolina.

If you should read these two fighting proclamations, it might be hard for you to believe that some years after, in 1837, when Hayne was in Nashville on business, Jackson heard about it and invited him to spend the day at the "Hermitage."

After several hours of conversation, Hayne rose to leave, saying, "I would say to you, with perfect frankness and sincerity that if in the discharge of official duties, circumstances have occurred—and many such, we both know have occurred—to shake our friendship, they are now and ever will be forgotten."

Jackson was so old and infirm that he could hardly stand; yet he rose to speed his parting guest with these words, "Governor Hayne, the kind, frank, and noble sentiments you have just given utterance to are those I truly feel, and from the bottom of my heart I sincerely reciprocate them."

He then went on to express his pleasure that their friendship was again restored and in glowing terms told Hayne how much he had valued him, ever since their first meeting in 1820.

Hayne was only too ready to accept any just compromise of the difficulties between South Carolina and the rest of the Union. It was with real pleasure that he used his influence toward the acceptance of the Clay Compromise, which stilled the excitement for a while, although of course it did not settle the question. When "the tumult and the shouting" died, Hayne did all he could to keep one group of South Carolinians from feeling bitter toward the other. It was a difficult task, for he had to wipe out the long story of difference between the nullification and the anti-nullification believers in his own state.

At the end of his term as governor, Hayne was elected mayor of Charleston and was very efficient in that office.

A great many critics feel that Hayne's work for railroads was the most important service he performed. In 1836 he became president of the South Carolina Canal & Railroad Company, which had been chartered in 1827 and had already built the longest railroad line in the world at that time. This line, which was 136 miles long, went from Charleston to the bank of the Savannah River opposite Augusta, where the small town of Hamburg was located.

From here the road could go two ways. It might run across Georgia to Chattanooga or Memphis, Tennessee. This route would avoid mountains, but it would serve Savannah as well as Charleston, and this would not be so good for Charleston. Calhoun was in favor of this first route.

The second way could branch to Columbia, and go

The "West Point," the second locomotive built in the
United States for actual service on a railroad. It was built
for the South Carolina Railroad and after several experi-

through Asheville and Knoxville to Cincinnati. This called
for a conquering of the Blue Ridge Mountains, and the
following of the turns and twists of the valley of the
French Broad River. This was the route Hayne favored.
It was his dream that his railroad should tap the shipping
of the Ohio Valley at Cincinnati. Through the magic of
travel the South and the West would come closer together.
His great dream was that Charleston should be a greater
shipping center than New York.

In his pleas for the adoption of the mountain route,
Hayne showed a remarkable knowledge of the social,
economic, and political conditions of South Carolina and
the nation. His plan was adopted by the directors of the
road. Mass meetings and conventions were held everywhere
to arouse enthusiasm for this large project. Charters were
obtained from the legislatures of South Carolina, North
Carolina, Tennessee, and Kentucky.

Hayne traveled all over the country, using the great

mental trials, it made the first excursion trip, as above, on Saturday afternoon, March 5, 1831.

From The History of the First Locomotives in America, *by William H. Brown, 1871.*

powers of his oratory to get subscriptions for the new road; but, try as he would, it was only in South Carolina that the subscriptions ever came up to expectations. The panic of 1837 made it impossible for even those who were most interested to pay for their stock when payment was due. The South Carolina legislature came to the rescue and made a loan which enabled the laying of a few miles of track. Today the Southern Railway travels over practically the exact route for which Hayne and his companions fought with the greatest enthusiasm and eloquence at their command.

In spite of all they could do, Hayne could not get enough money to build even the road-bed. It was a tragedy for him, but perhaps it was an even greater tragedy for the people of the South, who had to wait many weary years for his dream to come true.

The end came for him at the stockholders' meeting in Asheville in September, 1839. Unable to arrive at a decision, because tempers were high and discussion was heated, the meeting was adjourned to another time and place. It was a meeting which the president of the road, Robert Y. Hayne, was destined not to attend. Perhaps he never knew that they were whispering that terrible word—"Failure."

It may be that the reason Hayne could not control the situation at the meeting of the railroad stockholders on that September day of 1839 was that, even as the meeting began, he was a very sick man. Eight days later, on September 24, he lay dead in Asheville.

Was this remarkable man a likeable sort of person? His friends said he was a delightful companion, cheerful and cordial always. He was a great conversationalist, and he was sometimes called the "prince of common sense." He always stuck to what he undertook, just as, when he was a boy, he had plunged into a freezing creek after a deer he was hunting. Once he told his sister that people thought he was talented, but that this was really a great mistake. He felt that his success was based upon the fact that he applied himself with great zeal to what he had to do and that he stuck to it until the end.

Hayne was tall and large of limb. He had unusually broad and sturdy shoulders and chest. His strong, irregular features made his face seem somewhat heavy when in repose. An amazing change would take place when he was interested and alert. His light-gray eyes would kindle. His whole face would awaken. He would appear eager, intelligent, and vivid.

Hayne was temporarily entombed in the family burying ground of his friend James W. Patten, of Asheville, but his body was later moved to St. Michael's churchyard in Charleston, where it now lies. When the news of his death reached South Carolina the entire state and the whole South mourned his passing. Even his political opponents wrote messages of sympathy. On October 8, 1839, by unanimous resolution of the city council and the citizens of Charleston, it was decided that a monument should be erected to him in the center of the city square.

In his short life, Robert Y. Hayne proved the truth of the words:

"We live in deeds, not years; in thoughts, not breaths;
In feelings, not in figures on a dial.
We should count time by heart-throbs. He most lives
Who thinks most, feels the noblest, acts the best."

John Caldwell Calhoun
1782–1850

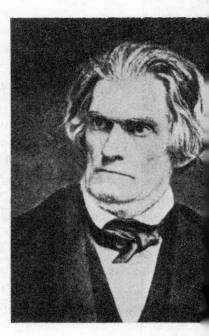

JOHN CALDWELL CALHOUN is often spoken of as "the greatest South Carolinian," because he truly stood for what South Carolina believed, and because he was a natural leader. Far outside of his own state, Calhoun's name is known. In some places it is hated; in others it is admired and loved. However people may feel about Calhoun, they must admit that he made history, not only in South Carolina but in all of the United States.

There is a tradition that the Calhoun family could trace its ancestry back to an Irish king, Conach, which accounts for the fact that sometimes John Caldwell Calhoun is described as "the descendant of Kings." At any rate, about 1733, three Scotch-Irish brothers arrived in America. By

---

John C. Calhoun. From a daguerreotype taken in 1844, when Calhoun was Secretary of State. This daguerreotype was sent to Europe and was the basis of the portraits by Eckhart and De Block. This daguerreotype has been called "the best likeness extant."

From the original picture in the library of William A. Courtenay, Charleston

slow stages, one of them, James, worked his way to the uplands of South Carolina and settled near the Savannah River. He and his family were sturdy frontier folk, who paid dearly for their right to develop a life in this new land. Catherine, James' wife, was killed by the Cherokee Indians in 1760 while some of her family watched in horror-stricken silence. Patrick Calhoun, the son of James and Catherine, carried the family sturdiness into the affairs of America.

John Caldwell Calhoun, who was next to the youngest of the five children of Patrick and Martha Caldwell Calhoun, was born March 18, 1782, in the only frame house in the region near Little River, Abbeville District, South Carolina. All of the other families in that neighborhood were still living in log houses. When Patrick Calhoun died, his son John was only thirteen, but he had already learned to share his father's belief that it was the chief duty of those who governed a country to see that the people who lived in that country were happy and safe.

John Caldwell Calhoun's education was crowded into about seven years. When he was fourteen years old, he was set to school under the famous Dr. Moses Waddel. Shortly after his arrival there, Mrs. Waddel died and the school was broken up for a time. Young Calhoun returned to his mother's plantation. Here an active, outdoor farm life restored his health, which had been weakened by too much reading and too little outdoor work and play. The time he spent in helping his mother manage her plantation gave him an interest in agriculture which lasted as long as he lived. After several years at home, his family decided that young John Caldwell should continue his education. He returned to the re-opened Waddel School, where he was graduated. In 1802 he went to Yale and was graduated from that college in two years. It seems quite suitable that he should choose as the subject for his graduation speech (which, by the way, he was too sick to deliver), "The Qualifications Necessary to Constitute a Perfect Statesman." Even then, his mind turned to statesmanship. Yale University considers him one of her most famous alumni. There is a monument to his memory on the Yale campus, and a building there has been named for him.

After a few months in the study of law, John Caldwell Calhoun was ready to practice in his native Abbeville District. This knowledge of law was helpful to him in later life, but actually he practiced his profession very little. Two years after studying law, he was elected a member of the state legislature, where he served for two sessions. He was so successful in the legislature that he was sent to the House of Representatives in the National Congress, taking his seat in 1810.

Another member of the House of Representatives has described how Calhoun looked as he took his place in Congress. He was six feet, two inches tall, with bushy, brown hair and piercing brilliant eyes. His features were strong and his face thin, in later life painfully thin. His clothes were plain and dark, and it was said one instantly knew that he was a country man and suspected that he was a great man.

Calhoun's mind was orderly, and he thought to the very end of each problem. One writer has described his mind as being a perfect filing system, with everything where it belonged and easily pulled out when needed. Early in his career Calhoun developed the remarkable manner of speaking which made him a leader in Congress. He never would learn the tricks of the orator of that day. When Calhoun spoke, people listened, because he spoke with force, sometimes with great feeling, always in a simple, direct manner.

Almost as soon as he arrived in Congress, Calhoun was put on the very important Foreign Affairs Committee, of which he later became the chairman. Through this committee, it became his duty to make the declaration of the War of 1812 against Great Britain. He himself has said that that was one of the proudest moments of his life, because it made the world recognize the strength of the United States of America. Those seven years in the House of Representatives made it clear that Calhoun was to lead a life of public service.

On January 8, 1811, he was married to Floride, daughter of John Ewing Calhoun.

When President Monroe went into office Calhoun was just thirty-six years old. The War Department was badly in need of reorganization and improvement. Calhoun was asked to undertake this task, and did it with marked ability. Under his direction the Department became a great deal more efficient. He set up a better plan for providing the army with food, equipment, ammunition, and medicine. Perhaps the most important service Calhoun gave as Secretary of War was in putting the department on a business basis by which he saved the United States $1,300,000 a year.

One of the interesting things about life in the United States is the idea that any boy may some day be president. Calhoun hoped that he might receive this honor, and it must have been a real joy to him when Pennsylvania nominated him for the presidency in 1822. He was more or less in the public mind as a presidential possibility for more

Calhoun addressing the Senate. One of the two panels
on the pedestal of the statue in Charleston.

than twenty years after that, though he never became president.

When John Quincy Adams of Massachusetts was elected president of the United States, Calhoun was elected vice-president, which made him presiding officer, or president, of the Senate. His seven years in this position were years of excitement for the United States. The famous Webster-Hayne debate came during that period; tariff was the great argument of those years, and there was much discussion of other important matters.

Calhoun's second term as vice-president came when his friend Andrew Jackson was president. It seemed certain that Jackson would do everything in his power to see his friend Calhoun elected president of the United States. Calhoun had proved his worth to the nation. Why did this great friendship suddenly come to an end? Why did Andrew Jackson use all his influence to have Martin Van Buren elected president? Calhoun's enemies had made a point of telling Jackson that Calhoun had not always acted as his friend and champion, when Jackson thought he had.

Jackson's temper was so aroused by this that he would not even listen to Calhoun's explanations. The friendship was forever at an end. Instead of helping Calhoun, Jackson opposed him.

When the tariff quarrel was at its height, Calhoun felt that all of his political ideals were concerned. Like Hayne, he feared having too much power in the hands of the central government. He wanted a careful understanding of the rights of the people, as guaranteed to them by the Constitution of the United States. He was eager to preserve the Union, if at the same time he could also guarantee to the people of the individual states all the rights which were

"Fort Hill," the home of John C. Calhoun, Clemson, S. C.

theirs under the national Constitution. Even his enemies admitted that Calhoun was a lover of the Union, but he loved more the rights of the separate states and of the South. A strong belief was being developed throughout the country that the rights of the states were the most important rights. This was known as "States' Rights." Calhoun became the great leader of the States' Rights party in the United States.

In order to protect States' Rights, he was eager to get down on the floor of the Senate and fight for his ideas. As a vice-president and presiding officer of the Senate he could not make speeches. He therefore resigned his office and became a senator. Robert Y. Hayne, you will remember, resigned his office of senator so that Calhoun could be elected to it. Some of Calhoun's greatest speeches were made at this time, perhaps the very greatest being the debate between Calhoun and Webster, when Jackson issued his proclamation threatening to send soldiers into South Carolina to force them to accept the tariff law.

The Clay Compromise temporarily settled the nullification trouble, as you have read in the life of Robert Young Hayne. Calhoun remained in the Senate, where for ten years he was a powerful fighter for States' Rights, especially as a protection for the weaker and poorer Southern states. Besides making speeches to explain his theory of government, he wrote several books on the subject.

Another great question which excited the United States at this time was that of slavery. Calhoun became one of the great defenders of slavery because he thought abolition would ruin the South, both white and black. He also thought that the question of slavery was a state matter and should be settled by the individual states without outside interference.

In 1843 Calhoun withdrew from public life, fully intending to spend the rest of his life in his beautiful home, "Fort Hill," near Pendleton, South Carolina. This home received its name from an old fort built during Revolutionary times by General Andrew Pickens. The fort had been placed there in order to make the Cherokees see the power of the white people.

When Calhoun was elected vice-president, he had expected to keep his family in Washington, but he had found this impossible on his small salary and decreased income from his plantation in South Carolina. It was at this time that "Fort Hill" became the Calhoun home. Here most of the family continued to live, although some member of it was always in Washington with Calhoun, who was very careful to stay on the job as long as the Senate was in session.

Lovely "Fort Hill" is now a shrine of South Carolina and of the nation. Located on the Clemson Campus, it has a beautiful view across the Seneca River to the misty Blue Ridge Mountains. In Calhoun's day the lovely rambling mansion (about which it was jokingly said that every time Calhoun went to Washington Mrs. Calhoun added a room) was surrounded by a most interesting "friendship garden." Here today may be seen a mimosa tree, which Calhoun loved because of its fragrance; there is a varnish tree, which Commodore Stephen Decatur brought from Madagascar; in that corner is a hemlock, which was given to Calhoun by his political enemy and personal friend, Daniel Webster; near by is an arbor-vitae, which expressed the friendship of Henry Clay.

Calhoun took a quiet enjoyment in being a South Carolina farmer, who was interested in scientific treatment of the soil and who enjoyed meeting with his friends in the Pendleton Farmers Society. He was not to be allowed these quiet pleasures for very long. When President Tyler went into office, he asked Calhoun to become his Secretary of State, so that again the South Carolinian took up his duties in Washington. He served successfully in this position. The most important event of his term of office was the annexation of Texas to the United States, an act of which he thoroughly approved. Again, after the Tyler administration, Calhoun retired to South Carolina to resume the life of a Southern planter. But once more he was called into public service. The country was again at a crisis, and Cal-

"Constitution Sideboard," made from the old battleship *Constitution* and given to Henry Clay, who presented it to Calhoun

houn's friends felt that his experience, power, and unselfish patriotism were needed in the Senate.

By this time John Caldwell Calhoun was an old man. For five more years he was to serve his country. All during this time he fought against what he thought was the injustice of abolition and for greater rights for the South. The climax of his great career as a senator came in the last speech he ever wrote. On March 4, 1850, as a sick, old man, he came into the Senate to talk to his fellow senators. This he was not able to do. Instead, he had to ask his friend James M. Mason, of Virginia, to read his speech for him. Many people have said that this was the most important speech made by a Southern leader before the outbreak of the Confederate War. In it Calhoun showed the horrors of the breaking up of the Union. He asked: "How can the Union be saved?" His answer was, "By observing justice for the South and living by the Constitution."

Henry Cabot Lodge of Massachusetts has described Calhoun as "the greatest man South Carolina has given to the nation." That in itself is no slight praise, for from the days of the Laurenses, the Pinckneys, the Rutledges, from the time of Moultrie and Sumter and Marion to the present day, South Carolina has always been conspicuous in peace and war for the force, the ability, and the character of the men who have served her and given her name its high distinction in our history.

On March 31, 1850, Calhoun died in Washington. Almost his last words were for "the South, the poor South." Honors above those usually paid to a senator were shown to him. Elaborate ceremonies were conducted in the Senate when those who had worked with him and those who had worked against him all combined to pay him honor. Throughout their senatorial careers Daniel Webster and John C. Calhoun had opposed each other's ideas. Therefore the tribute of Webster is of double interest to us. He said that although he had always opposed Calhoun's political arguments, he had realized that he was a truly great man.

If ever a man was loved, admired, and respected in South Carolina, that man was Calhoun. For many years his word was all that a South Carolinian wanted to know. Why did this great love exist between Calhoun and the people of his state? Through his long career of forty years he thought, first and foremost, not of himself and his own ambitions, but of the needs and desires of his state. Few men of

America could equal Calhoun in fineness of character and brilliance of mind.

When South Carolina had to select two, and two only, of her unforgettable sons to be memorialized in Statuary Hall, Washington, D. C., the first choice was John Caldwell Calhoun.

Today, as has been truly pointed out, few of us can remember the names of the presidents of the period between 1820 and 1850, but we do remember its three great senators, Calhoun, Clay, and Webster.

One of his strongest opponents summed up Calhoun's life in these words: "Mistaken he was often, but he never did anything consciously that he thought was wrong or low."

Joel Roberts Poinsett

1779–1851

"OH! SUSAN, I'm so glad you thought about buying this lovely red plant for Mother's Christmas present. I think she'll like it."

"Yes, I've heard her say that she thought poinsettias were the prettiest Christmas decoration in all the world. Their lovely red flowers make her feel Christmasy from top to toe."

"Poinsettias?" asked their little visitor. "Is that what you call those pretty red flowers? Where did they get that funny name?"

"That's not a funny name, Gretchen. They are named for Joel R. Poinsett, who brought them to the United States from Mexico. But that's not all he did. He was a great man in lots of ways and—I'll tell you all about him if you want to know. . . ."

A flower named for Joel Poinsett really should have

Joel R. Poinsett.

From a portrait by J. W. JARVIS, *owned by the City of Charleston.*

glowingly bright leaves, for his life was glowingly bright, too. Poinsett explored the world and gathered all sorts of interesting knowledge from places where few Americans had ever been before. Five presidents, Madison, Monroe, John Quincy Adams, Jackson, and Van Buren, gave him difficult and interesting tasks to perform for the nation. He was a great traveler, a congressman, a diplomat, and one of the best secretaries of war we have ever had.

Born in Charleston, South Carolina, March 2, 1779, Joel Roberts Poinsett was the son of a prominent doctor, Elisha Poinsett, and his wife Ann Roberts, a cultured English lady. The Poinsetts were French Huguenots and young Joel Roberts combined some of the best traits of both his French and his English ancestors. Shortly after the Revolutionary War the whole family went to England, where they stayed until Joel was about nine. Upon their return to Charleston, Dr. Poinsett decided to send his son to Timothy Dwight's Academy in Connecticut.

It might be said that Joel R. Poinsett's entire life, and everything that happened to him, was based in some way upon the condition of his health. From the time he was a little baby, he was very delicate. He could not stand extremely cold climates, nor was he well unless he spent a great part of his time outdoors. The cold climate of Connecticut was unhealthy for him; so he was removed from Dr. Dwight's school and sent to a very fine private school in England.

No one could know that this young boy was later to become the companion of kings; but surely the lessons he learned in meeting and moving in the best society of England helped him when he entered the drawing rooms of the crowned heads of Europe.

There were two especial loves in Poinsett's school life, languages and military science. He learned French, Spanish, Italian, and German·so that he could speak them almost as well as if he had always lived in the countries where they were spoken. Later he added Russian to his list of languages. In traveling around the world, his knowledge of languages was a great help to him, for he could see below the surface of things and could talk without an interpreter.

Joel R. Poinsett as he looked when he started out on his travels.

From a miniature by MALBONE.

Poinsett wanted to go into the army, but his father did not favor it. Instead, young Poinsett decided to study medicine and went to the famous medical school in Edinburgh, Scotland, to be trained. Again the climate was too severe for his delicate health, and he had to seek more sunshine.

A long sea trip to Lisbon, Portugal, and a nice lazy time in the sunshine of southern Europe completely restored his health. His physicians told him that a doctor's life would be too much of a strain, and so at last he began in earnest the study of military affairs.

When he was twenty-one, Poinsett returned to his native Charleston. He wanted to enter the United States Army, but his father persuaded him to begin the study of law.

This profession proved to be uninteresting to the young man, who was still eager to see the world and learn more about military affairs. Again young Poinsett's health was affected by the long hours he had spent indoors. His real interest lay in going places and seeing things, at the same time regaining his health.

When he was just twenty-two the handsome, charming young Charlestonian started out on his travels. For ten years he went to the far corners of the earth. The United States owes a big debt of gratitude to Poinsett, for he was almost an unofficial ambassador to many countries. He went into places where the United States was only a name; he visited most of the great leaders of the day and talked to them of their problems, their hopes, and their dreams. His own culture, education, and tact made him a welcome visitor wherever he went, and the United States became far more popular because this young citizen had made a good impression. After he had visited most of the known, and some of the unknown, places of the world, Poinsett was asked what his deepest impression was. He gave this interesting answer: "What I have seen in Europe has made me more enthusiastic about America."

Certainly Poinsett had a chance to compare the countries of the world. On his first trip he traveled through France, Italy, Sicily, Switzerland, Germany, and Austria, and in each country he talked to the people, lived among them, and found out what really went on, not just what the tourists of today might see.

It was a sad young man who suddenly cut short his travels and hastened home. He had just heard that his father had died and that his only surviving relative, his sister Susan, was dying. Charleston could hold only bitter memories for him, and so as soon as he finished attending to the business affairs which were necessary, now that he was the only Poinsett left in South Carolina, he again set out to forget his grief. This time he visited the northern section of the United States, Canada, and New England. He wrote that the beauty and the glory of Niagara Falls was almost more than he could bear.

But he still had some European travel to catch up on. And so in 1806 he reached the city of St. Petersburg, Russia. The Czar, Alexander I, welcomed him cordially. In fact, young Poinsett was actually embarrassed by the amount of attention which was shown him. There is a story that the Czar never tired of hearing Poinsett tell of the United States, its system of government, and the wonderful future which the young American expected it to have. On one occasion, so enthusiastic did the ruler of Russia become about America that he turned to Poinsett and said, "Sir, you are right and if I were not an Emperor I should become a republican." But, interesting as Poinsett found his visit to St. Petersburg, there was a great deal more of Russia that he wanted to see. When he asked permission for his party of nine to make the trip into the wild and unknown parts of Russia, the Czar at first did not grant it for fear that the visitors would never come back alive. He was finally persuaded to allow them to go if they would take with them a guard of honor to protect them on their journey.

Can't you imagine these nine young travelers and their Cossack guard getting into dangers and being thrillingly rescued? Once in crossing the steppes their horses were stolen. Most of the party were in favor of getting along as best they could and saying nothing. But Poinsett insisted upon visiting the Khan of the tribe and demanding their horses back. Imagine the surprise of the Khan when this young American walked in, uninvited and unwanted. The camp was in a turmoil. First Poinsett had to explain who he was. He was an American, a citizen of the United States. The Khan had never heard of the United States. It took a lot of explaining, and among the explanations was the one, carefully recorded in the history of the tribe, that Thomas Jefferson was the Shah of the United States! Poinsett got his horses, the Khan had a delightful visitor, and the tribe learned about the United States. When the travelers returned to St. Petersburg only three of the nine were alive.

Spring at Joel R. Poinsett's summer home in Greenville County. It was probably designed by Robert Mills. The marker was attached recently.

From a photograph by Carl Julien

The Czar's delight in the young American finally led to the offer of a position of colonel in the Russian army. Poinsett declined the offer with thanks, for he felt that his services should be only for his own country.

It seemed to Poinsett that war with England was sure to come, and so in 1808 he hurried home. In his hope of being given an important position in the army he was disappointed. War was actually delayed until 1812, and when it did come Poinsett was in South America performing another service for the United States.

President Madison wanted to know exactly what was going on in South America. He needed a confidential agent to report to him, and he chose Poinsett for this important mission.

Some of the countries in South America were fighting for their independence from Spain. Would they succeed? What should the United States do? The President needed someone who knew the language, who was a patriotic American, and who could be counted on to do the right thing. Poinsett was the man.

The first report sent by Poinsett was from Rio de Janeiro. Later he traveled to Buenos Aires and in Argentina; finally he undertook the dangerous and unusual journey across the Pampas and over the Andes Mountains to Chile. Thrills, excitement, and danger followed each other in quick succession while Poinsett was in Chile. Finally he took command of a portion of the Chilean army and marched against the Spanish and Peruvian forces, in order to rescue the officers and men of eleven captured American whalers, which had been taken when a false report was sent that the United States was at war with Spain.

Even after all this adventure, Poinsett was not by any means ready to settle down. Soon after his return to this country, he decided really to "see America." This time he and two friends started out on a long trip to the West. They covered 2,100 miles, practically all of it on horseback. His friends thought that it would be dangerous to travel beyond Pittsburgh, but Poinsett left them and went a great deal farther alone. It was on the return part of this trip that he was the guest of Andrew Jackson in Nashville; and perhaps at that time Jackson became impressed with the South Carolinian, to whom he later entrusted such delicate and important work.

As soon as Poinsett returned to South Carolina from his western trip, he entered the state legislature, where he served for two terms. His great interests were in better roads, bridges, canals, and improvements. He appreciated, as did few others, how necessary it was for a state to have easy means of travel. In 1818 he became a member of the commission on Internal Improvements of South Carolina and in 1819 was made the chairman of that body. To him is credited the building of the famous "old state road." Parts of it are in use to this day.

. Having served successfully in the state legislature, Poinsett was sent to Congress, where he served from 1821 to 1825. Much more of a doer than a speaker, Poinsett is recorded as having made only four long speeches. One was in favor of recognition of the Spanish American republics, which had won their independence from Spain, and another was in behalf of a better military organization for the United States.

His congressional career was interrupted for about a year when he went on another secret mission, this time to Mexico. His report to President Monroe proved to be so correct and his knowledge of Mexico, gained by months of travel, so full, that he was appointed our first minister to that country. As minister to Mexico, Poinsett had three big tasks to perform. He was to make stronger the ties of friendship between the United States and Mexico, our nearest Southern neighbor. He also had to protect the citizens of the United States and their belongings in Mexico, and he

S. R. Poinsett

The flag scene in Mexico City. From *Joel R. Poinsett, Versatile American*, by J. Fred Rippy.

was to establish closer and better trade relations and business dealings between the two countries.

He honestly did his best to be fair to everybody and to all parties in Mexico. He had many difficulties, and many of his plans did not go as he wished. Finally, after about four years, he asked to be recalled.

Before he left Mexico, Poinsett had one of the most exciting experiences of his career. On one occasion, when the quarrel between the aristocrats and the common people of Mexico became very intense, a mob gathered in the street and were about to attack the home of one of the rich ladies in Mexico City. She and some of her friends asked that Mr. Poinsett protect them in his house. Although he was not really in favor of the aristocrats, and had been rather badly treated by them, he agreed. When the mob heard that the people they hated had taken refuge in the home of the American minister, they started for it. They were determined to get their enemies, if they had to pull down the very walls of Poinsett's home. Poinsett and his secretary stepped out on a balcony and threw the United States flag out to the breeze. Standing under the protecting folds of the red, white, and blue, he explained to the people what the flag was and why anyone who asked for protection from a mob was safe under it. He managed to quiet the people and saved those who had trusted to his protection. It was a very courageous thing to do, for the "thousands who were thirsting for his blood because he had balked them of their revenge" might not have listened. Poinsett taught them to respect the flag of his country.

Throughout his travels Poinsett never lost his interest in science and history. Wherever he went, he collected the historical oddities of the country, as well as plants, flowers, and other interesting specimens. So big was this collection when he died that it was divided between the Charleston Museum and a society in Philadelphia.

No sooner had Poinsett returned to America from Mexico than he found himself in the midst of another difficult situation. South Carolina was in a heated quarrel over nullification. There were two parties, the Nullifiers and the Unionists. Poinsett was always enthusiastically in favor of the Union and he became one of the leaders of that party in South Carolina. In fact, he was asked by Jackson to take charge of the plans for organizing the South Carolina Unionists against the Nullifiers. Jackson had declared that if necessary he would send soldiers into South Carolina to make them obey the law of Congress. Poinsett

Aztec ceremonial stone yoke brought from Mexico in 1822 by Poinsett.

armed the Unionists to carry out Jackson's orders if that became necessary. Fortunately the fact that Congress compromised the dispute by lowering the tariff prevented bloodshed. This was the Clay Compromise, of which you read in the lives of Hayne and Calhoun.

Perhaps after the nullification trouble, which narrowly avoided becoming a bloody war among South Carolinians, Poinsett felt that he was ready to settle back and let someone else attend to the affairs of the world. Quite late in life he married Mary Izard, widow of Poinsett's friend, John Julius Pringle. After their marriage the Poinsetts retired to Mrs. Poinsett's rice plantation near Georgetown. Here this globe-trotter found quiet, happiness, and contentment, and plenty of time for reading, scientific study, and good conversation with his many friends. He became intensely interested in agriculture and made a study of scientific farming.

Poinsett warned the people against the danger of one crop and begged them not to depend on cotton alone. He became

A Walk in Poinsett State Park, the only park in South Carolina named for an individual man.

one of the early speakers for what has become so familiar to us today as "rotation of crops."

A man like Poinsett was not long to be allowed the joy of sitting back and watching the world go by. When President Van Buren selected Poinsett to become his secretary of war, the South Carolinian reached the height of his career, the great opportunity for which his study and experience had best fitted him. Poinsett was one of the best-trained and best-equipped secretaries of war that the United States has ever had. Not only did the secretary of war have to attend to the War Department but he had many other tasks. Some of the things which he was supposed to do were to supervise all the internal improvements, that is, roads, canals, bridges, etc. He was responsible for the equipping of all exploring expeditions. He had to take charge of all the mineral resources which belonged to the United States. Indirectly he was responsible for the Indians who lived in this country and he performed a great service for the red men in arranging affairs so that they could be sure of receiving certain rights. But it was in the army itself that Poinsett performed his greatest service. During his four years as secretary he practically made over the form of the army. During this time a general staff was created. In addition to the creation of the general staff, Poinsett greatly improved the artillery. West Point, the training school for the officers, received much better equipment and introduced a more varied and useful course of study.

Perhaps the greatest service that Poinsett rendered as secretary of war was the introducing of the plan which is still used in the United States army. He thought that the way to have a successful army was to supply it with a great many highly trained, experienced officers. These officers would have little trouble in training men to fight under them when such soldiers were needed at short notice. Poinsett believed this to be so necessary that he sent some American officers to be trained in what was then the most famous military school in the world, one run by the French government. This plan of Poinsett's was based on the fact that in the United States men are not forced to serve in the army as they are in a great many other countries. He believed that a volunteer army was the right kind and that it could best be handled in this way. The experiences of America in the World War showed that his plan of a group of highly trained officers to teach "rookies" was a good one.

After his term of office as secretary of war, Poinsett again retired, dividing his time between the plantation near Georgetown and his summer home in Greenville County under the shadow of the Saluda Mountains.

This time Poinsett had really retired from public life although he did, unofficially, express his opposition to the Mexican war and to the secession of South Carolina from the Union.

Poinsett's scientific knowledge led him into doing more than just collecting items of interest. In 1805 he had been one of the men who started the Academy of Fine Arts in Charleston. Twenty-five years later he helped to found the National Institute for the Promotion of Science and Useful Arts in Washington, D. C. He worked tirelessly to have the money which was left by Mr. Smithson accepted by the United States government, and it is said that, more than any other one man, Poinsett decided what the Smithsonian Institution should become. It is now one of the greatest museums in the world.

A recent book has been written called *Joel R. Poinsett,*

The Anderson Homestead in Sumter County where Poinsett died.

From a sketch by Miss M. Virginia Saunders

Versatile American, which means that he was a man of many talents and that he could do many things well. It is said that he had traveled more than any other man in America up to his time. He knew thoroughly England, France, Switzerland, the Italian and German states, Sweden, Russia, Spain, Portugal, Cuba, Porto Rico, Mexico, and South America. From his knowledge of these countries, he believed that the system of government of the United States was the best in the world, and he earnestly hoped to extend it to the countries of Central and South America. Among the things he worked for was a compulsory education for everyone in the United States.

Throughout a long life Poinsett was always dogged by ill-health and had to overcome many difficulties. At the age of seventy-two, he tried, for the last time, the cure which had worked so often in the past. He was ill, and travel would cure him. However, when he arrived at Stateburg, South Carolina, his condition had become so serious that his dear friend, Dr. William Anderson, who shared with him his interest in flowers, persuaded him to rest at "Hillcrest," the Anderson home. Here on December 12, 1851, the rich, full life of Joel Roberts Poinsett came to an end. He is buried in the Anderson plot in the cemetery of the lovely little Episcopal Church in Stateburg. Today there is no Poinsett in South Carolina, but we do have many reminders of him in the glowingly beautiful poinsettias, which at Christmas time turn our thoughts to Joel Roberts Poinsett, who brought them to us from Mexico.

James Louis Petigru

1789-1863

IN THE spring of 1919, at the end of the World War, Woodrow Wilson, the great American president, whose boyhood home was in Columbia, was in Paris to fight for the ideals which he held and which he thought were representative of his people. The men who represented France, England, Italy, and Japan did not agree with him, and he stood almost alone, a towering figure, fighting for international good will. Heart-sick, saddened, he asked the postmaster of Charleston to cable to him the epitaph on the grave of James Louis Petigru. Did he, fighting his lone fight for an ideal, want to be reminded of this other giant, this South Carolinian who also fought alone for his ideals? Petigru, though he saw his children, his kinsmen, even his wife, joining hands with the opposing forces, was true to his beliefs and ideals. For this, he was honored by those who opposed him most. Here, in part, is the epitaph for which Woodrow Wilson cabled from France:

James L. Petigru.

From a copy of a portrait by THOMAS SULLY.

"Unawed by Opinion,
Unseduced by Flattery:
Undismayed by Disaster,
He confronted Life with antique
Courage:
And Death with Christian Hope:
In the great Civil War
He withstood his People for his Country:
But his People did Homage to the Man
Who held his Conscience higher than their Praise:
And his Country
Heaped her Honours upon the Grave of
the Patriot,
To Whom, living,
His own righteous self-Respect sufficed
Alike for Motive and Reward."

Yet James Louis Petigru's fame does not rest upon the high positions he held, for there were none. His memory is held dear to the world, not because he was a great general or an inspired leader. He was neither. He was the greatest private citizen South Carolina has ever produced. His is a place unlike that of any other.

Born in Abbeville District on May 10, 1789, this son of William and Louise Pettigrew [1] was given the names of his two grandfathers. The James was in honor of his father's Irish-American father, while the Louis was for his mother's French-Huguenot minister father, Jean Louis Gibert.

James Louis was one of several children in the Pettigrew family. There was little money with which to support them. William Pettigrew was not so much interseted in making money as he was in reading books. Mrs. Pettigrew had many difficult household tasks to perform, and young James

---

[1] This name was *Pettigrew*, until James Louis changed it, as told later.

Louis helped her as much as he could. Naturally there were many jobs for him to do, and not much chance for an education. Many of his neighbors thought he was smart to read so much, but others, who passed him on the road when he was reading aloud, put him down as a bit "queer." They probably thought that their own sons had the right ideas.

On the left is the Petigru family coat-of-arms. On the right is Petigru's seal, with a little crane, *petit grue*, believed to have been designed as a joke by Captain Thomas Petigru, U. S. N.

They were interested in hunting, fishing, and swimming. Who remembers those boys today?

A willingness to work and the ability to tell a tale clearly and quickly gave young Petigru the chance to attend Dr. Moses Waddel's famous school at Willington, which he entered in 1804.

After two years under Dr. Waddel, Petigru entered the South Carolina College, finishing his course with the class of 1809, when he was graduated with first honor. During his stay in Columbia, Petigru had earned his expenses by teaching at the Columbia Academy, but even with this, he could scare up only enough money to buy one regular meal a day. Fortunate indeed was he when a dinner invitation gave him another meal. How doubly tragic it was, then, when he had to refuse an invitation because of "insufficient clothing."

At some time while he was in college, young James Louis changed the spelling of his name from the Irish *Pettigrew* to the French *Petigru*, in the belief that the name was really from two French words meaning "little crane."

When James Louis Petigru had left home to go to school, it was from "Badwell," the family farm in Abbeville District. "Badwell" had become the family home when James Louis was eleven. Here he spent the happiest days of his boyhood. Always it was for him the home of greatest delight.

After his graduation from college the young man returned to "Badwell" to find the family sunk even deeper into debt. Was his newly acquired learning to be used only in pushing a plow? An uncle urged him to go away and try to be a success in life. Young Petigru replied, "I will never desert my mother." Mrs. Petigru, however, showed him that it was not desertion for him to better his fortunes and be able to help her more. Upon her advice he secured a position teaching in a school in St. Luke's Parish near Beaufort, South Carolina. At the same time he studied law in the office of Mr. William Robertson, a prominent lawyer of Beaufort. For a short time he also taught in Beaufort College.

Petigru was admitted to the bar in 1812 and began the practice of law. Coosawatchie, a little town between

Charleston and Savannah, was the place in which court was held for Beaufort District. Here Petigru carried on his early practice. He reported that for three years he was without a legal brief, which meant that he had no important cases. That was a startling contrast to the record of later years, for then his name appeared in a great many cases, as lawyer for one side or the other. His comment in the briefless days was that he took his "revenge by studying the harder," which may account for his later success.

This learned lawyer was always at the call of young, inexperienced lawyers and probably saved them from many serious mistakes. One of his own youthful errors taught him not to promise a client too much. One day a man came in to ask Petigru about collecting a claim. The young lawyer brashly assured him that of course he could collect. The client told him to sue, and the verdict was against him. "Don't worry. We'll appeal and certainly collect," gayly assured Mr. Petigru. When Petigru lost the appeal, he was too ashamed to admit it to his client and reached into his own almost empty pockets and paid the claim himself.

In 1816, without his request or knowledge, the legislature elected him solicitor, or state lawyer, for Beaufort District.

Just five years after he began the practice of law, Petigru was invited by James Hamilton, Jr., to become his law partner in Charleston. In 1819 the invitation was accepted and Petigru moved to Charleston, where he made his home until the end of his life.

When Robert Y. Hayne resigned as attorney-general of South Carolina in order to enter the United States Senate, Petigru was elected attorney-general in his place. He liked this type of work and would probably have continued in it indefinitely, if his friends had not persuaded him that it was his duty to resign and become the Union Party candidate for state senator. This was during the wildly exciting campaign of 1830. Petigru disliked politics and never took part unless he felt it to be a sacred duty. As far as the senatorial campaign was concerned, Petigru might have kept his legal office. He was defeated. A few weeks later, however, he was more fortunate in being elected to fill an unexpired term in the House of Representatives. Perhaps his fellow-lawmakers would not have liked the description of them written by Petigru to his sister: "The members are making as much noise as idle boys in a country school when the master is out."

A short time in the legislature was enough for Petigru. He was eager to return to his beloved law. To him the law was, first and foremost, a means of justice. He would not stoop to legal tricks to win a case. His earnest belief that the law could bring about justice and mercy, added to his great knowledge and hard work, made him known as the finest lawyer of his day. Even now he is ranked as the greatest legal mind South Carolina has ever produced. It is quite fitting that the law school at the University should be called Petigru College.

For more than forty years he was the recognized head of the South Carolina bar. This is a remarkable record for anyone, but it is even more surprising when we realize that, during that time, he was politically opposed to almost every great leader in the state. His fame as a lawyer spread over the entire country. Whenever visitors came to Charleston they made a point of meeting him, for it was nice to be able to say: "While in Charleston I met Mr. Petigru," somewhat as we might say, oh so casually, "When I was in Washington, I met the President."

No matter how badly Petigru needed money, and there were times when he needed it desperately, some of his clients could not pay him a fee. A friend, or someone in need, or one who had befriended him in his early life, was not allowed to pay him for his services. Distress of any kind went straight to his heart. In behalf of black or white, rich or poor, free or slave, Northerner or Southerner, the great legal talents of James Louis Petigru were at the disposal of anyone who needed them, provided the case was honest and honorable.

As Petigru's practice grew to enormous proportions, he had many men associated with him as well as numerous young students. The greater part of his legal life was spent in his office, located on St. Michael's Alley. The building, shaped somewhat like a Greek temple, looked out on a lovely garden, planted by Petigru, so that as he looked from his window he could refresh his soul by gazing at the flowers or evergreen shrubs. This garden was his walking space. Back and forth over the paths he would go, sometimes talking aloud to himself. His friends knew this as a signal not to interrupt, for he was either arguing a case to himself or soothing his tired nerves by repeating his favorite poems.

Petigru was truly a great lawyer, but there are records of other great lawyers whose lives might have proved inspiring to Woodrow Wilson. No, it was not only as lawyer that Wilson thought of Petigru. It was as the brave man who withstood his friends and family for what he thought was right. The great, unchanging belief of Petigru was that the Constitution of the United States was the greatest plan of government ever known to the world. Such a belief gave him a deep love for the nation and the Union. About nullification, for which he could find no reason in law, morals, or

The First Baptist Church, Columbia, where the Secession Convention was held.

common sense, he wrote, "I am devilishly puzzled to know whether my friends are mad or I beside myself."

Although he was violently opposed to secession he was hopeless of being able to do anything to stop it. Once, while in Columbia, he was stopped by a stranger who asked if he would point out the insane asylum. Pointing to the Baptist Church, where the Secession Convention was in session, Petigru said, "There it is." We may think this funny today, but it was a matter of real heart-break to Petigru, and sometimes he could not help showing his sorrow. When the bells of St. Michael's rang out the news of Secession, Petigru thought it was the signal for a fire. When told that it announced Secession, he exclaimed, "I tell you there is a fire; they have this day set a blazing torch to the temple of constitutional liberty and please God we shall have no more peace forever." We know he felt that he was a man alone, for he wrote to his sister, Mrs. Jane North, to whom he took all his troubles, of the queer feeling he had when he was sad while all others were celebrating the attack on Fort Sumter.

Should you think that to take the position of district attorney was an act of heroism? President Fillmore asked many men to be district attorney. None of them was brave enough to accept. He persuaded Petigru to do so after he had appealed to him in the name of his country and for the sake of the president. In regard to this, President Fillmore wrote, "I regarded it then and do now as an act of moral heroism such as very few people are capable of performing and which justly entitled him to my thanks and the gratitude of the people. He was truly a noble man and we shall scarcely look upon his like again." Nothing could more surely point the way in which the public opinion was turning. It took actual heroism to stand for the Union. Yet there was never any doubt about Petigru's attitude. In March, 1861, President Lincoln sent two of his friends to Charleston to find out if it were true that there was a strong feeling for the Union there. These gentlemen reported that the only admitted Unionist they could find was Petigru.

It is hard to be opposed to everything done by your best and dearest friends, and it is hard to be different from all those around you. Petigru knew every such pain, but he "held his conscience higher than their praise." Many unhappy experiences came to him during the war period, but none more distressing than when he was called upon to give information to a Confederate court about property owned by some of his Northern clients. According to the law of the Confederacy, this property was liable to be seized, and anyone could be called upon for information. Petigru refused to become what he called "an informer," standing upon his rights as a free man, with the God-given privilege to choose between right and wrong. The court ruled against him, but he was repaid for his stand by a letter from his friend, Alfred Huger. Mr. Huger wrote to thank him for his stand and remarked that Heaven had provided men like Petigru to protect the weak and those not there to protect themselves.

South Carolina Hall, Charleston, where the Ordinance of Secession was signed.

It was not until he met the beautiful Miss Jane Amelia Postell, daughter of a near-by planter, that Petigru fell deeply in love. His suit with the lovely Jane was successful and they were married on August 17, 1816, at the home of her grandfather near "Badwell." Dr. Waddel performed the ceremony. Although Mrs. Petigru was an invalid for the greater part of her married life, they had a happy home and the great lawyer enjoyed his home and the care of his children.

Fortunately a great many of the delightful letters from Petigru to his children have been saved, and we can see for ourselves the care of their training and education. Once he wrote to his daughter Sue, "French is indispensable in polite society," and said that she should know other languages also, "especially Spanish, the stateliest daughter of the common parent of them all," by which he meant Latin. Another letter warned his daughter about the horrors of poor handwriting, a theme which interested him greatly.

Education, in the usual sense, was not his only concern for his children, for just after Susan's marriage to Henry C. King of Charleston, he wrote to her hoping that she would be happy and asking that she make a good wife to Henry, for, said he, "I have often said that I should be as much chagrined to turn out a bad wife from the nursery as to send a student from the office to be rejected."

Once when another daughter, Caroline, who was the wife of William A. Carson, had to get away in order to regain her health, there was no one who could take her. Petigru threw aside his heavy business cares and escorted her, her baby, and the nurse to White Sulphur Springs, Virginia, and stayed with her until she was well. The series of letters written from Virginia to his wife show that he was always devoted and sympathetic.

His love and care for his wife and children did not make him less attentive to the needs of his mother and sisters. He had always had a great affection for "Badwell," and the first money he ever earned was used to build a home there for his mother, which was also later used by his sister, Mrs. North. Every summer he went to visit her and to forget his cares in a joyous vacation on the old farm, where he would delight to show that he had not forgotten how to guide a plow. The place itself became a haven of delight to him, and on it he lavished much loving care, a great deal of money, and untiring interest. His letters about forestry and farming have a strangely modern sound.

In 1843 Petigru planned a magnificent avenue of white oaks at "Badwell" to serve as a memorial to him after his death. For twenty years, in spite of disappointments and failure, he kept on with the planting of white oaks in his avenue. An English gardener was imported to attend to the care of the trees, but today there are only a few straggling oaks of his memorial left. The fame of Petigru himself has lasted better than the trees. Once, just before his death, Petigru was greatly distressed that a Negro had chopped off some of the limbs of his precious trees. He could not get over the wanton destruction of such an act. Each of the trees had been dedicated to one of his friends, and in his mind had become the impersonation of that friend. The Negro had practically chopped off the arms and legs of his friends, right before his eyes!

Into his family came the terrors of war. For them it was a personal tragedy in every way. Mrs. Petigru was thoroughly

Petigru's spring at "Badwell."

From a photograph by Carl Julien

in sympathy with the South; Sue's husband was killed while serving in the Confederate army; Petigru's own son died while wearing the Confederate gray. General Johnston Pettigrew, a cousin very dear to James Louis Petigru, was a high ranking officer in the Confederate forces. Only James Louis Petigru and his daughter, Caroline Carson, were in sympathy with the Union.

Nothing could better show Petigru's fine attitude than that he should take his grandson to meet General Robert E. Lee. In presenting the young boy to the General he said, "I beg to present to you my grandson, who in after years will remember that he has had the honor of shaking the hand of so great a man as General Lee." Could this have been the same grandson who some years later appealed to General William T. Sherman for collection of a claim for a silver pitcher, looted from a bank in Columbia? In answer to his letter Sherman wrote, "There is no family anywhere for which I would like to manifest love and respect more than for that of James Louis Petigru of Charleston."

Although Petigru was doomed to stand almost alone because of his strong views on nationalism, in most other things he agreed with his neighbors. Although no abolitionist, he did not like slavery. In fact, though he had slaves himself, it was his hope that slavery would slowly be done away with. With conditions as they were, he felt that the happiest lot of the Negro was to belong to a kind master who would be interested in caring for him. An ardent free soiler, he was opposed to carrying slavery into the new states. He believed that slavery would slowly become a forgotten custom.

In the midst of his political difficulties he wrote to his daughter, "If one is to be proud of anything it should be of self-control, and of acting well." This was his theory of life, and upon it he ordered his conduct. His manners were warm, hearty, friendly. He had the happy faculty of being cordial and friendly without losing his dignity. Everyone loved him. No matter how violent the battle was, he lost no honors and no friends. There was probably no more ardent leader for secession than Robert Barnwell Rhett. A tribute from him to the leader of the Unionist party means a great deal. Rhett wrote, "My friend in early manhood, my better friend in advanced life, whom neither time nor fortune, private duties nor troubles, nor the angry public contests and differences of more than thirty years ever induced to say to me an unkind word or to do an unkind act." Another friend wrote that Petigru was so generous that he was one man who had truly earned Webster's description of a lawyer, "One who works hard, lives well and dies poor."

People might disagree with Petigru, but no one could doubt his personal honesty and fineness of character. A land speculation deal into which he had entered with his friend Hamilton turned out very badly. In fact, Petigru was finally ruined by this financial failure. He found himself not only without any money, but owing thousands of dollars. It was a dreadful experience for a man fifty-three years of age, with a large family to care for, and many responsibilities. He wrote to his sister shortly after this disaster: "I am in hope that I may clamber over this mountain in my path, though I can never expect to rake and scrape enough to retire as I once hoped to do, when too old for the stage."

His creditors offered to compromise and let him pay part of the debt, which they would then cancel. He refused all such suggestions, saying, "Give me time and I will pay the last dollar for which I am liable." It took terrific effort and tireless work, which carried him all over the country, but at last he could thank God that every dollar of his debt was paid.

It was no easy road which Petigru traveled. A glimpse at his daily schedule will convince us that he did more than a normal share of work. Early in the morning he would go to the market in an effort to find some choice bit of food with which to tempt the appetite of his invalid wife. After an early breakfast he would go to the office and work until about three o'clock, when he came back for dinner, usually bringing a friend along. A good dinner and good conversation prepared him for his return to the office, where he worked late, often until midnight, and sometimes until dawn would streak the sky above beautiful Charleston Harbor.

One of the greatest contributions Petigru made to his

state was the service he rendered in putting all the laws of
the state in order. In 1859 the legislature decided that the
laws of South Carolina should be put in order, or codified,
and selected Petigru for this very difficult task. Although
he was politically opposed to most of the members of the

Duelling pistol made especially for James L. Petigru by
James L. Happoldt.

legislature he was reëlected by that body until the com-
pletion of his task in 1863.

Fortunately we have a first-hand description of the appearance of this remarkable man. Mr. Daniel Pope, who was
both a pupil and a friend of Petigru, has described him. He
has told us that his elastic step and erect carriage made him
appear much taller than he actually was, while his powerful
muscles made him seem larger. His strong, massive chin and
magnetic dark eyes gave an effect of dignity, character, intelligence, and interest. Perhaps the most characteristic
thing about him was the vein, high up on his forehead. Usually unnoticed, it swelled out when he was highly excited
or angry. Mr. Pope declared that this vein was a danger

signal which said to all who knew him, "Look out for the engine when the whistle blows." His hands were considered unusually beautiful and he was supposed to have been somewhat vain about them. But his voice was the unforgettable quality of his personality. "Such a voice! At times it was shrill and discordant as the notes of a bagpipe. I have heard it in the pathetic as soft as the breathing of a lute . . . I have heard it on occasion roll like the swell of cathedral organs . . . I have heard it in passion crash like the blast of a bugle."

There were many happy aspects of Petigru's life, for he had, even in the darkest hour, the ability to find pleasure in little things. Just at the time that his daughter Caroline was going to make her debut, or, as he put it, "At the very time when other people brush up and look as smart as they can, to bring out a daughter," the Petigrus were without a carriage for the first time in fourteen years, and for twenty years their house had never looked so gloomy and shabby. Instead of bemoaning the situation, Petigru joyously remarked that Caroline never complained, but was busy and happy all the day long. Perhaps it was this keen appreciation of the good in everything which made Petigru write his sister that he hoped her "little farm was smiling."

There were two complete lacks in Petigru's life. He had absolutely no eye for color and no ear for music. He adored dancing, but was regarded as one of the worst dancers in all social history. While he was a student at the South Carolina College, a Mr. Sudor opened a dancing school in which Petigru was one of the first to enroll. Try as he might, he never was able to execute the pigeon-wing, which was the pride of the teacher's heart, nor could he learn the stately minuet.

Petigru's dancing was of such a peculiar type that the ladies often laughed at him in spite of themselves. Once, seeing the signs of such a laughing spell coming on, he turned to a friend and said: "The ladies think I am dancing for their amusement, whereas I am dancing altogether for my own." Perhaps one reason that he could not dance was that he had no ear for music. Once he heard a young lady playing on her guitar and complimented her sincerely on the beautiful music she had been making. Imagine his surprise when she said, "I was only tuning my guitar, I haven't played anything yet."

Petigru had expressed the desire that he should die in harness, and his wish was granted. He was ill only a short time before he died at the home of his old friend, Judge King, in Charleston, and was buried in St. Michael's churchyard next to the grave of his son. The whole city mourned his passing. The civil and military authorities, the rich and the poor, black and white, attended his funeral. The Charleston Bar Association met immediately after his death and passed resolutions of sympathy. They also ordered that a portrait of the great lawyer be hung in the library of the Court of Appeals of Charleston.

His daughter, Caroline Petigru Carson, lived for many years in Rome. She paid tribute to the father, whom she adored, by erecting a monument to him. On it she wanted to put the words which should tell the world how great a man he was. Friends offered to raise funds for the erection of the monument, but she jealously held that privilege for herself. Having little money, she painted; and when she was too ill to do that she lay on her back in bed, knitting overshoes, which she sold. She saved every penny she could earn for two years, until she had enough to purchase the

Caroline Petigru Carson, the daughter who worked for years to perfect the epitaph on her father's grave.

From a painting made when she was eighteen years old by THOMAS SULLY

proper stone. Her own words were the foundation of the beautiful epitaph, but she received assistance from some of the greatest writers of the day. Through their help the famous epitaph, as it now stands, was finished, and the monument was erected in St. Michael's churchyard.

Petigru has been called the greatest private citizen that

South Carolina ever produced. It has been said of him that though he rarely held a high public office, he was a great statesman; though he was never actually made a judge, he was truly a great lawyer and a great judge. Though he never wrote a book, his life is a book for all to study. Though he never started a charity, he was a true and a great-hearted charitable person. Some day, when we visit the Protestant cemetery in Rome, we might go to the grave of his daughter, Caroline Carson, "daughter of James Louis Petigru," to show that we too remember her father, who has become one of the unforgettable sons of South Carolina.

James Henley Thornwell

1812—1862

IN THE careers of men of small beginnings and great endings there is a touch of magic, a bit of the old fairytale."

All of us remember the story of the boy who, in order to win the princess of his dreams, had to climb the mountain of glass. Every time he took a step forward, he slipped back two! Rich men with horses and helpers had failed and had given up the task as hopeless, but not our hero. He had nothing but his two hands and feet, a brave heart, and the determination not to let anything stop him before he reached the top. It was a long weary pull, and all his friends told him that he would never get to the top of the Glass Mountain. Day after day he tried, little by little he climbed, and then one glorious day he reached the pinnacle and received his reward. He had won the hand of the beautiful princess—fame and fortune.

That youth might well have been named James Henley

James Henley Thornwell. *From the portrait by* SCAR-BOROUGH

Thornwell, for he too climbed the "glass mountain" of life. He too started with little except his own courage and the determination to make something fine of his life. His friends told him, time and again, that he could not succeed, but he smiled and climbed, little by little, ever higher. At last he too reached the pinnacle of the mountain, to claim "the hand of the princess" and to become one of South Carolina's unforgettable sons.

James Henley Thornwell was born in Marlboro District, South Carolina, on the upper reaches of the Peedee River. He was the son of Martha Terrel and her husband James Thornwell. James, Sr., was a man of generous disposition, whose home was always open to his friends. He spent whatever he made as plantation overseer for Christopher B. Pegues, and when he died in 1820, he left nothing to his family. Mrs. Thornwell, who was of good old Welsh stock, found herself in unfortunate circumstances. She had no money and no place to turn for help. She was a woman of deep religious feeling, a good mind, and a strong will, and she decided that her small children should have an opportunity to develop into fine men and women. True, they had nothing, but she made up her mind that her children should have an education and a good home, and should be brought up as God-fearing citizens.

Not long after the father's death, a kinsman, Captain John Terrel, who lived near Level Green in Marlboro District, took the family to live near him. Young James, who was nine years old when his father died, was put into school at Level Green. Here he had the great good fortune to come under the eye of a teacher who saw that James had a fine brain and a grim determination to succeed. He would study far into the night when others were asleep, and when the daily lessons were done, he would go on reading. He read many volumes of history and literature, lent to him by kind neighbors.

Three gentlemen of Cheraw became interested in seeing that young Thornwell received an education. General James Gillespie and his brother, with Mr. William H. Robbins, became his foster-fathers and helped him to educate himself. Mr. Robbins took young Thornwell into his own home and allowed him to attend the Cheraw Academy. After two years here, he was considered ready to enter the South Carolina College.

James Thornwell's fame as a student had gone ahead of him, and when he applied at the South Carolina College for entrance into the Junior Class, everybody thought that he was sure to pass the examinations with high honors. The Cheraw Academy considered him their prize pupil. But by

The University of South Carolina during Thornwell's presidency.

some freak of the mind, probably because he was nervous, young Thornwell did not pass all of his examinations. Perhaps a great many young men would have given up. The Glass Mountain was proving hard to climb. But there were no such words as "give up" in Thornwell's mind. He went home, studied, and in a few months stood another examination, this time passing with high honors.

We must remember that Thornwell was going to college at the expense of his foster-fathers. Evidently he was very careful not to spend more money than was necessary. Once Mr. Robbins wrote to scold him because he was spending too little. Thornwell's answer gives a pretty good idea of how he felt about spending other people's money. He wrote, "What's economy in one man is parsimony [stinginess] in another. . . . We must accumulate before we can spend and not spend before we can accumulate." He was always careful not to impose on the kindness of his friends.

That young James Thornwell had a mind of his own was shown even before he entered college. Mr. Robbins, one of his foster-fathers, was a prominent lawyer in Cheraw and had planned to have his young ward become a lawyer also. In order to make him familiar with legal terms, he had taken James into his office and had taught him how to copy and draw up legal papers. When the time came for Thornwell to decide on his profession, Mr. Robbins told him of his plan for him, and of his joy at the thought of having Thornwell with him, handling his business and helping him as he grew older. It was a hard thing for Thornwell to tell his friend "No," after all that Mr. Robbins had done for him. He appreciated the wonderful opportunity he had been given and felt that he should do whatever was asked of him, but his heart was set on becoming a preacher.

In a remarkable letter which the young boy wrote to Mr. Robbins, explaining how much it hurt him to disappoint his benefactor, he stated, "I have determined to adopt theology as my profession." Fortunately Mr. Robbins was willing for him to follow his own ambition.

James Thornwell was just eighteen years old when he entered the South Carolina College in triumph. Some of his professors of that day said that his mind worked "with the steadiness of a fine piece of machinery." Not satisfied with having only the small vocabulary which he could learn at a country school, Thornwell studied the finest of English writers and memorized large portions of the King James' version of the Bible, Shakespeare's plays, and Milton's poetry. He soon was said to have the largest vocabulary in college. His greatest interests, outside of his studies, lay in debating and in taking part in the programs of the literary societies. He liked Latin and Greek, but his real delight was in the classes on philosophy, where he could learn how and what the great leaders of mankind had thought.

He was not an "old stick-in-the-mud" by any means. Whenever there was fun to be had, James Thornwell could be counted on to enter into it. He was never rowdy and never dissipated, but he liked a healthy, clean, good time as much as any boy on the campus.

In 1831, at the age of nineteen, James Henley Thornwell was graduated from the South Carolina College with the first honors of his class. The youth had climbed a long way up the Glass Mountain. In those days the first-honor man gave a speech called a Salutatory, or Salutation (Greetings), every word of which was written and delivered in Latin. It was a great triumph when Thornwell stood up, as the head of his class, to greet his class and his fellow students.

Main building of the Presbyterian Theological Seminary.
This building, in which James H. Thornwell taught, was
designed by Robert Mills.

From a photograph by Carl Julien

They hardly recognized him as the student who has been described by one of his friends in these very uncomplimentary terms: "In December, 1829, there came to the South Carolina College a most unprepossessing looking youth—short, sallow, wearing a long coat to the heels, exciting merriment of his fellow students by his absurd appearance."

Of that first appearance on the campus of the college one of his classmates wrote, "In personal appearance he was perhaps the most unpromising specimen of humanity that ever entered such an institution. Very short in stature, he was shorter by a head than he became later in life, very lean in flesh, with a skin the color of old parchment, his hands and face as thickly studded with freckles as the Milky Way with stars, and an eye rendered dull in repose by a drooping lid. Such was the youth when first seen striding over the campus, arm in arm with a friend six feet high, as if burlesquing his own littleness by contrast."

Before his death that funny-looking boy was to become president of that very same college and one of the greatest preachers America has known.

After graduation Thornwell wanted to remain at the South Carolina College to do graduate work. He had planned to continue his fourteen hours a day of hard study, earning enough by coaching to pay for his simple living expenses. Unfortunately not enough coaching jobs developed, and he was forced to take a position as teacher in Sumterville.

Perhaps you are asking what had happened to Thornwell's determination to become a minister? It was lying quietly in his mind, waiting until the right opportunity should come. While teaching he happened to read a book

which in all of his reading had not fallen into his hands
before, *The Westminster Confession of Faith*. That book
and his own strong religious feeling made him decide to
join the Presbyterian Church, which was not the church to
which his family had belonged, and he became even more
determined to be a preacher.

In 1834 Thornwell entered the famous Andover Theological Seminary. The views taught in this Massachusetts
school were a little too advanced for his ideas, and he withdrew. He went to Harvard and spent a few months there
studying Oriental languages, especially Hebrew, which he
found very enjoyable. He also liked German literature and
wrote home that there was nothing which had given him
greater pleasure than to have the free use of the enormous
Harvard and Athenaeum libraries. He could browse among
the books there as long and as late as he wished.

Before his visits to the North—which he found cold, both
mentally and according to the weather man—he had returned, when just past twenty, to his old school in Cheraw
to become a teacher where he had not so long before sat as
a pupil. In 1833 he had announced that he was going to become a minister and had been fortunate enough to be taken
under the care of the Presbytery of Harmony, who had
interested themselves in seeing that he was given a chance
to do what he wished.

After his return from Harvard, he was licensed, on November 28, 1834, to preach in Presbyterian churches, and
he served as pastor of several churches in Lancaster District.
An amusing story about him tells that while preaching at
Lancaster, Thornwell rode a fleet horse named "Red Rover"
and rode it with the style which was due to a horse of such
good breeding and fine spirit. One of the members of his

church wrote, "It gave our pastor the appearance of being
a little fast," and then went on to remark that he sold the
horse when he was married.

It had taken James Henley Thornwell twenty-five years
to climb part way up the Glass Mountain. He might well
have thought that he was nearing the top when in 1837 he

One of the cartoons popular in the South during the political upheaval just preceding the Confederate War.

was elected professor of philosophy at the South Carolina
College. His classes were crowded, and he was considered
the most successful professor on the campus. At heart he was
still a preacher, and so, when the call came in 1840 for him
to minister to the Columbia Presbyterian Church, he resigned, to take up his duties there. Once he said of himself,
"When I'm preaching, I'm a teacher; when I'm teaching,
I'm a preacher." It is therefore not surprising to find that in

1841 he returned to South Carolina College. This time he was both teacher and preacher, for he was a professor, and he also served as chaplain of the college. Except for a short time when he was minister of the Glebe Street Presbyterian Church in Charleston, Thornwell spent the rest of his life in Columbia.

Perhaps he would not have called it the top of the Mountain, but it seems to us that when James Henley Thornwell was elected president of the South Carolina College he had reached the pinnacle of his success. He might well have shouted, "Eureka!" or "I have found it!" He, the boy of small beginnings, had scaled the heights.

At that time there were 190 students in the college, a small number compared with the nearly 2,000 who now attend. But we must remember that there were other difficult problems for Thornwell to solve. He had to make the people see that the college was really on the side of religion, which some had doubted since the days of Thomas Cooper. Then, too, the business affairs of the college were not in the best shape.

In order to get ideas for running the college, Thornwell visited Harvard and Yale and studied their ways of doing things.

In 1843 President Thornwell wrote a very remarkable letter to Governor Manning about the duty of the state to educate its people. He thought that the state was responsible for the education of her sons and daughters. He believed that it was perfectly possible for religion to be a part of a state school. He further pointed out that history teaches that one of the greatest dangers in any state comes from a division among its own people. These divisions, he said, became more terrible whenever the religious element entered into them and he begged his people never to let religious quarrels enter into their lives. He stated that every dollar which the state spent to educate her people was a good investment. When the people who attended public schools or state-owned colleges grew to manhood or womanhood, they would have been trained to serve wisely and for the best good of all the people. Ignorant rulers make for bad government—education is one way of having good government.

But Thornwell was never entirely happy at the college. His old ideal of devoting his entire time to religion still burned brightly. Also, he was "burning the candle at both ends," and finally his worn-out body demanded a rest. The doctors advised a sea voyage, and on May 19, 1841, he left New York by sail-boat, arriving in Liverpool, England, on June 6, having made a "quick" trip, in nineteen days. His interesting diary and his letters to his wife have been preserved, and from them we can gain an idea of his loneliness and of his interesting experiences in foreign lands. From Paris on the last day of July, 1841, he wrote, "I candidly believe that America is the first nation on the globe; and all through the continent of Europe the American flag is honored and respected. . . . I am proud of my nation and prouder still after having seen others."

Not only was Thornwell proud of his nation but he was equally proud of his state. On the journey home after this trip to Europe, he traveled by carriage from Charlotte, North Carolina, to Lancaster, South Carolina. As the carriage crossed the South Carolina line, he suddenly got out and knelt upon the soil of his native state, kissing it reverently with his lips. This was not a silly gesture, but a sincere expression of his deep and passionate love for the state which had given him birth, a love which was felt by many South Carolinians of that day. Some years later his health was again bad, and for the second time he was ordered to Europe. This time, however, he was a member of a congenial party, and his letters were cheerful and showed that he was far less lonely than he was on his first trip.

At last the Presbyterian Church decided that they had loaned their great scholar to the state of South Carolina long enough. They knew that the hard work he was doing was too much for him, and "they recalled the loan and saved the man." In 1855 Thornwell resigned the presidency of the South Carolina College to become a professor in the Presbyterian Theological Seminary, in Columbia. For seven years he served the Seminary. These were perhaps the seven best years of his life, for although he was not well, he was at last doing the thing for which he was best fitted. While he was a professor at the Seminary, he also again served as preacher of the First Presbyterian Church in Columbia, so that he was happily combining the teaching and the preaching of religion.

We have spoken of the letters which Thornwell wrote to his wife, but nothing else has been said about this delightful woman. On December 3, 1835, Nancy White Witherspoon became the wife of the young Presbyterian preacher. She was the daughter of Colonel James H. Witherspoon, former lieutenant-governor of the state of South Carolina and a prominent citizen of Lancaster. A woman of rare grace and beauty of character, Mrs. Thornwell proved to be the ideal wife. Several children were born to them and brought joy and sorrow into their lives. Thornwell's joy in them is shown in the very fine letters he wrote them. The sorrow came with their death at too early an age. His son, Gillespie, who was under age, enlisted in Confederate forces and was killed in service. His beautiful young daughter died when she was only twenty years old, just a few days before she was to have been married. Still another tragedy came into the lives of the Thornwells when a son, just nine years old, died from typhoid fever.

Perhaps few men ever had more friends than Thornwell. Men like Robert W. Barnwell and the Reverend Dr. Stephen Elliott delighted to call him friend. But young people, especially, were drawn to him. His students spoke always of his absolute fairness. To them he was the perfect umpire. He never did become a handsome man, though in later years he outgrew the very unattractive appearance described when he was a boy. As an orator he could hold an audience spellbound for hours, but he would never allow himself to become cheap. He had a cold, clear manner of reasoning, which was softened by his love for the beautiful. His friends said that he actually suffered when he heard incorrect English. He was very solemn in the pulpit, but he was a joyous, delightful companion out of it.

The old saying, "The busy man always finds time to do something else," was certainly true of Thornwell. In addition to all his other duties, in 1847 he became the editor, at Columbia, of the *Southern Presbyterian Review*, a magazine in which he could express his views. Between 1847 and 1860 he attended ten of the annual assemblies of his church. In 1847 he was elected moderator (presiding officer), the youngest man ever to be so honored by his church. One of the very large churches in Baltimore invited him to become its pastor in 1845, but he could not leave the University at the time without a year's notice, and so the matter was delayed. When the year was up, the Presbyterian Church of

Thornwell College, University of South Carolina. Named in honor of James Henley Thornwell.

South Carolina would not allow him to leave, and so South Carolina kept her great teacher.

Although Thornwell was opposed to having the church take any part in affairs outside of religion, and though he sincerely hoped that it would be possible to keep the Union unbroken, he was a leader in having the Presbyterian Church of South Carolina endorse secession. When the Confederacy had actually been formed, Thornwell became one of the leaders in organizing the Presbyterian Church of the Confederate States. He became famous for his writings explaining the Southern point of view. A most terrible picture of war is painted in an address he made before the soldiers of the Confederate Army in 1862. This speech, which he called

"Our Danger and Our Duty," foretold the terrible things which would happen to the South during Reconstruction if the North should win the war.

The work done by Thornwell for education and religion was appreciated outside of Carolina. Within one week in the year 1846, three colleges (Jefferson, Hampden-Sydney, and Centre) gave him the degree of Doctor of Divinity, honors which he well deserved and deeply appreciated.

Long before he became an old man, overwork, illness, and the excitement of war brought to an end the life of this great preacher, teacher, and leader. The last days were spent in the home of his friends, Mr. and Mrs. W. E. White in Charlotte, North Carolina. He had gone there in connection with his duties and was taken ill while visiting the Whites. On August 1, 1862, he died. The president of the railroad set aside a private car to bring his body back to Columbia. A great throng of sorrowing people attended his funeral and his burial in Elmwood Cemetery. A beautiful, gleaming white marker shows the love and affection of the people of his state for this man, who, as a boy, started with nothing at the foot of the Mountain, and by his own will and determination climbed up the steep, glassy slopes to the pinnacle of success.

Index

Gadsden and, 90–91; explained, 113–14; John Rutledge and, 114
North, Mrs. Jane, sister of Petigru, 326
Nullification defined, 283; Calhoun's views on, 283–84; Poinsett's attitude toward, 312; Petigru opposed to, because it would injure the Union, 324–25

"OLD STONE CHURCH," 186; picture of, 183
Oliphant, Dr., teacher in Charles Town, 204
Olive plants, introduced in colony, 7
One-crop system, Poinsett warns against, 314
Orangeburg, S. C., 149
Oranges, in S. C., 44
Oratory. *See* Public speaking
Ostenaco. *See* Austenaco
Oswald, Richard, friend of Laurens, 78
Otis, James, 90
Oucconastotah, and Governor Bull, 60–61
Outacite, friend of Thomas Sumter, 142; picture of, 143
Oxford University, 128, 190
Oyster Point, site of Charles Town, 13

PAINE, THOMAS, 92–93
Paints, oil, 241
Palette, Washington Allston's described, 241
Palmetto Society, 278
Parker, Thomas, married Mary Drayton, 139
Parsons, James, Charles Town lawyer, 109
Partisan bands, defined, 147; effectiveness of, 150; importance of, 163
Patten, James W., of Asheville, friend of Robert Y. Hayne, 288
Pawley's Island, 229
Peagues, Christopher B., 339
Peale, Charles, portrait of Washington painted by, 105; portrait of Christopher Gadsden painted by, 107

Pendleton, S. C., 296
Pendleton Farmers Society, 298
Peronneau, Elizabeth (Mrs. William Hayne), mother of Robert Y. Hayne, 275
Pettigrew, General Johnston, cousin of James L. Petigru, 330
Pettigrew (Petigru), William, father of James L. Petigru, 319; change of spelling of, 319, note; 321
Pettigrew (Petigru), Mrs. William, mother of James L., 319, 321
Petigru, Caroline, daughter of James L., 328; picture of, 326; debut of, 334; efforts of, to erect father's monument, 335–36
Petigru, James L., life of, 318–37; picture of, 318; voting ticket of, facsimile, *frontispiece;* epitaph of, 319
Petigru, Susan, daughter of James L., 328
Petigru coat-of-arms and seal, pictures of, 320
Petigru's spring at "Badwell," picture of, 330
Philosophy, as a study, 342, 346–47
Piano, Mills' formula for tuning, 272
Pickens, Andrew, father of Andrew Pickens, 173, 174
Pickens, Andrew, life of, 173–86; picture of, 173; leader of Partisan band, 147; in Cherokee War, 161; mentioned, 117, 149, 163, 297
Pickens, Andrew, Jr., governor of S. C., 182, 184
Pickens, Anne, mother of Andrew Pickens, 173
Pickens, Ezekiel, son of Andrew Pickens, 182
Pickens, Francis W., grandson of Andrew Pickens, 184; picture of, 185
Pinckney, Colonel Charles, father of Charles Pinckney, 204

DATE DUE

MAR 20 '75 NOV 20 '75			
GAYLORD			PRINTED IN U.S.A